The Currency of Cultural Patrimony

Contemporary Hispanic and Lusophone Cultures

Series Editors
L. Elena Delgado, University of Illinois at Urbana-Champaign
Niamh Thornton, University of Liverpool

Series Editorial Board
Jo Labanyi, New York University
Chris Perriam, University of Manchester
Paul Julian Smith, CUNY Graduate Center

This series aims to provide a forum for new research on modern and contemporary hispanic and lusophone cultures and writing. The volumes published in Contemporary Hispanic and Lusophone Cultures reflect a wide variety of critical practices and theoretical approaches, in harmony with the intellectual, cultural and social developments that have taken place over the past few decades. All manifestations of contemporary hispanic and lusophone culture and expression are considered, including literature, cinema, popular culture, theory. The volumes in the series will participate in the wider debate on key aspects of contemporary culture.

17 Regina Galasso, *Translating New York: The City's Languages in Iberian Literatures*

18 Daniel F. Silva, *Anti-Empire: Decolonial Interventions in Lusophone Literatures*

19 Luis I. Prádanos, *Postgrowth Imaginaries: New Ecologies and Counterhegemonic Culture in Post-2008 Spain*

20 Liz Harvey-Kattou, *Contested Identities in Costa Rica: Constructions of the Tico in Literature and Film*

21 Cecilia Enjuto-Rangel, Sebastiaan Faber, Pedro García-Caro, and Robert Patrick Newcomb, eds, *Transatlantic Studies: Latin America, Iberia, and Africa*

22 Ana Paula Ferreira, *Women Writing Portuguese Colonialism in Africa*

23 Esther Gimeno Ugalde, Marta Pacheco Pinto and Ângela Fernandes, eds, *Iberian and Translation Studies: Literary Contact Zones*

24 Ben Bollig, *Moving Voices: Poetry on Screen in Argentine Cinema*

25 Daniel F. Silva, *Empire Found: Racial Identities and Coloniality in Twenty-First-Century Portuguese Popular Cultures*

26 Dean Allbritton, *Feeling Sick: The Early Years of AIDS in Spain*

27 Ana Fernandez-Cebrian, *Fables of Development: Capitalism and Social Imaginaries in Spain (1950-1967)*

28 María Chouza-Calo, Esther Fernández and Jonathan Thacker, eds, *Daring Adaptations, Creative Failures, and Experimental Perfomances in Iberian Theatre*

29 Anna Tybinko, Lamonte Aidoo and Daniel F. Silva, eds, *Migrant Frontiers: Race and Mobility in the Luso-Hispanic World*

30 Tess C. Rankin, *Feeling Strangely in Mid-Century Spanish and Latin American Women's Fiction*

The Currency of Cultural Patrimony

The Spanish Golden Age

ROBERT BAYLISS

LIVERPOOL UNIVERSITY PRESS

First published 2024 by
Liverpool University Press
4 Cambridge Street
Liverpool
L69 7ZU

This paperback edition published 2026

Copyright © 2026 Robert Bayliss

Robert Bayliss has asserted his rights to be identified as the author of this book in accordance with the Copyright, Designs and Patents Act 1988.

All rights reserved. No part of this book may be reproduced, stored in a retrieval system, or transmitted, in any form or by any means, electronic, mechanical, photocopying, recording, or otherwise, without the prior written permission of the publisher.

British Library Cataloguing-in-Publication data
A British Library CIP record is available

ISBN 978-1-802-07448-2 (hardback)
ISBN 978-1-80596-573-2 (paperback)

Typeset in Borges by
Carnegie Book Production, Lancaster

Contents

Introduction: The Cultural Patrimony of the Spanish Golden Age   1

1. Lope de Vega and the Performance of Spanishness   41
2. Don Quixote de la Mancha, 'Made in Spain'   81
3. Repatriating the Cid: Spanish Cultural *Reconquista* in the Era of Globalization   111

Conclusion: The Spanish Golden Age and Empire, Then and Now   137

Bibliography   157

Index   169

Introduction

The Cultural Patrimony of the Spanish Golden Age

¿Qué me importa lo que Cervantes quiso o no quiso poner allí y lo que realmente puso? Lo vivo es lo que yo allí descubro, pusiéralo o no Cervantes, lo que yo allí pongo y sobrepongo y sotopongo, y lo que ponemos allí todos. Quise allí rastrear nuestra filosofía.

[What do I care what Cervantes wanted or did not want to put there and what he really put there? What is living is what I find in it, what I put there and superimpose and write under it, and what we all put there. I chose there to trace our philosophy.]

Miguel de Unamuno, *Del sentimiento trágico de la vida*, 269[1]

By foregrounding its utility for addressing problems in modern Spanish society, this passage from Miguel de Unamuno's *Del sentimiento trágico de la vida* describes a mode of engagement with *Don Quixote* that will be shown in these pages to be far from unique among his compatriots—except perhaps for the self-awareness that it reflects, and for its explicit renunciation of any claims to pursue a better understanding of the novel itself or the early modern society that it represents. By putting aside such claims to historical authenticity or philological fidelity, Unamuno articulates what is generally unsaid about Spain's relationship with its cultural Golden Age: *Don Quixote* and other Spanish literary "classics" from the sixteenth and seventeenth centuries retain their value in subsequent eras insofar as they remain useful for negotiating Spain's evolving and emerging cultural circumstances. To be sure, the complexities of twenty-first-century Spain are quite different than those of Unamuno's era, but the persistent utility of the Spanish Golden Age has been perhaps the most constant and stable feature of Spanish culture since these words were written.

---

1 Unless otherwise noted, all English-language translations of Spanish-language citations are my own.

This book examines Spain's relationship with the cultural artifacts of its Golden Age with a purpose different than Unamuno's, which is to argue that based on recent scholarship in early modern Spanish studies, the broader academic field of Hispanic literary and cultural studies stands much to gain from its scrutiny. More specifically, I argue that the cultural narrative of a Spanish Golden Age through which early modern Castilian cultural production renders a cache of national literary "classics" makes the study of how those artifacts have been used in the twentieth and twenty-first centuries a powerful heuristic tool for understanding the cultural complexities of contemporary Spain. While Unamuno's generative hermeneutics are tied to his own particular notion of *intrahistoria* (a conception of shared cultural experience that eschews chronology and authorizes him to deduce from the *Quixote* what the moment demands), my point of departure is that, within Spain, Golden Age literature is inscribed in a national interpretive tradition and reception history that treats it as cultural patrimony. As participants in a nationalized interpretive community, contemporary Spanish consumers of products tied to this "classical" period of their cultural history engage with Golden Age literature in a discursive ecosystem that accommodates their contemporary perspectives and interests, but that is also carefully curated by public cultural institutions and corporate media. All of these participating elements—cultural producers, consumers, and institutions—shape and contest the meaning of Golden Age cultural patrimony, effectively rendering that *patrimonio* a powerful reflection of its *patria*.

By speaking of Spain as a singular collective entity (e.g., Spain's usage of Golden Age literature) I do not mean to suggest that there is universal buy-in or unanimous agreement among all Spaniards regarding this cultural narrative. To be sure, the increasingly polarized and divisive political climate of the present century is inhospitable even to the kind of *cultura de consenso* [culture of consensus] that Luisa Elena Delgado describes in her prescient book, *La nación singular: Fantasías de la normalidad democrática española (1996–2011)*(19), as a tenuous and fragile collective agreement to agree among Spaniards, notwithstanding the unresolved divisions and problems that such an agreement would pretend to erase. As I write these pages in 2023, the notion of Spain held by the ruling Socialist government as a pluralistic *nación de naciones* [nation of nations] reflects but one layer of a complex cultural climate in which so-called peripheral nationalisms, among many other contentious problems, challenge the very idea of Spain as a contiguous culture, and in which even the public display of the Spanish national flag anywhere in the country can be considered a divisive political act. It is therefore inevitable that cultural artifacts of the Spanish Golden Age will be engaged in contradictory ways in this environment, according to the positionalities and political dispositions of those who engage them. The cultural narrative in which Golden Age texts are inscribed is now especially fraught with contradictions, as are efforts by individual Spaniards and Spanish cultural institutions to maintain, curate, and update that narrative to better meet their needs.

"Spain" is therefore used in this book to describe not a consistent or coherent subject position, but rather a cultural and geopolitical space in which historical memory and cultural identities are under continual revision, and in which all participants who engage with Golden Age cultural patrimony must account for its claims to cultural authority or privilege. In this contested space the efforts of Spanish artists, entertainment industries, and cultural institutions influence how Spaniards understand "their" Golden Age and experience the period's literary texts, albeit in often contradictory and inconsistent ways. "Spain" is also used in this book to describe the diverse Iberian publics who consume and react to these engagements, as members of Spanish society and as consumers of cultural production to which those artists, industries, and institutions must appeal. If we consider the Spanish Golden Age to be a kind of mirror to be held up to Spanish society, wherein each reference, invocation, or adaptation of its patrimony can be read as a kind of cultural barometer, it is difficult to imagine how current engagements with or deployments of this patrimony could not reflect the deep divisions within Spanish society today between generational, geopolitical, socioeconomic, religious, racial, and ideological positionalities.

Another way to understand the notion of Spaniards and Spanish cultural institutions participating in the continual curation of a Golden Age cultural narrative is to employ the terminology of conceptual and textual "grids" coined by André Lefevere in the context of translation studies. Lefevere explains that the translator must access the grids tied to the linguistic communities of both the original text and the target culture for whom the translation is being realized in order to ensure that their work fully captures and conveys the full range of cultural references and sociolinguistic nuance in the source text. To export this concept to the subject of this book, we can consider the twenty-first-century adaptation and commemoration of a seventeenth-century literary text to constitute that text's "translation" from an early modern sociohistorical and linguistic context to the context in which contemporary Spaniards now experience it. Filling in the gaps between these two historically situated conceptual and textual grids, we will see, is subject to the perspective, positionality, and even the politics of those doing this translational work, and to the missions of the cultural institutions sponsoring it.

In simple terms, Lefevere's concept of a "conceptual grid" entails all of the extratextual and paratextual discourses that accompany a literary text in the real-world experience of the reader, or in other words the packaging, marketing, and presentation of the text in a synchronic cultural context. In the case of the eight-hour televisual miniseries adaptation of the first part of *Don Quixote* aired on Spanish public television (RTVE) in 1991, elements of the conceptual grid included trailers aired on television, advertisements in print and digital media, interviews with the series' production team (producers, adaptors, directors, actors, etc.), and reviews published in print media or aired on radio or television. Meanwhile, a "textual grid" entails the linguistic markers that link texts together in a shared discursive practice and thus condition the reader's experience, as when a fairy tale begins with "Once upon a time...," or as when a Golden Age *comedia* concludes with the conventional perfunctory request for the public to forgive its flaws. The distinctive linguistic features of the early modern Castilian language and the historical distance conveyed by them to a modern Spanish audience also contribute to the Golden Age's textual grid, as do the footnotes and glosses embedded in modern critical editions of Golden Age texts, most often as interventions to bridge the historical distance between early modern author and twenty-first-century reader.

All of these conceptual and textual elements accompany each instance of a contemporary Spaniard's experience of a Golden Age literary text, and together they combine with all other such elements from all other such engagements with Golden Age cultural patrimony experienced by contemporary Spaniards to constitute a discursive ecosystem whose curation will be examined in this book. When one takes into account the longstanding use of this patrimony since well before Unamuno's generation, whether to support political causes, to foster cultural identities, to educate the national citizenry, or to promote box office or bookstore profit margins (among many other possible reasons too numerous to name here), it becomes clear that the sheer banality and ubiquity of the Spanish Golden Age in contemporary Spanish culture makes the prospect of their exhaustive catalogue as overwhelming as Borges's Library of Babel. For very practical reasons, in these pages I will not attempt to document or account for the immense totality of data contributing to Spain's curation of a cultural environment in which the Golden Age continues to thrive. Instead, I will attempt to illuminate this environment's development and some of its key features and implications in order to inspire further study. I also argue for the value of prompting scholars of early modern Spanish literary and cultural production to be more explicitly aware of our own participation as curators in this discursive ecosystem.

In Spain, increasingly frequent references to Golden Age cultural artifacts as *patrimonio cultural* [cultural patrimony] are indicative of how these conceptual and textual grids are configured to convey upon this literature what Pierre Bourdieu would call cultural capital, an intangible value promising access to privileged social status to those who attain knowledge of it. Especially since the Spanish Civil War (1936–1939), the cultural capital of the Spanish Golden Age has been intertwined with national identity: because it is understood to capture some dimension of a shared Spanish national heritage, to consume the period's cultural production (or some modern or postmodern simulacrum thereof) is to participate in the "imagined community" of which the nation is comprised.[2] Of course, this status of cultural prestige can also be considered something of a self-fulfilling prophecy: cultural capital simultaneously stimulates and justifies the investment of public funds to curate these conceptual grids through institutions like the Real Academia Española [Royal Spanish Academy, henceforth RAE], the Instituto Cervantes, the Compañía Nacional de Teatro Clásico [National Classical Theater Company, henceforth CNTC] and the International Classical Theater Festival in Almagro. For these and other cultural institutions, the Spanish Golden Age is not unlike Dulcinea is for Don Quixote, whose chivalric fame and glory are directly proportional to her beauty and virtue. Just as the knight errant regularly insists that others praise and venerate her so as to elevate his own status in turn, these institutions structure engagements with Golden Age patrimony that they hope will stimulate support for further funding of similar engagements.

However, as we will examine in greater detail in Chapters 2 and 3, these cultural institutions cannot claim exclusive influence over the grids that they construct and curate around the Spanish Golden Age, nor can they control for the reception of Golden Age literary texts by the consumers of a Spanish nation that is more diverse and pluralistic than these institutions have traditionally acknowledged. My study of the contemporary cultural dynamics informing these institutions, including the political turnover in their missions and leadership as the ideological pendulum of the government continues to swing dramatically from right to left, suggests that this patrimony constitutes a privileged realm in the perpetual struggle among Spaniards to define their nation. A complicating factor, as we will learn especially in Chapter 3, is that the cultural capital afforded to the Golden Age can also be monetized in the neoliberal free market—it can be leveraged to generate revenue in the entertainment industry, or to sell goods

---

2 The notion of the "imagined community" to describe nationhood was originally developed by Benedict Anderson.

and services in marketing campaigns, for example—in ways that may not align with public cultural institutions or the politicians who fund them.

Filmax's 2007 animated film *Donkey Xote* is but one example of a private industrial intervention into this discursive ecosystem or conceptual grid. To appeal to young Spanish viewers more familiar with *Shrek* than with *Amadís de Gaula*, the film's screenwriter (Ángel Pariente) and director (José Pozo) opt to replace the chivalric intertexts for which Don Quixote's madness is blamed with a tapestry of visual intertextual references to American films by Disney and Pixar. This decision makes sense from an economic perspective, but it is also indicative of the extent to which the cultural literacy of Spanish children has merged with that of other wealthy, industrialized nations with access to digital media. Moreover, the significant changes in plot and character made by the film to accommodate this digital-native audience will further contribute to a generational understanding of and appreciation for *Don Quixote* that is more globalized (i.e., that is decreasingly distinguishable from how children of the same generation experience the story of Don Quixote across the industrialized world) and therefore less "Spanish," despite its strategic domestic marketing as a product inextricably tied to Spanish national identity. This example is indicative of how a cultural landscape can be influenced by globally circulated digital media in ways that alter the conceptual grid in which twenty-first-century Spanish experiences of the Golden Age are situated. One problem that this book diagnoses, then, is that what the societal mirror of Golden Age cultural patrimony reflects has become increasingly difficult to pin down in the digital era.

A further problem within the discursive ecosystem that nurtures the cultural narrative of the Spanish Golden Age emerged with the transition to democracy at the end of the 1970s: after four decades of politically motivated and ideologically informed curation by the Franco regime, in no small measure supported by the philologists employed at Spanish public universities and regulated by a strict censorship regime, a fault line would emerge between the treatment of Golden Age patrimony in popular culture and in academic discourse. Chapter 2 examines this divergence in greater depth in the case of the discourses surrounding *Don Quixote* in the twenty-first century, but here it is important to establish in broad terms the ways in which the academic study of Spanish literature and culture and the narrative of a Spanish Golden Age are mutually formative—in other words, to establish that until this popular-academic divergence emerged after Franco, the cultural narrative and the field of study had enjoyed a mutually beneficial and symbiotic relationship. While during the Franco era this patrimony was used by both the regime and its exiled opponents as a centripetal cultural force pointing to a shared national ontological essence, the cultural aftermath of the regime subjected the cultural narrative of a Spanish Golden Age to a confluence of centrifugal cultural forces that challenge its longstanding essentialist nature and homogenizing effect. As a consequence of this pluralistic turn, deployments of Golden Age literature have required this narrative's continual revision according to evolving circumstances of an increasingly diverse society. In political terms, the regular oscillation between conservative and liberal governments in the democratic era have even further complicated the narrative, insofar as political power includes control of the public cultural institutions that exercise the greatest influence, through cultural programming and academic funding, on the conceptual grids surrounding each deployment of a Golden Age literary text.

The Spanish Golden Age: A History

The Spanish Golden Age's entanglements with the Academy stretch back to even before the nineteenth-century development of the modern academic units dedicated to the study of national languages and literatures. Indeed, the term itself can be said to be the product of the Academy, as its earliest usages are attributed to early members of the RAE in the eighteenth century. Nicolás Marín notes a reference in 1736 by Alonso Verdugo to a *siglo áureo*, the first of several such references by Verdugo and his colleagues during the *siglo de luces* that suggest an implicit consensus that, at least in the context of lyric poetry, the sixteenth and seventeenth centuries were understood to be an era of artistic achievement superior to that of their contemporary neoclassical poets.[3] No eighteenth-century treatise from the RAE or anywhere else offers a direct and comprehensive narrative of what was meant by *Siglo de oro*, but the term's occasional reference invariably expresses cultural nostalgia for it, as a kind of foil with which to unfavorably compare to Enlightenment-era cultural production.

Notwithstanding these sporadic references, a coherent narrative of a literary Golden Age based on aesthetic criteria and tied to a notion of national character was initially stimulated from without, fed by the cultural headwinds of Romanticism beyond the natural borders of the Iberian Peninsula. Barbara Becker-Cantarino attributes the initial usage of the term to denote a more nationalistic Spanish cultural narrative to the

---

3 Alberto Blecua ("El concepto del Siglo de Oro") examines a number of late eighteenth-century references to an early modern *siglo de oro* of Spanish literature, primarily articulated to critique what was considered the inferior poetry of the neoclassical era, based on a vague notion of *buen gusto*.

"Romantic hispanophilia" expressed by Friedrich Schlegel and other German intellectuals at the turn of the eighteenth century.[4] Evidence that this new usage had spread beyond the continent can be found in the American Hispanist George Ticknor's three-volume *History of Spanish Literature* (1849), which uses the term to identify a discrete phase of Spain's cultural history in terms that largely echo those of the German Romantics, who admired early modern Spanish poetry, prose fiction, and theater for its reflection of an authentic national *Volksgeist*. During this midcentury period, a variety of intellectuals in Europe and North America contributed to a developing narrative of Spanish cultural history that identified an early modern Golden Age as its epicenter.[5] As Alberto Blecua notes, the chronological parameters of the term remained flexible to accommodate fluctuating tastes and ideologies of its users, with different voices centering the era on either the sixteenth or the seventeenth century, or what is now commonly called either the Spanish Renaissance or the Spanish Baroque.

By the latter half of the nineteenth century this narrative had taken root in Spain itself, where Agustín Durán and other writers heavily influenced by Romanticism further developed a *Volksgeist*-based understanding of the Spanish Golden Age that tied literary expression to a Spanish national character or essence.[6] Its impact on the historiography of Spanish literature extends to Marcelino Menéndez y Pelayo, often considered the "father" of modern Spanish literary historiography, and to Unamuno's *fin-de-siècle* concept of *intrahistoria* and beyond. As academic units dedicated to the study of languages and literatures emerged in institutions of higher learning in Europe and North America during the final decades of the nineteenth century, the Spanish Golden Age was embraced in an academic climate eager to identify national literary traditions and canons from within a decidedly Eurocentric paradigm. Indeed, while American institutions were in part motivated to promote Hispanism for practical, economic reasons (as James

---

4 Becker-Cantarino situates this "hispanophilia" in a broader continental contest, in which German intellectuals sought to reverse the underappreciation of Spanish culture among Enlightenment-era French intellectuals: "By the end of the 18th century, Spain was becoming the country of romantic yearning for German writers; a 'golden legend,' a *leyenda aurea*, was supplanting the stern 'black legend'" (122). See also Anthony Close's seminal study, *The Romantic Approach to Don Quixote*, for a clear presentation of this cultural development.

5 For a detailed chronology of Hispanism's development in North America during the nineteenth century, see James Fernández, "Longfellow's Law," which foregrounds the strategic economic motives behind the promotion of the field.

6 Diana Arbaiza's *The Spirit of Hispanism* examines this development from a transatlantic perspective, and with a focus on the field's entanglements with economic policies in the nineteenth and twentieth centuries.

Fernández argues), Spanish institutions encouraged the field for motives that have been characterized by Diana Arbaiza as "a nationalistic discourse of imperial nostalgia" (3).

By this time, the RAE had evolved from an eighteenth-century Enlightenment society narrowly focused on the regulation of language usage to a nineteenth-century nation-building cultural institution whose expanded mission included the publication of definitive editions of "classic" Spanish literary texts from the Golden Age.[7] By the end of the Spanish–American War in 1898, after which Spain ceded possession of its most important remaining colonies (Cuba, the Philippines, and Puerto Rico), the RAE and the network of Spanish universities whose faculty constituted its membership had fully embraced a *Siglo de oro* narrative that would prove to be invaluable for cultural programming and educational curricula in the aftermath of that disastrous war, and indeed through the Franco dictatorship (1939–1975). In this way, as Christopher Britt-Arredondo has argued, the *fin-de-siècle* "Quixotists" (Unamuno, Azorín, Ortega y Gasset, et al.) developed such a compelling reading of Cervantes's hero as a national allegory that they can be said to have unwittingly sown the discursive seeds of fascism. After the Civil War (1936–1939) this narrative maintained its coherence beyond Spain as well, in part due to its reinforcement by the mass exile of anti-fascist Spanish academics to Europe and to the Americas, many of whom sustained this nostalgic cultural narrative as they joined the faculty at major universities in their adopted countries.

The Spanish Golden Age: A Metahistory

Especially among Hispanists in North America, the term "Golden Age" gradually fell out of favor in the waning years of the twentieth century for a variety of reasons, chief among them a desire to approach early modern cultural production more dispassionately than the term's implicit cultural narrative would allow.[8] It was replaced by terms meant to be more precise—for example, the MLA's "sixteenth/seventeenth century Spanish Drama" division—or, as with the most prevalent term "early modern,"

---

[7] The RAE's canonization and dissemination of standard print editions of the Spanish "classics" began as early as 1780 with a four-tome illustrated edition of *Don Quixote*, but the production of definitive editions of Golden Age texts would accelerate over the course of the nineteenth century.

[8] For informative discussions of the shift away from "Golden Age" to designate the field of study, see Margaret Greer ("Thine and Mine"), Barbara Mujica ("Golden Age/Early Modern Theater"), James Parr ("A Modest Proposal"), and Allison Weber ("Golden Age").

more engaged with the related fields of Comparative Literature and English, French, and Italian studies of the same period. Regardless of the reasons for this shift in nomenclature, it reflects the field's general divestment of the nationalistic narrative exploited by Franco, which in turn has created a critical distance over the last three decades from which the concept of a Spanish Golden Age can now be re-examined more dispassionately. As with many such issues in terminology, the shift says more about the field of study than it says about its object, but other developments in literary and cultural studies since the 1980s have also prompted an expansion of the Golden Age canon (for example, the recovery and study of women writers) that the Franco-era nationalistic paradigm likely would have resisted. Philologists in Spain, notably, continue to use the term *Siglo de oro* and the synonymous adjective *áureo* [golden], for reasons that will be more evident after reading this book. The term also remains the preferred historiographical label for other cultural institutions like the Instituto Cervantes, the Biblioteca Nacional de España [National Spanish Library], and the Spanish ministries of Education and Culture.[9] As will be examined in greater depth in Chapter 2, Spanish institutions remain invested in the notion of a Spanish Golden Age to this day because they are publicly funded organizations participating in a discursive ecosystem curated with support from the Spanish government. As the citation above from Unamuno indicates, Spanish intellectuals have relied upon this term to understand and define their nation at least since the definitive collapse of the Spanish Empire at the end of the nineteenth century.

Approaching the problem from outside of Spain and from within an international academic field no longer invested in the implicit cultural narrative of a Spanish Golden Age affords a critical distance to perceive the need not for a history, but for a *metahistory* of the Spanish Golden Age. Rather than trace the historical events that shaped early modern cultural production, this book revisits the history of the Golden Age *since* the early modern period in order to fully inform an analysis of its functionality in the twenty-first century. As a symbol of past cultural splendor, as a repository of cultural heritage deeply embedded in contemporary identities, and as a kind of analogy for purposes of charting national paths forward during moments

---

9 Spanish government ministries are regularly reorganized and renamed when government authority is transferred from one political party to another. As of 2023, the relevant institutions are the Ministerio de Educación y Formación Profesional and the Ministerio de Cultura y Deporte.

of crisis, Spain has engaged with both the idea of a *Siglo de oro* and the artists and artifacts associated with it continuously since the eighteenth century.[10]

In recent years, the term "cultural patrimony" has become the Spanish government's preferred term to describe these engagements, but the notion that a culture's practices and products should be preserved for posterity and treated as its material and/or intellectual property can be traced back at least to the medieval period.[11] Indeed, as the flourishing of cultural production intensified during the Golden Age itself, the Spanish monarchy began the practice of appropriating or commissioning texts and theatrical spectacles—and memorializing them in the archives—to solidify the historically novel concept of a unified Spanish state and to promote an essentialized cultural notion of Spanishness, as well as to project the power and cultural splendor of the Spanish Empire to its colonial subjects and to the foreign gaze. From its inception, the very idea of "Spain" has been articulated through the curation of its early modern cultural production, which eventually would be synthesized into a national (and at times a nationalist) narrative meant to articulate a shared Spanish cultural identity, both to project externally and to foster cultural cohesion among domestic audiences. The historian Henry Kamen has noted the pervasiveness of this narrative in the Spanish cultural imaginary:

> One of the most extraordinary aspects of Spain's sixteenth century is that many Spaniards are still living in it. In a sense, they have never left it. The sixteenth century has dictated a good part of their ideas and aspirations, their vision of the past and of the future. Pick up any newspaper, any novel, and you will find echoes of the sixteenth century somewhere. When politicians wish to make sense of their policies, they look backwards to it for inspiration. It was an age that created, and is creating, Spain, not only because of those who still yearn for it but also on account of those who feel they must reject it passionately. (*Imagining Spain*, 4)[12]

---

10 Francisco Abad Nebot and Alberto Blecua ("El concepto de Siglo de Oro") offer more detailed histories of the term.

11 As Eric Ketelaar has argued, the preservation and treatment of written records in medieval European monasteries offer early evidence of what Ketelaar terms "the paradigm of *Patrimoine*," which would gradually develop in more secular contexts to include material objects and cultural practices in the eighteenth and nineteenth centuries.

12 Kamen's focus on the sixteenth century, I would argue, is due to his perspective as a historian, from which the geopolitical power of the Spanish Empire peaks before many of the literary texts associated with the Golden Age were produced.

While my argument is less concerned with the early modern period than it is with the use of that period's cultural production in subsequent centuries, there are aspects of early modern Spanish history that can inform our understanding of later uses of the period's cultural artifacts in subsequent centuries, insofar as the (con)textual preconditions of Golden Age cultural products can explain their propensity for being appropriated in subsequent eras as cultural patrimony. Today we still feel the unforeseen consequences of early modern Spain's unique literary and cultural environment, which George Mariscal famously characterizes as "an intense rivalry between competing discourses" (*Contradictory Subjects*, 3), as this environment fostered and favored modes of cultural expression that have proven to be quintessentially protean, adaptable, and therefore exportable to future cultural circumstances, however remote they may be to the sixteenth and seventeenth centuries.[13]

Therefore, while this book does not attempt to provide an exhaustive account of early modern Spain, the historical circumstances informing the discursive climate of the period are germane to our understanding of what the Spanish Golden Age has come to mean today, in an era in which Mariscal's concept of a discursively "competitive" climate could be equally applicable, albeit with some adjustments. While Mariscal's analysis of early modern Spain focused on competing models of subjectivity and subject formation, twenty-first-century discursive battles are more frequently discussed in terms of the ontological status of the nation. According to Mariscal, Cervantes and Quevedo explore emerging notions of the subject that challenged more traditional views long bolstered by inherited social hierarchies, with the participation of subversive discourses like picaresque fiction in the erosion of a social order under threat from emerging economic forces. Scholarship since the 1990s has deepened our understanding and broadened our awareness of the variety of discourses in competition, especially in light of Barbara Simerka's observation that "reception, like production, is significantly influenced by the competition among discourses" (11). This turbulent discursive climate may not map perfectly onto contemporary cultural circumstances in Spain, but it did stimulate a mode of literary representation that both navigated early modern

---

The cultural narrative of a Golden Age of cultural production, which is generally considered to extend to the last decades of the seventeenth century (often to the death of Pedro Calderón de la Barca in 1680), outlasted this geopolitical and economic power, which waned in the final years of the sixteenth century.

13 This theoretical approach to early modern Spain is largely indebted to Raymond Williams, whose *Marxism and Literature* explores the intersection of what he terms dominant, residual, and emergent discourses.

cultural tensions and yielded a depository of texts that, some 500 years later, retain their ability to speak to contemporary Spaniards and to be valued as cultural patrimony. The cultural and symbolic capital of the Spanish Golden Age today, to again borrow Bourdieu's terminology, is tied not just to the era of its original production but also to the problems of that era as manifested in the literary discourses it produced. Regardless of how well or poorly those problems translate to a twenty-first-century context, the discursive tensions, ambiguities, and ambivalences generated by them remain embedded in what twenty-first-century Spaniards now read, according to their contemporary conceptual grids, as their cultural patrimony.

While early modern cultural problems such as those identified by Mariscal may not translate easily to contemporary Spanish society, this book examines how the curation of these grids by cultural institutions and media industries does often entail the search for equivalencies and points of applicability as points of access to engage contemporary Spanish audiences. To cite one example that Chapter 1 describes in greater detail, a revival of interest in Lope de Vega's play *Fuenteovejuna* in the aftermath of José Luis Rodríguez Zapatero's presidency (2004–2012) capitalizes on Lope's treatment of sexual violence to synchronize with efforts by Zapatero, Spain's self-described first *presidente feminista* [feminist president], to reform Franco-era domestic violence laws. If we were to limit our inquiry to the ways in which the CNTC's production of *Fuenteovejuna* in 2016 enhanced our understanding of Lope and his historical moment, we would miss the opportunity to explore equally valid questions about the CNTC itself and its participation in curating the Golden Age conceptual grid—including how the production is informed by its own twenty-first-century political context (and by the rise in feminist activism that it inspired).

A formulation of the competitive discursive dynamics at play in twenty-first-century Spain that seems similar to Mariscal's early modern analysis is Sebastian Balfour's diagnosis of a "discursive civil war" (179) in the aftermath of landmark legislation in 2007 known as the *ley de memoria histórica* [law of historical memory]. This law, which in hindsight appears to signal the beginning of the end of what Delgado calls Spain's transition-era *cultura de consenso* [culture of consensus], reversed a so-called *pacto de olvido* [pact of forgetting] negotiated in the aftermath of Franco's death in 1975 for the sake of national unity. The 2007 law effectively authorized the victims (and their descendants) of both the Civil War and the ensuing Franco dictatorship to seek justice and compensation for human rights violations, notwithstanding the predictable pushback from conservative politicians and pundits. The law also met with considerable resistance from the left for, among other things, failing to explicitly repeal the 1978 *ley de amnistía* [amnesty law], and for being more symbolic and less materially and legally consequential. More importantly, it opened a discursive space in which longstanding political tensions reemerged.

The consequences of this discursive battle are still in progress, but Spain's persistent political polarization reflects a society in which many of the questions that the 1978 constitution claimed to answer remain unresolved. Is Spain a federation of semi-autonomous regions controlled by a strong central state, or is it a "nation of nations" comprised of so many peripheral national identities? Is the separatist movement in Catalonia indicative of a fraying national political system, or is it merely a reflection of longstanding political tensions and the inherent messiness of democratic governance in a pluralistic society? Does the discovery of political corruption undermine the functionality of the Constitution itself? After four decades of democracy, can the ideas and ideologies of the far right (currently voiced through the political party Vox) be peacefully accommodated? To the extent that Spain's ongoing discursive contests (like the countless contests before it tied to Spain's ontological status) will appeal to some kind of national or shared cultural history, cultural artifacts of the Spanish Golden Age will invariably be deployed, just as they were during the Civil War itself, as evidence for diametrically opposed arguments.[14]

Regardless of what originally may have inspired it, the competitive discursive climate of the early modern period yielded texts whose discursive malleability would leave them ripe for multiple and often contradictory readings both then, as popular and elite cultural products, and now, as "classics," a slippery term which in these pages will refer to cultural artifacts that have assumed the function of cultural patrimony. After their historical displacement from the discursive context in which they were originally composed, these "Golden Age classics" demonstrate a remarkable ability to resonate with new readers, spectators, or consumers when reinserted into new contexts, regardless of the historical distance or changed cultural dynamics separating them. These artifacts, treated in this book with a focus on literary texts, elude the irrelevance normally acquired with the passage of time, long after an author's intended or imagined audiences have died off; indeed, given the institutional functionality of cultural patrimony, I argue that the utility of the Spanish Golden Age has only increased with

---

14 See, for example, Jason Parker's "Recruiting the Literary Tradition: Lope de Vega's *Fuenteovejuna* as Cultural Weapon during the Spanish Civil War," which examines productions of Lope's play in support of both sides of the conflict, as well as David Rodríguez-Solás's *Teatros nacionales republicanos: la Segunda República y el teatro clásico español*.

the passage of time. These revived, de- (and re-) contextualized artifacts paradoxically come to represent metonymically that remote, otherwise ill-defined past according to contemporary Spanish cultural imaginaries. In this way, Golden Age classics perform a function of shared cultural memory not unlike Unamuno's notion of *intrahistoria*. This performative functionality of Golden Age literary texts requires their continual re-contextualization in the current moment, in other words their re-inscription into contemporary narratives or, to use Hans Robert Jauss's terminology, their continual reorientation according to each generation's horizon of expectations. Insofar as they work to confirm what one projects from the present onto the past, the classics are a tautology; however, their continual re-use in new contexts and for often contradictory purposes suggests that their selection from among the countless number of other texts in circulation during the early modern period was no accident, but rather due to their protean exportability.

The original discursive climate of Golden Age Spain, then, is an important element in any thorough explanation of the ways in which its cultural artifacts have proven so prone to acquire new resonances, interpretations, and uses for the Spaniards who would engage and deploy them since the early modern period. To be clear, this book does not articulate the claims of historical transcendence or cultural universality often attributed to Golden Age classics, such as those made in the twentieth century that persist in the discourse of cultural institutions to this day, but rather explores the history of those claims as a function of their accumulated cultural currency. Understanding this currency, I would argue, allows for the study of the classics' ongoing deployments in contemporary Spain to contribute to our broader understanding of the cultural economy in which they circulate. In short, this book revisits the Spanish Golden Age both as cultural production and as a cultural process, if we accept that the production of the historical concept of a *Siglo de oro* is itself continually evolving, contingent upon the needs of those invoking and deploying it and upon the communities who identify with it, but also inevitably reflecting the acquired "baggage" of its earlier uses.

The Spanish Golden Age: A Methodology

Anglophone Golden Age studies—or, as we are more likely to call the field today, early modern Peninsular Spanish Studies, Iberian Studies, or "Hispanism"—has for decades featured historicizing or neohistorical studies among its principal theoretical modes, the exhumation of the early modern archives to create an ever-expanding "thick description" of the historical context from within which Golden Age classics like *Don*

Quixote were created.[15] While Golden Age philology in Spain has engaged in recovering and providing cultural and linguistic context for the Golden Age canon since the nineteenth century, scholars elsewhere would join them (from diverse theoretical perspectives) in this work to recover information about early modern Spain in order to elucidate the classics in the final decades of the twentieth century. What these diverse approaches share, I would argue, is a synchronic mode of studying the material past adjacent to the curation of Lefevere's notions of textual and conceptual grids discussed above, but with a key difference: while Lefevere's "grids" are the translator's task for rendering the translated text accessible to contemporary (and often commercial) readers, this synchronic academic approach—even when practiced by "Golden Age enthusiasts" who would promote an appreciation of the classics in contemporary cultures—presumes that prevailing or popular understandings of the past, often transmitted through decontextualized transmissions of the classics themselves, lack the historical rigor or contextual "thickness" that such scholarship provides. This difference may appear to be minor in theory, but its realization in practice shows a fundamental divergence in orientation between one that orients the reader through historical analogies and relative equivalencies (through Lefevere's "grids") and one that supplements the reader's awareness of historical information that would otherwise be inaccessible to the reader and their contemporaries. Put more simply, Lefevere's "grids" aim to show continuity between author and reader, while much of recent Golden Age scholarship works against the contemporary cultural grain by identifying deficiencies in popular understandings of the cultural past in order to supplement them as a remedy. The critical introduction to a new printed edition of a literary classic, whether explicitly neohistorical (as is prevalent in Anglophone scholarship) or philological (as is prevalent in the Spanish Academy), inevitably aims to inform the reader of from whence (and from whom and where) the primary text came, presumably to foster a greater appreciation and deeper understanding of the text in question, but nonetheless to somehow correct the contemporary misunderstandings of the text that have resulted from lacking such contextual information. As I explain below, a key problem with this synchronic approach lies in its implicit assumption that the historical past can be recovered from the scholar's objective and

---

15 My use of the term "thick description" invokes its usage by Stephen Greenblatt and other scholars associated with the New Historicism in North America and with Cultural Materialism, its analogue in the United Kingdom. The term was originally coined by the cultural anthropologist Clifford Geertz.

ahistorical vantage point, as if modern scholars are not themselves limited by their own historical experiences and positionalities.

While this synchronic scholarship continues the important work of filling the gaps between early modern and contemporary cultures, this book posits the need to reflect more critically on how inseparable that transmission of information is from the modern academic contexts from which it is articulated. The very idea of an historically distant Spanish Golden Age hermetically sealed off from contemporary Spanish and Hispanic cultures is itself a problem, and for two principal reasons: first, it presumes an ahistorical and objective vantage point from which we may achieve a disinterested critical understanding of Cervantes and his contemporaries, and second, it implies that the meaning of the literary text is complete once it has been written and published, regardless of the kinds of overwriting and underwriting described by Unamuno at the beginning of this introductory chapter. This perspective implies a secondary, derivative status for new or alternate interpretations developed throughout the remarkable afterlife of Golden Age cultural artifacts—a delegitimization that is common in studies of literary and filmic adaptations, against which Linda Hutcheon argues persuasively in *A Theory of Adaptation*.

I argue that even if we were to succeed in the quixotic mission of analyzing Spanish Golden Age literature exclusively from a position of ahistorical omniscience and with a focus on its early modern production, we would still miss important aspects of what that literature means to Spaniards today, and what kind of cultural role it plays in contemporary Spanish society. The afterlives of these texts are driven by cultural, political, and economic forces that do in fact directly implicate students of contemporary Iberian cultures, insofar as we are interested or invested in the political, ideological, and cultural winds of contemporary Spain, and insofar as how we understand the Spanish Golden Age is directly impacted by how contemporary Spaniards understand it. Historicizing scholarship can only benefit from reflecting more critically on how it is inevitably, even if unwittingly, inflected by what has happened *since* the Golden Age. If these classics are often mechanized in contemporary political and cultural discourse, especially when cultural identities and political causes are at stake, we would do well to raise our awareness of the extent to which our work participates in those discursive contests.

In other words, the Spanish Golden Age is not over, and this book proposes that its diachronic study offers a unique and largely untapped source of insight into the often confusing state of cultural and political affairs in Spain today. In an era in which the bulk of scholarly attention is paid to the country's peripheries, in which the notion of "nationalism" is generally treated in the plural—as in Catalonian, Basque, or Galician nationalisms—deployments of the "Golden Age classics" offer a unique angle into the ways in which contemporary Spaniards across all of the nation's autonomous regions and cultures view their common cultural heritage—or, conversely, how they view a heritage imposed upon them by a colonizing Castilian hegemony that they disavow or resist.

While each invocation of the concept of a Spanish Golden Age is specific to the needs of its deployers and consumers, what they all share in common is an appeal to the cultural capital that it has acquired over the centuries (and continues to acquire) as a metonym for the very idea of Spain—an intrahistoric (if not anachronistic) notion of Spanishness whose reinforcement can be as explicit as a national holiday (such as the *Día del Libro* treated in Chapter 2) or as subtle as a "flagging" in the spirit of Michael Billig's *Banal Nationalism* (such as the impression of Cervantes's portrait on Spanish currency, or the naming of public buildings and spaces after Golden Age figures like Lope de Vega that I explore in Chapter 1). My reading of contemporary uses of the Spanish Golden Age, then, implies an understanding of culture not unlike that of George Yúdice's paradigm of "culture as resource," in which production is understood as more than the simple creation of commodities: cultural products, in this instance the texts that are now called "Golden Age classics," are extracted or "absorbed into an economic or ecological rationality, such that [their] management, conservation, access, distribution, and investment" become the objects of scrutiny (1). The aim of this book, then, is to outline the complexities and agencies of such cultural extractivism and to demonstrate their importance for understanding what the Spanish Golden Age means to (and can teach us about) Spaniards today.

The Spanish Golden Age: A Diachrony

This book's holistic focus on Spain comes at an opportune time for the field of Peninsular Hispanism or Iberian Studies, in which recent scholarship has overwhelmingly directed its attention to those centrifugal forces—e.g., globalization, peripheral nationalisms, gender identities, and ethnicities—that frame the notion of a single Spanish nation as tenuous and besieged. This predilection for pluralism and diversity has done important work since Paul Julian Smith voiced impatience in 2000 that Spanish Cultural Studies remained an underdeveloped field of study; we now better understand the complexities and tensions that inform ongoing economic, political, and cultural crises in Spain today, even as those crises and tensions have intensified and have grown more complex since Smith's complaint at the turn of the century. Given Spain's history within the last hundred years, it has been vital for Hispanists to study the nation's emergence from the Franco dictatorship with special attention paid to the peripheral identities and counterhegemonic cultural practices that the regime had repressed. Moreover, scholars operating under the diverse and multidisciplinary lens of Iberian Cultural Studies have assumed such a centrifugal focus in response to a tradition of scholarship, particularly in the realm of literary studies, that was complicit in this repression and marginalization of the voices and perspectives of Spanish cultural "outliers," as Luis Martín-Estudillo and Nicolas Spadaccini have argued, insofar as that tradition presumed a stable and culturally homogeneous Spain. The need to discover and tease out the cultural and discursive faultlines underlying a nationalistic master narrative of Iberian cultural cohesion is only greater in light of the fact that, especially in Spain, that narrative depended on "old assumptions in connection with the imperialistic and/or colonialist dynamics that supported many of the efforts associated with Hispanism" (7). The field's longstanding complicity (and indeed its investment) in the institutionalization of a monochromatic Spanish cultural history, which from a decolonial perspective could rightly be called a function of the coloniality of knowledge, explains the current splintering of Iberian Studies into the study of so many Spanish nationalisms.

In the wake of these important and necessary centrifugal efforts since the turn of the century, however, important critical voices have emerged to question whether the pendulum's pluralistic counter-swing away from homogeneity might be approaching its apex, and whether the time is right to rethink the very idea of Spain—an inherently centripetal question—in light of the newly recognized complexity and diversity that we continue to study. The work of scholars like Luisa-Elena Delgado and Cristina Moreiras-Menor have begun to ask the important question underlying this book: what does "Spain" mean when considered from this complex, contested, and reconfigured landscape? While no simple or single answer can account for the many voices and perspectives negotiating such a question, it does offer a useful direction for inquiry into the resonances and uses of the Golden Age in contemporary Spain, which in turn can delimit the cultural cacophony to a more concrete discursive field as its object of study.

The *Siglo de oro* is a convenient point of access to see how different individuals and communities sharing the label "Spanish" understand the very idea of Spain, and to see the extent to which any consensus remains amid the constant negotiation of peripheral nationalisms and marginalized identities, the demographic changes resulting from an immigration boom since the turn of the twenty-first century, and the economic and cultural tensions associated with integration into the European Union. This book examines the ramifications of these and other recent developments in Spanish society in the context of cultural production, both public (state sponsorship and subvention, cultural programming, and institutions) and private (media of the entertainment and publishing industries, tourism). While the Golden Age and its artifacts have enjoyed a long tradition of deployment by the Spanish government in times of calamity, the current era of seemingly perpetual economic crises poses new problems for realizing such an approach; conversely, the same cultural dependence on Golden Age revival in times of national emergency creates opportunities for private enterprise to feed this dependence for profit. Some of these privately funded efforts have proven more economically sustainable and profitable than others, which is itself a way of measuring the fickle and fluctuating appetites of Spanish consumers for all things *Siglo de oro*. As the cultural ground in Spain continues to shift, we may better understand its evolving and problematic nationalism(s) and implicit national, regional, and local identities by looking to how the classics are deployed in these cultural negotiations.

Looking at contemporary appropriations of the Golden Age classics seems at first to be a relatively straightforward project, oriented around such basic questions as which classics are being deployed, who is deploying them (and why), and in what ways are the original cultural artifacts adapted to work within the media of contemporary Spain and in order to appeal to a twenty-first century audience. These questions echo Linda Hutcheon's *A Theory of Adaptation*, in which she approaches the adaptation of an earlier cultural artifact as a process, so as to avoid the facile contrastive analyses that have traditionally dominated scholarship on filmic and televisual adaptations. For Hutcheon, the film adaptation is neither inferior nor superior to the original, but rather a product of a cumulative adaptive process that yields something altogether different, albeit necessarily defined by its dialogic relationship with its source material. Her approach informs this book's analyses of twentieth- and twenty-first-century adaptations of Spanish Golden Age classics in Spain, which are treated here as more than mere curiosities that previous generations of scholars would consider novel "distractions" from the more serious work of early modern historicized scholarship or the analysis of more "original" contemporary Spanish cultural production. I also argue that Hutcheon's model requires updating and qualification when applied to the Spanish Golden Age to account for the fact that, with few exceptions, the continual revival of early modern narratives over the centuries creates so many intertexts with which any new adaptation must engage.[16] This book supplements both historicized early modern studies and the study of contemporary cultural production by arguing for their interdependence, and by demonstrating the utility of literary classics as a kind of barometer for comparing discreet historical moments according to their usage.

Hutcheon's model for adaptation studies (i.e., adaptation as intertextual process) yields productive answers when applied to this book's object of analysis. For example, the animated film *El Cid: La leyenda* (2003), directed by José Pozo and produced by the Filmax animation company, invites the kind of process-oriented approach for which Hutcheon argues. Filmax takes the source material from Guillén de Castro's seventeenth-century *comedia*, *Las mocedades del Cid*, and adapts it to the codes and aesthetic sensibilities of the animated films of the Walt Disney Corporation. The fact that the animated *Cid* film targets an audience of young children makes the utility of Hutcheon's theory immediately apparent: the contextual questions guiding her approach lead us to identify not only the film's specific demographic target but also the process through which the Golden Age *comedia*'s content is encoded so as to appeal to that audience. While Castro's play focuses on the dilemma of balancing familial honor against personal desire, Pozo elides the violence and simplifies the conflict so as to present a more accessible case of good vs. evil. Complete with animal helpers, a would-be feminist Jimena and a slithery and emasculated antagonist, the Moorish king Ben Yussef, this film does at first glance lend itself to Hutcheon's process-oriented approach very well.

But when one digs deeper, the answers provided by such an approach are incomplete for a number of reasons, not the least of which is the revisionist history implicit in the film, particularly as it relates to the representation of the Muslim Other and the military and sexual violence that the Moorish antagonist embodies in the film. There is more to this cultural representation than would meet the eye if we were armed only with Hutcheon's "dialogic" approach, which presumably would be limited to the direct comparison between an original "source" and its adaptation.

---

16 Examples of such exceptions would include the recent discovery, editing, and publication of Lope de Vega's comedy *Mujeres y criados* by Alejandro García Reidy (and its subsequent stage production by the Fundación Siglo de Oro in several Spanish and American venues), as well as the numerous publications, translations, and stage productions of *comedias* written by women during the early modern period. In all of these cases, the cultural capital of the Spanish Golden Age is still central to their realization, but their recovery/discovery in recent decades means that they lack the same diachronic trajectory and accumulated significations as the narratives under scrutiny in this book.

In order to understand the cultural baggage beneath the surface, we need to weigh the Moorish Other's representation by Guillén de Castro against the playwright's Valencian identity—an identity with far stronger cultural ties to Al-Andalus than Castilians had ever experienced. Castro's play appeared in Madrid's public theater scene in an era when Castilian cultural hegemony over Valencia was relatively new, especially in the realm of theatrical praxis, in which a longstanding and thriving Valencian theater industry had only recently exercised a formative influence on a young Lope de Vega while he lived there in exile from Castile. Lope's development of an *arte nuevo* would eventually stimulate Madrid's eclipse of the Valencian industry and dramaturgy, and it would inspire a new generation of Valencian playwrights (including Guillén de Castro) to abandon their city, if not their native dramaturgy, for Castile. These internal early modern cultural tensions regarding regional and linguistic identities within the emerging Spanish nation are now better understood by scholars thanks to neohistorical and philological scholarship, and they undermine a Spanish cultural will-to-homogeny emanating from its Castilian center of political and economic power that motivated many of the ideologically conservative and culturally centripetal deployments of the Spanish Golden Age over the centuries, including those of the Franco dictatorship.

A full account of *El Cid: La leyenda* must also include cultural tensions in Spain tied to the presence of Muslim cultures in Iberia that predate the idea of Spain, that were exacerbated in Guillén de Castro's own lifetime by the *morisco* expulsion in 1609, and that persist today in the form of immigration from northern Africa. Between the Golden Age and the twenty-first century, a longstanding tension evolved regarding the place and displacement of Muslim communities in Spain, not to mention the many cultural representations of those communities. To understand the full cultural ramifications of this adaptation, we must take into account the longstanding obsession with *limpieza de sangre* [blood purity] in Spanish culture as one consequence of that tension, not to mention the fact that the Cid was the Franco regime's cultural icon of choice, which led to a cultural association with the regime's ideology and its essentialist notion of *Hispanidad*, with racial purity and with cultural fascism.

The problem is further complicated by a tradition of foreign adaptations of the Cid legend, from Corneille's *Le Cid*, which encoded the narrative into an emergent neoclassical mode of Tragedy in France, to Anthony Mann's film *El Cid* (1961) starring Charlton Heston, which reconfigured Corneille's presentation of Rodrigo as a conflicted hero torn between duty and desire according to the conventions of heroism specific to the midcentury Hollywood "epic" genre of films like *Ben Hur* and *Sparticus*. In what I call in Chapter 3 the legend's "repatriation," the Cid eventually returns to his country of origin after having acquired all of these different treatments, each version fully aware of and in dialogue with its predecessors, bearing vestiges of the discursive features circulating amid the increasing tides of globalism to the point of washing back ashore to the Iberian Peninsula, as if the Cid's patrimonial value has been internationally validated in the process. By the time the legend was picked up by Pozo and Filmax at the turn of the current century, an earlier repatriation had already been realized for young audiences: *Ruy, el pequeño Cid* was a one-season animated series written for Spanish public television (TVE1) but animated by the Japanese company Nippon Animation in 1980, effectively adding another layer of generic filtering (this time the visual representation and narrative structure of Japanese anime) to the legend's accumulated baggage. Pozo and Filmax developed a feature-length animated film based on a Cid legend that was inflected by all of these foreign discursive currents, which themselves reflected both a foreign perspective on Spanishness inevitably impacted by the so-called "Black Legend" and by the needs of foreign adaptors to "universalize" Rodrigo de Vivar for their international audiences and according to their own discursive contexts. The diachronic and cross-cultural evolution of the Cid's legend, in other words, is repatriated or comes back to Spain with new layers of signification acquired overseas, but also with the persistent autochthonous "Golden Age" cultural currency that had inspired the Valencian Guillén de Castro to write his *comedia* four centuries ago.

Accounting for the acquired layers of signification of a Golden Age text over time requires an approach that examines not only the early modern original text and its latest adaptation or redeployment, but all relevant points in between them as well. The Spanish Golden Age is treated here as a *diachronic* rather than a synchronic problem, with each revival of the period or its artifacts inevitably inflected by its previous invocations. Such diachronicity shares Hutcheon's goal of pushing the field of Cultural Studies beyond the implicit subordination traditionally associated with adaptation studies, in which adaptations are treated as approximations of original literary sources unworthy of our attention in their own right. This progressive approach, I would argue, actually works in the same spirit as neohistorical scholarship's thirst for contextual thick description—a quest which, as noted above, often finds itself working against the grain of popular (mis)understandings of Spanish history as it is at least in part acquired through the decontextualized circulation of the classics. In both cases, textual analysis aims to inform our understanding of the text and its dialogic relationship with the context in which it was produced. The adaptations of literary classics such as those studied in this book are more complex than those explicitly examined as case studies of adaptation in Hutcheon's book, because in the case of a work like *Don Quixote* it is not only the original text that is adapted, but also the tradition of adapting and interpreting it over the centuries since its original composition.

In short, what is needed to achieve this kind of diachronic perspective on the Spanish Golden Age is to be found at the intersection of historicized early modern scholarship and contemporary Cultural Studies. The emphasis of the former on what Louis Montrose has termed "the historicity of texts and the textuality of history" ("New Historicisms," 392) allows us to situate Spanish Golden Age literary texts in their original discursive and ideological contexts, which include considerable philosophical, economic, theological, and geopolitical upheaval (imperial expansion and economic crisis, the Protestant Reformation and Catholic Counter-Reformation, Renaissance Humanism, and the emerging Enlightenment, to name a few of many such elements), and in the more recent contexts of their adaptation and consumption, whether they be the culture wars of Enlightenment-era neoclassicism, nineteenth-century Romantic articulations of nationhood, the nostalgic conservative ideologies of the Franco regime, or the cultural polarization that led to the Civil War and that has returned in the twenty-first century. Historicized scholarship can inform our understanding of the functionality of Golden Age patrimony in constructing what Henry Kamen calls a "myth" in his book *Imagining Spain*—that is, as a projected narrative of historical, geopolitical, and cultural cohesion that was forged in early modern Iberia to provide ideological fuel to the State's efforts to rally its subjects around an ambitious imperial project, as scholars including Patricia Grieve, Barbara Fuchs, Anthony Cascardi, and even José Antonio Maravall have argued.

Thanks to recent historicized scholarship we now know more about the engagement of early modern literary texts with their original cultural contexts than ever before, which positions us well to address the role of the institutional stakeholders in cultivating the Golden Age's present-day conceptual grid, which in turn informs Spaniards' understanding of and experiences with their cultural patrimony. To be sure, my own professional and personal positionality as an Anglo-American male writing from an institution of higher learning across the Atlantic will place limits on the depth of experience that can inform my understanding of this patrimonial relationship, but I also benefit from the privilege of critical distance that this positionality affords me.

To illustrate the benefit of this critical distance, I would point to how political developments within Spain have invariably resonated in the work of philologists employed at Spanish universities. For example, what was seen at the time as a fundamental re-casting of the narrative through which the Spanish Golden Age was understood emerged just after Franco's death: the school of sociocultural analyses of early modern Spain instigated by José Antonio Maravall and José María Díez-Borque. Their post-Franco scholarship, which would profoundly influence a generation of Hispanists and continues to resonate in today's critical conversations on the topic, read Golden Age theater synchronically as a propagandistic tool of the emerging early modern Spanish absolutist state—not, as Spanish scholarship during the dictatorship would have it, as a populist expression of the very essence of *Hispanidad*. It is surely no coincidence that this new (and arguably more cynical) narrative would emerge just after the end of a regime known for media censorship and fascistic institutional control, as Spanish scholars during the transition to democracy participated in a broader reassessment of the cultural icons and symbols that had been deployed for decades at the service of the autocratic state. Perhaps once Maravall and his generation enjoyed the requisite civil liberties and academic freedom to critically examine the regime's use of the Spanish Golden Age and its cultural artifacts, they could not help but perceive a similar kind of ideological deployment at play in the seventeenth century itself; alternatively, one could argue that the participation of these scholars in their own cultural experience of the transition to democracy inevitably influenced their reading of cultural history. Franco's use of the Spanish Golden Age, as either narrative would have it, was a revival of the same utility for which it had been patronized by the monarchy in the first place. Simply put, the Spanish Golden Age came to mean something altogether different during the "transition" period, just as the very idea of Spain (and of being a Spaniard) evolved in complexity during the same period, and just as it continues to evolve in complexity today, after four increasingly turbulent decades of democracy.

At the same time as early modern Iberian Studies on both sides of the Atlantic have become increasingly informed by historicized research and perspectives, scholars in the field of contemporary Spanish cultural studies have expanded their objects of inquiry in ways that have led, albeit somewhat incidentally, to the critical scrutiny of some contemporary adaptations of the Spanish classics. Marsha Kinder's work on Spanish Cinema (in particular her seminal monograph *Blood Cinema*) reflects a broader awareness in the field of Spanish Cultural Studies of the presence of the Spanish Golden Age in contemporary Spanish culture and cultural memory: the object of her study, mid-twentieth-century Spanish Cinema, is informed by a kind of essentialist and atemporal (intrahistoric?) Spanish aesthetic involving melodrama, the blending of realism and fantasy, and cultural obsessions with ritual sacrifice—elements whose presence Kinder links to the Spanish Golden Age as if to prove their autochthony.

Kinder's use of the Golden Age in this way is symptomatic of much of the work in Spanish Cultural Studies at the turn of the current century that references the Golden Age—above all as a kind of "intrahistorical" depository of cultural symbols whose utility is defined by how they inform contemporary cultural production. According to Barry Jordan and Rikki Morgan-Tamosunas, this field of study examines "the sort of stories we pick up and tell each other about who we are" (3), which is to say that it reads culture (particularly in terms of the narratives selected and privileged by artists and consumers) as the site where local and national identities are forged, negotiated, and challenged. As Spanish Cultural Studies has blossomed into a dominant mode of scholarship in Iberian Studies, its methodological flexibility has increased to accommodate the kind of problems that this book addresses: a diachronic study of the afterlives of narratives written centuries ago. This flexibility permits us to learn more than was allowed by its earlier "presentism," a term used by Mariscal ("Can Cultural Studies Speak Spanish?," 237) to describe the field's bias toward synchronic studies of the "original" cultural production of a given period, or toward newly authored narratives arising as a consequence of contemporary circumstances.

The Spanish Golden Age: A Field

By presenting this diachronic analysis of the Spanish Golden Age, I join a growing chorus of scholars interested in the re-interpretations and re-castings of early modern Spanish cultural artifacts, most of whom have pursued this interest in the form of journal articles or published essays dedicated to a specific adaptation.[17] Monographs by Bruce Burningham (*Tilting Cervantes: Postmodern Reflections on Baroque Culture*) and Duncan Wheeler (*Golden Age Drama in Contemporary Spain: The Comedia on Page, Stage and Screen*) are two examples of scholarship taking deeper monographic dives into the complexities of the Spanish Golden Age in the twenty-first century, from very different angles. Among the most recent monographs sharing this terrain, Elena García-Martín's *Rural Revisions of Golden Age Drama: Performance of History, Production of Space* stands out for its attention to the experience of Golden Age patrimony within local Spanish communities, an approach that in this book informs Chapter 1's examination of Lope

---

17 For two outstanding examples of this scholarship on Golden Age, see Esther Fernández and Cristina Martínez-Carazo's article, "Mirar y desear: la construcción del personaje femenino en *El perro del hortelano* de Lope de Vega y de Pilar Miró," and Christopher Oechler's "Dictating Aesthetic and Political Legitimacy through Golden Age Theater: Fuente Ovejuna at the Teatro Español, Directed by Cayetano Luca de Tena (1944)."

de Vega's cultural footprint in local communities. The field of Golden Age *Comedia* performance studies, no doubt fostered by the journal *Comedia Performance*, has seen a steadily growing body of scholarship concerned with the theatrical production and reception of early modern Spanish cultural patrimony in the contemporary Hispanic world and beyond. This growing body of scholarship suggests that the academic bias against adaptation studies diagnosed by Linda Hutcheon in 2006, at least in the realm of Hispanism, is fading.

While the frequency and substance of adaptation studies tied to the Spanish Golden Age has increased substantially over the last decade, I would argue that the field's developing concern for contemporary adaptations and stage productions of Golden Age texts has not yet congealed into a concrete articulation of what Hispanism stands to gain from such studies. What remains to be done—and what this book aims to contribute—is the kind of panoramic study of the broader cultural currents affected by Golden Age cultural patrimony that can inform our readings of each specific appearance of a Golden Age classic, allowing us to see it as but one participant in an ongoing negotiation of a national cultural imaginary, through a shared conceptual grid constructed by the totality of this patrimony's contemporary uses. My underlying argument, then, is less a coherent narrative of one particular way in which Golden Age patrimony is utilized than it is an examination of the complexities involved in these cultural phenomena, and an argument for the promise of future studies to illuminate many of the vexing questions that continue to occupy the broader field of Iberian Studies. It plots the various ways in which the cultural authority of the Spanish Golden Age is used today, but through an historicized awareness of its use in the past, both during and since the early modern period, as part and parcel of any full account for the diverse and often contradictory purposes it serves in the present. Therefore, this book engages Hutcheon's mode of adaptation studies with Spanish Cultural Studies and historicized early modern Spanish Studies in order to forge a productive dialogue and fill the gap between synchronic (historicized) scholarship and the contemporary cultural deployment of Spanish Golden Age patrimony. Both the New Historicism and Cultural Studies are inherently elastic and flexible fields, and both attempt to situate text within context in a way that, as Patrick Brantlinger and others have argued, invites their comparison. The critical conversation in which this book participates is evidence of a field that is increasingly interdisciplinary, and that is increasingly occupied with pushing beyond the ossified divisions of Hispanism that developed over the course of the twentieth century. Among these inherited demarcations is the tendency of both contemporary and early modern Hispanists to conceive their work in only synchronic terms: even methodologically progressive publication venues like the *Journal of Early Modern Cultural Studies* established themselves primarily through scholarship that applied the methods of Cultural Studies to the early modern period in a synchronic fashion—that is to say, with less concern for how our modern-day experiences of Golden Age patrimony are invariably impacted by the ways in which this patrimony has circulated in modern (and postmodern) cultural contexts.

This myopia is itself a symptom of how, regardless of how progressive and current our theoretical vocabulary may be, the study of any culture's "classics" must swim against the cultural currents that made them "classics" in the first place—currents, that is to say, with a tradition spanning centuries of reverence and admiration for the cultural artifact and its creator. Cultural Studies counters this malady by examining the complex power dynamics within any given culture, and by urging that we move beyond the more traditional academic focus on producers of culture (authors, artists) and hegemonic cultural institutions so as to consider consumption as a form of agency and even resistance. Particularly since the end of Spain's dictatorship in the 1970s, this broader perspective on culture has led to our understanding of the complex array of global, national, and local forces involved in how Spaniards experience and participate in their national culture. As Ann Cvetkovich and Douglas Kellner have argued, globalization's full scope and cultural impact is only understood when studied at the level of local community experience.

An excellent example of this local/national/global dynamic may be found in the annual International Classical Theater Festival held in Almagro, a small village on the outskirts of Ciudad Real in Castile. The festival names itself *Internacional* and recruits production companies and theater troupes from around the globe, many of which filter their performances of Golden Age *comedias* through the cultural conventions and discursive practices of their cultures of origin; indeed, even Spanish productions in the festival are aesthetically informed by global theatrical practices, as evidenced by regular participating groups like the Joven Compañía [Youth Company], a pedagogically oriented offshoot of the CNTC. The festival forms part of a summer circuit of similar homages to Golden Age theater publicly funded and coordinated by virtually all levels of government, from the municipal to the national, as an effort to preserve and foster appreciation for the *Comedia* as Spanish national cultural patrimony. What becomes immediately clear upon attending this festival is the crucial role of local *cofradías*, schools, and even Almagro's small municipal government in the coordination and execution of the event. These local participants are essential to the festival's logistics in hosting a public of festival attendees larger than the town itself, and this small community has enthusiastically embraced and invested in the cultural experience it provides to that public, while also taking advantage of that patrimony to generate desperately needed tourism revenue.

In this way, this book's panoramic and diachronic study of the Spanish Golden Age examines the ever-increasing impact of globalization on autochthonous cultural production, accelerated in the digital information age, while recognizing both the importance of political, cultural, and economic forces in Spain and the value of studying the experience of this patrimony in local communities. As David Morley and Kevin Robins explain, "Globalisation is like putting together a jigsaw puzzle: it is a matter of inserting a multiplicity of localities into the overall picture of a new global system" (116). Their observations in the context of a globalized Britain in the 1990s are equally applicable to the context of twenty-first-century Spain, especially in terms of how local cultural experiences, including those with clear nationalistic implications, are packaged for consumption in globalized markets like the international tourism industry. Cultural Studies' "turn to consumption" has sparked greater interest than ever in the inherent complexity of distinguishing between the global, national, and local layers of cultural production, a problem with which Annabelle Sreberny and others have wrestled. This book's approach to patrimonial cultural production is meant to prompt the field to rethink how we can more concretely incorporate the local, national, and global dimensions of cultural production and consumption as inevitably intertwined but still discrete and distinctive dimensions of cultural life. For our purposes, Lawrence Grossberg's description of the work of cultural studies seems especially appropriate: "describing how people's everyday lives are articulated by and with culture, how they are empowered and disempowered by the particular structures and forces that organize their lives, always in contradictory ways, and how their everyday lives are themselves articulated to and by the trajectories of economic and political power" (4).

The Spanish Golden Age, Adapted

The complexities of contemporary cultural analysis noted above are certainly evident in the long line of cultural products and programming that provide the conceptual grid in which the Spanish Golden Age is consumed today—a grid as diverse (politically, ideologically, and culturally) and open to interpretation as is Spanish national identity itself. While in the nineteenth century the Golden Age constituted a set of classical texts whose adaptation or *refundición* was the battlefield in an ongoing culture war, and while in much of the twentieth century it was a favored source of narratives used to ideologically nurture the people according to a conservative mode of nationalistic reductivism, in the first decades of the current century we see the conceptual grid curated for the consumption of Golden Age patrimony as a continued practice by cultural institutions and agents, but with far less unanimity or consistency than in previous eras. Today the Spanish Golden Age is viewed from a landscape in which the line between fact and fiction, between truth and spin, are every bit as blurry as they were to Cervantes, as William Eggington has argued. Golden Age adaptations are still judged by some critics according to their "fidelity" to the original, but consumers of Spain's contemporary globalized media are now comfortable with eschewing such rigidity and accepting cultural products that bear much weaker resemblances to an original "source" cultural artifact, including works of historical fiction like the *Capitán Alatriste* novels that place contemporary narrative structures in a Golden Age historical context. Like Spain itself, the Spanish Golden Age is a more fluid, flexible, and contested cultural space than ever before.

This flexibility, I would argue, is less a matter of choice than of economic necessity; it stems from the need for economic and cultural sustainability within a society and economy shaped by the powerful forces of globalization, resulting in a process of repatriation or of reconciling this patrimony with those forces. While the literary artifacts of the Spanish Golden Age have been a mainstay of the tourism industry at least since the midcentury development period of the Franco regime, their incorporation into the mainstream media only began to gather cultural steam in subsequent decades. The regime's state-run television apparatus had broadcast a long series of televisual adaptations of Spanish and European "classical theater" under the title *Estudio 1*, but as Duncan Wheeler argues, the increasingly complex media landscape after the dictatorship would take some time to recognize the Spanish Golden Age as a viable consumer product. Children's cartoon versions of *Don Quixote* notwithstanding, the "high culture" of the classics had generally not been a particularly strong niche for the film and television industries until the 1990s—an ironic testament to how successfully and pervasively Franco had appropriated the symbolic value of the Spanish Golden Age.

Because of this lingering association with a regime whose memory was treated with caution by the new democracy, it would be nearly a decade before the entertainment industry's repatriation of the Golden Age classics could begin in earnest, carefully curated by the state through efforts like the creation of the CNTC in 1986. In 1991, an epic serial adaptation of *Don Quixote* was screened by Televisión Española [TVE], after years of development originally fostered under Pilar Miró, the director of the public TVE in the late 1980s and Directora General de Cinematografía [General Director of Cinematography] during the early years of Felipe González's presidency (1982–1996). The screenplay for the *Quixote* miniseries was adapted by Camilo José Cela and directed by Manuel Gutiérrez Aragón, in what might be called the "preservationist" spirit with which Golden Age classics were treated by the heavily state-subvented television and film industries during the initial transition to democracy. Pilar Miró's efforts would continue after leaving the state-run media, when in 1996 she directed the film adaptation of Lope de Vega's play *El perro del hortelano*. This film's commercial success and critical acclaim (including seven *premios Goya*) stimulated further cinematic adaptations of Spanish Golden Age narratives, including the picaresque novel *Lazarillo de Tormes* in 2000 and another *comedia* by Lope de Vega, *La dama boba*, in 2006.

These more recent film adaptations, however, reflect a changing cultural landscape in which Golden Age classics are often approached more innovatively, albeit with mixed results. Both adaptations suggest a stronger influence of the contemporary cinematic codes and conventions through which their original literary texts are filtered, as Chapter 3 will explain. To borrow a concept from Stuart Hall, the adaptations are "encoded" in contemporary cinematic conventions in order to better match the contemporary Spanish public's frames of reference. The title of the *Lazarillo* adaptation is appropriately changed to *Lázaro de Tormes* as the protagonist's famous childhood is narrated by him as an adult and woven into a romantic plot that has little to do with the original picaresque text. In order to produce the sympathetic male hero with whom the viewer can identify, the ironic presentation of a paranoid and dishonored cuckold in the original is replaced with an honest, hardworking young man whose oral testimony of his *mocedades* [youthful exploits] entertains the town's children, woos the beautiful woman who would become his wife, and even liberates him from legal jeopardy. Despite the shady arrangement of their marriage inherited from the original novel (arranged by an *arcipreste* as a cover that would allow her to continue her illicit affair with him), Lázaro's oral performance of the novel's later *tratados* in court eventually wins her heart and procures his acquittal of unspecified charges. As we will see in Chapter 1, Manuel Iborra's 2006 adaptation of *La dama boba* works in a similar spirit by creatively filtering Lope's original *comedia* through the codes of the contemporary Hollywood romantic comedy, with an emphasis on the female protagonist's attainment of a "happily ever after" marriage after a coming-of-age experience that features her sexual awakening and fulfillment.

This trend in the current century of more creative or "loose" Golden Age adaptations being more overtly shaped by the codes and conventions of contemporary media is especially evident in children's entertainment, such as the Filmax adaptation of the Cid legend noted above (and to be examined further in Chapter 3), in which the tried-and-true formulae of Disney's animated films adjust the medieval legend to more familiar territory for a young Spanish audience raised on American entertainment. Along similar lines, Filmax's *Donkey Xote* (2007) features Rucio, Sancho Panza's famous *asno*, in a style of animation that makes no effort to hide the influence of Hollywood: promotional posters and DVD cases feature the statement "De los productores que vieron *Shrek*" [By the producers who saw *Shrek*]. The influence extends to the film's narrative, in which Rucio's "impossible dream" is to someday be a horse, as he helps Don Quixote defeat the *Caballero de la Blanca Luna*—only to discover that this apparent antagonist is in fact Dulcinea herself in disguise, an echo of Tirso de Molina's cross-dressing *Don Gil de las calzas verdes* and countless other Golden Age *comedias* that featured women assuming male identities to access the agency that early modern Spanish society denied to their gender. In *Donkey Xote*'s climactic scene, Rucio realizes his dream by serving as Don Quixote's horse in a joust that Dulcinea had organized as a test of Don Quixote's merit and loyalty. This intertextual dialogue between Cervantes's classic novel and the animated films of Pixar and Dreamscape is but one of many recent examples in which Golden Age narratives are repatriated via a discursive reboot for savvy consumers of the global children's entertainment industry.

If the practice of assuming a less "archaeological" reverence and taking greater creative license with Golden Age narratives constitutes a trend in more recent adaptations and repatriations, it also prompts us to rethink what the Spanish Golden Age means to Spaniards, young and old, as the Spanish entertainment industry continues to develop and compete on a global scale. Films "Made in Spain" still do not generate the majority of the country's box office revenue, but the current cultural interest in all things *Siglo de oro*—an interest both curated and fostered by Spanish cultural institutions and media industries—is implicated in the efforts to close the gap. The Spanish film and television industries, which since the 1980s have evolved in an economically multinational and discursively globalized direction, have repatriated Golden Age narratives through the conventions of popular Hollywood genres in a long list of examples beyond those already noted here, including the biopics *El Greco* (2007) and *Lope* (2010), with striking parallels between the latter and *Shakespeare in Love* (1998) that I have studied elsewhere.[18] The *Capitán Alatriste* novels set a very contemporary

---

18 Robert Bayliss, "Lope enamorado: Patrimonio cultural y cine posnacional." *Hispania* 98.4 (2015): 714–25.

blend of intrigue and action in the remote period of the seventeenth century, where well-known historical events and figures interact with the fictitious title character as he solves a series of mysteries and protects Spain from its enemies. In television this taste for the Spanish Golden Age is no less evident, as evinced by series such as *Isabel*, *Águila Roja*, and *El Ministerio del Tiempo* and feature-length productions like *Cervantes vs. Lope* and the film adaptation of Arturo Pérez-Reverte's *Capitán Alatriste*. Further complicating this landscape of Golden Age Spanish cultural production is the development of production studios in Spain by multinational streaming services, including Netflix (which funded the final seasons of *El Ministerio del tiempo* after its cancellation by TVE) and Amazon (which produced two seasons of its original series *La leyenda del Cid* in 2020-2021). While the critical and commercial success of these "Golden Age revivals" has been inconsistent, it is beyond question that they reflect a cultural turn to history that is itself tied to complex questions surrounding historical memory, a cultural and political problem with which the field of contemporary Spanish cultural studies continues to grapple.

The Spanish Golden Age: An Argument

This book articulates what I call the "currency" of the Spanish Golden Age, a reference both to the present-day meanings or interpretations being applied to the period's literary texts—in other words, how Spaniards currently understand them—and to the cultural and symbolic capital conveyed upon them by being inscribed in its cultural narrative—their function as a kind of currency denoting value that can be monetized, as when copies of commemorative editions of *Don Quixote* are sold, or when money is invested in its adaptation to film or to theatrical performance. This diachronic, historically informed study of the Spanish Golden Age as it has come to be understood in contemporary Spain attends to the myriad local, national, and global forces informing that currency. While every chapter takes into account the complex matrix of these cultural forces, each one will focus more heavily one area of the equation—the local in Chapter 1, the national in Chapter 2 and the global in Chapter 3. Taken as a whole, they demonstrate the potential for future scholarship in all three dimensions, along with the importance of considering them in tandem as we work toward a better understanding of their interconnectedness.

Local experience is the point of departure for Chapter 1 ("Lope de Vega and the Performance of Spanishness"), which focuses on Golden Age theater and the figure of its "founding father" and most successful playwright, Lope de Vega. Even during his own lifetime, Lope's name constituted a brand of excellence that extended beyond the theater industry—a point emphasized by the 2016 exhibition at Madrid's Casa-Museo Lope de Vega [House and Museum of Lope de Vega] with the slogan *Es Lope*, which the organizers' website explains as a reference to the seventeenth-century phrase *es de Lope* ["It is of Lope," or "as good as Lope"] used to denote "todo aquello que era 'muy bueno'" [all things that were "very good"].[19] Lope's name and likeness are so diffuse in contemporary Spain as to invite comparison with Michael Billig's notion of "banal nationalism": each passing reference to the playwright constitutes a subtle "flagging" whereby Spaniards are reminded of their nation's Golden Age—and by extension, their own place in that cultural legacy. Beyond the long tradition of educational and cultural programming to celebrate the *fénix*, the continued presence of "the Lope brand" is ubiquitous on the level of daily experience in the names of public spaces and private businesses in local communities throughout Spain, but especially in his native Madrid.

Set in the midst of such local pageantry, the performance of Lope's most canonical *comedias* has remained one of the few constants in Spanish culture during the last two centuries, even when paradoxically used to argue both sides of a contentious debate. Among the most compelling Spanish productions of *Fuenteovejuna* in this century, for example, are those involving local causes, especially in the case of the small rural town from which the play takes its name. Fuente Obejuna's regular production of the play in its town square, like the similar example of the annual classical theater festival in Olmedo (the setting of Lope's famous *El caballero de Olmedo*), demonstrates the ways in which Lope's cultural capital is leveraged to celebrate local identities and to generate tourism revenue during increasingly challenging economic times.

Lest we lose sight of how these local deployments are not immune to Spain's increasingly polarized political landscape and culture wars, I would cite the controversy in the summer of 2023 surrounding a planned performance of Lope's *La villana de Getafe* in Getafe (a Castilian *villa* now incorporated into the larger metroplex of Madrid): after a preview of Marcos Toro's production, with a set design featuring unambiguous phallic and vulvar sculptures and a homoerotic performance that included a passionate kiss between two female characters, local municipal government officials from the alt-right Vox party banned the production as an inappropriate public spectacle.[20] While similar prohibitions by conservative local officials across Spain of films and public

---

19 https://casamuseolopedevega.org/en/activities/recitals-and-shows/94-actividades-en/historico-de-actividades-en

20 "Vox pide retirar 'un falo y una vulva de considerable tamaño' de la obra de teatro 'La Villana de Getafe' de Lope de Vega." https://www.elmundo.es/madrid/2023/07/04/64a3b66be9cf4a343d8b45a1.html

art expositions had become too numerous to count that summer, the Getafe injunction against *La villana de Getafe* stood out for journalists and cultural critics for its symbolic cultural significance: local conservative governance had gone so far in its campaign of censorship as to ban Lope de Vega. In a public statement during the controversy, a statement from Vox defended the prohibition: "Resulta incomprensible por qué se ha decidido perverter la obra de teatro de Lope de Vega, la cual en ningún momento incluía este tipo de escenas en las que, además, han participado niños" [It is incomprehensible why it was decided to pervert Lope de Vega's play, which never included this kind of scene in which, moreover, children are present].[21] For his part, Toro defended his production on social media, "con ánimo de abanderar un pacto político que proteja y refuerce el tejido cultural de nuestro país" [with the motive of championing a political agreement that would protect and reinforce the cultural fabric of our country].[22] Regardless of where one falls in this polemic, this recent example shows us how cultural controversies and flashpoints only grow more intense when the cultural patrimony of the Spanish Golden Age is invoked.

In order show how the use of Lope as a kind of brand name synonymous with "Spanishness" takes on even more striking implications for local identities when studied in the context of competing peripheral nationalisms, Chapter 1 also examines the cultural dynamics at play surrounding recent performances of several of his plays in the autonomous region of Valencia. These performances reveal how the Valencian community embraces both a local autonomous culture and a geopolitical "Spanish" identity: Lope's five-year residence in Valencia while in exile from Castile allows the community to celebrate its own contribution to the multicultural tapestry of Spanish national identity through its self-inscription in the conceptual grid of Golden Age patrimony. The inherently political nature of modern theatrical production (most often dependent on local and national governmental support) and the inherently ambiguous political function of the theater in the seventeenth century converge in Spain to make Golden Age theater a powerful political and cultural tool. At the same time, as has been made clear with cinematic adaptations of *La dama boba* and *El perro del hortelano*, the contemporary revival of Lope's work is fraught with the cultural baggage acquired through its previous deployments, particularly during the Franco

---

21 Paula Baena, "Vox denuncia que el Ayuntamiento de Getafe exhibe un pene gigante en una obra de Lope de Vega para niños." https://okdiario.com/madrid/vox-denuncia-que-ayuntamiento-getafe-exhibe-pene-gigante-obra-lope-vega-ninos-11222131

22 https://twitter.com/MarcosToro5/status/1676460882178588674

regime—a nationalistic association between Golden Age theater and the Falange that continues to impact the performance and reception of his work, and against which cultural institutions like the CNTC must contend.

If the first chapter focuses on the "local," Chapter 2 ("Don Quixote, Made in Spain") emphasizes the "national," by way of the Spanish Golden Age's strategic deployment by various cultural agents to project an image of national cohesion across its diverse autonomous regions, and in turn for the sake of Spain's cultural image abroad. I argue that this dual engagement with Cervantes's masterpiece to project national cohesion and coherence both internally among Spaniards and externally to the outside world is no coincidence, but rather a reflection of the consubstantial nature in Spanish history of colonial expansion and national actualization. Simply put, since before the existence of any political entity resembling what we now call Spain, the acquisition of territory through military conquest of a non-Christian Other has been linked to the consolidation of identities and interests into a coherent and unified community. In this way, the construction of a conceptual grid in which to experience *Don Quixote* echoes the medieval geopolitical narrative known as the *Reconquista* [Reconquest], which to this day remains a cultural narrative used in right-wing political discourse to explain the birth of the Spanish nation.[23] *Don Quixote*'s use in modern Spanish history entails service to the Spanish state both in articulating a national character or essence (see Unamuno above) and in presenting *Hispanidad* for foreign consumption. This foreign-and-domestic usage is not unlike the parodic presentation of folkloric stereotypes used to sell Spain in Luis García Berlanga's classic 1953 film *¡Bienvenido, Mr. Marshall!*, in which a small *pueblo* in Andalucía becomes so committed to presenting a simulacrum of Spanishness to attract foreign investment that it actually transforms itself into the representation it was asked to project.[24] In keeping with this pattern, Spain's experience of globalization effectively turns the projected image of Spain as seen from without into a reflective and self-affirming cultural narrative that informs national identity.

Cervantes's novel has been appropriated by and adapted to every medium of communication available, from the painter's canvas to the silver screen. While it shares with Golden Age theater a rich legacy of political engagement, such as Pablo Picasso's famous rendition of the knight errant and his

---

23 See Marc Esteve del Valle and Julia Costa López for an analysis of Vox's use of the *Reconquista* trope in Spain's 2019 elections.

24 Justin Crumbaugh elaborates on this reading of *¡Bienvenido Mr. Marshall!* in his book *Destination Dictatorship: The Spectacle of Spain's Tourist Book and the Reinvention of Difference*.

sidekick (sketched while in exile due to his own leftist political affiliations), it furthermore has been an important piece of propaganda for a nation that struggled throughout the twentieth century to establish its place in the legacy of Western culture. The English term *quixotic* is indicative of how globally pervasive the literary figure of Cervantes's protagonist has become, and it reflects a more general global perception of Spain as unique, paradoxical, and idealistic. This perception was carefully crafted during the dictatorship's midcentury *desarrollismo* or period of development in the 1960s, and its continued deployment since the establishment of democracy is illustrative of the inextricable linkage between Spanish national identity and the image of itself that Spain has chosen to disseminate in the global marketplace (again, through the collective local experiences such as are the subject of Chapter 1). An examination of several film adaptations and the character's evolving role in cultural programming and promotional materials connected to the tourism industry—culminating in the 2005 and 2015 anniversary celebrations of the novel's publication—makes clear that Don Quixote's symbolic value persists, if in a more complicated way as Spanish national identity is itself complicated by economic and political crisis, integration into the EU, the ascendency and legitimization of autonomous peripheral nationalisms, and increasing levels of immigration.

The third and final chapter ("Repatriating the Cid: Spanish Cultural *Reconquista* in the Era of Globalization") elaborates on these complexities by studying how the "classics" have remained an enduring force in print, film, and televisual media in the context of globalization. While the focus in Chapter 2 on the "national" implies the "global" in terms of *Don Quixote*'s role in projecting an image of Spanishness abroad, this chapter takes a more explicitly global focus in its tracing of the literary figure of the Cid, an originally medieval creation immortalized by Guillén de Castro's Golden Age play *Las mocedades del Cid* (first published in 1618) that has undergone a wide array of international transformations, as is discussed above, before being repatriated in Spain. The 2001 animated film *El Cid: La leyenda* filters the legend through the discourses and conventions popularized by the Walt Disney corporation, while an ongoing popular Spanish live-action series "Made in Spain" for Amazon Prime, *La leyenda del Cid*, demonstrates the increasingly slippery identity of "Spanish" cultural production in the digital age. These adaptations invite an examination of how the patrimonial value of the Golden Age is capitalized in a global economy, and how the industries involved in contemporary cultural production dictate the terms of that conversion.

More importantly, this chapter suggests the inherent complexity of Spain today as it comes to terms with its fascist past while also embracing a transnational European (as well as a trans-Hispanic) identity, itself a tenuous negotiation of the various pressures of the international community, multiculturalism (as understood in both foreign and domestic contexts), and post-Franco peripheral nationalisms. That the global film industry has spawned a Spanish production of the Cid (Franco's favorite literary figure for purposes of political appropriation) in which the legend's traditionally Christian-nationalist narrative is innocuously "Disneyfied" in an adaptation targeting young children is indicative of the extent to which the global marketplace and its implicit strategies of representation have increasingly muddied the waters of Spanish cultural patrimony, presumably for profit. This chapter argues that a number of other Golden Age-themed film productions since 2000, in the era of what is often called "postnational" cinema, reflect how Spain's notions of cultural patrimony and identity are inextricably linked to the discursive currents of globalization. These currents and the Golden Age artifacts that circulate through them are further complicated by the recent trend of historical fiction set in the Golden Age, including the biopics *Lope* and *El Greco*, the Shakespeare-Cervantes comedy *Miguel y William*, the best-selling *Capitán Alatriste* novels, and popular television series like *Isabel*, *El Ministerio del Tiempo*, and *Águila roja*.

These narrative repatriations participate in a broader relationship between Spain and its Golden Age that is as old as the nation itself. Its continued evolution is increasingly unforeseeable and often contradictory, not unlike Spain's political and economic stability. As the quotation from Henry Kamen cited above suggests, Spain is and will forever be obsessed with the period, less because of anything that actually happened or was produced during it, and more because it projects a myth of natural unity and ontological stability that seems increasingly less connected to the political and cultural tensions that Spain and its autonomous regions are experiencing today. The nation's desire for unity and national identity, to the extent that such a desire exists, is projected nostalgically on the Golden Age, despite the fact that the very notion of a Spanish Golden Age as we understand it today did not actually exist in early modern Iberia. At the same time, the Golden Age is capable of representing both a jingoistic national essence and the Castilian cultural hegemony against which peripheral positionalities are articulated. The *Siglo de oro*, then, truly can be said to function as a mirror to contemporary Spanish society, just as Lope de Vega argued of his *comedias* in the seventeenth century, at the conclusion of his treatise known as the *Arte nuevo de hacer comedias en este tiempo* [*New Art of Writing Comedies in These Times*]—before "these times" had become "those times," and an object of nostalgic reflection posthumously bedazzled with the "golden" and "classic" attributes that we now use to define it.

Humanae cur sit speculum comoedia vitae,
quaeve ferat juveni commoda, quaeve seni,
quid praeter lepidosque sales, ex cultaque verba
et genus eloquit purius inde petas,
    quae gravia in mediis occurrant lusibus, et quae
    jucundis passim seria mixta jocis;
    [...]
    Oye atento, y del arte no disputes,
    que en la comedia se hallará modo
    que, oyéndola, se pueda saber todo.
[Lope de Vega, *Arte nuevo de hacer comedias en este tiempo*, ll. 377-82, 387-89]

[Comedy is a mirror of human life,
Showing the truth of both young and old,
Offering subtle wit crafted with words
From which the species speaks more purely,
What grave matters should be shown,
With what pleasure here and there mixed with mirth;
[...]
Listen carefully, and do not dispute this art,
that in Comedy a way will be found
so that, hearing it, you can know everything.]

CHAPTER ONE

Lope de Vega and the Performance of Spanishness

An article appearing in *La vanguardia* in July 2015 announced a formal recognition of *hermanamiento*—what in the U.S. would be called a relationship as "sister cities"—between Almagro and Fuente Obejuna, based on the two communities' shared identification with Spanish Golden Age theater, known in Spain simply as *teatro clásico*, and in particular with its most famous practitioner, a *madrileño* named Félix Lope de Vega Carpio. In this press release, Fuente Obejuna's mayor, Silvia Mellado, explained the decision to formalize the intermunicipal relationship as based on "los lazos que nos unen culturalmente gracias a Lope de Vega y al profundo amor que ambos pueblos sentimos por el teatro" [the ties that unite us culturally thanks to Lope de Vega and the deep love that both communities share for the theater].[1] During the waning years of the Franco regime, architects unearthed an authentic seventeenth-century *corral de comedias* in Almagro, a small Castilian village near Ciudad Real, and in 1978 the village began hosting a classical theater festival featuring the restored *corral* that has continued uninterrupted, all the while attracting ever-increasing numbers of international tourists, for the last four decades. The even smaller Andalusian village Fuente Obejuna, situated near Córdoba and best known as the setting of Lope de Vega's famous tragicomedy *Fuenteovejuna*, has featured "locally sourced" amateur productions of the eponymous play since the 1990s. In 2015 this quintessentially local production, "*Fuenteovejuna* en Fuente Obejuna," was performed for the first time outside of the village—in the Almagro festival. As *La vanguardia* explains, Fuente Obejuna hopes to leverage this newly formalized relationship with Almagro as it attempts to organize and launch its own classical theater festival in the near future. Mellado explains this development as a logical next step in her community's

---

[1] http://www.lavanguardia.com/cultura/20150701/54433662244/almagro-y-fuente-obejuna-se-hermanan-a-traves-del-teatro.html

"apuesta por la cultura como base sólida para la prosperidad de los pueblos" [bet on culture as the solid base for the prosperity of these people].

Such a cultural (and theatrical) turn by these local communities reflects more than mere resourcefulness in the face of ongoing national economic crisis and dwindling federal funds for local municipalities, although the choice of the term *prosperidad* does reflect the fact that their celebration of Spanish Golden Age theater has resulted in significant material gain. But even if we were to accept the cynical premise that local municipalities are merely cashing in on the classics, their cultural supply only functions according to popular demand, both within those communities and among the thousands of Spaniards who flock to them each year in order to see their classics performed at their uniquely "authentic" venues. Beyond the regular appearance of Golden Age *comedias* in metropolitan theaters across the country, the people of Spain (and a smaller but growing number of international theater enthusiasts) now fill seats at a series of similar festivals each summer in towns such as Mérida, Olmedo, Olite, and Alcalá de Hernares. Almagro's infrastructure, which for 50 weeks each year supports only its regular population of 9,000, is stretched beyond capacity each July as upwards of 60,000 people attend the festival. Clearly these small communities have converted the cultural capital of the Spanish Golden Age into an economic capital dispersed across all economic strata, from taxi drivers to business owners, but especially to those connected with the tourism industry. Betting on culture, to borrow Mayor Mellado's phrase, has proven to be good business.

This chapter will attempt to explain this demand for classical Hispanic theater by focusing on its most prolific and popular playwright, Lope de Vega. After situating contemporary Spanish appetites for all things Lope, the study of his most canonical play, *Fuenteovejuna*, will show that its evolving performance history reflects a broader cultural history informed by the extreme political turmoil that has seen the Spanish government oscillate from secular democracy to religiously doctrinaire dictatorship and back again. Because *Fuenteovejuna* was consistently deployed as a celebration of Spanish cultural patrimony at each point of this tumultuous political trajectory, each performance or adaptation adds a layer of complexity to the diverse ways that contemporary Spaniards have come to understand the play and its author, as each cultural generation inherits not only Lope and his works, but also all of the uses of his name and works that have occurred in the intervening years. With each new production of *Fuenteovejuna* in contemporary Fuente Obejuna, we will see, a new layer of meaning is grafted onto this evolving narrative—a layer through which the footprints of previous adaptations are reshaped to speak to contemporary local concerns, most recently concerning the role and treatment of women in Spanish society.

"Made in Spain": The Lope de Vega Brand

In an article published in the Spanish newspaper *El mundo* in January 2015, Ramón Valdés and Elena Di Pinto describe 2014 as a banner year for enthusiasts of Lope de Vega in Spain, despite the fact that no official cultural programming had been designed to make it one. "Y de repente llegó un Año Lope de Vega. Así, espontáneamente y por coincidencia, sin programarlo ni planearlo, sin sociedades conmemorativas ni presidentes de honor, 2014 se convirtió en un Año Lope de Vega" [And suddenly the Year of Lope de Vega arrived. Spontaneously, and by coincidence, without cultural programming or planning, with neither commemorative societies nor honored presidents, 2014 became a Year of Lope de Vega].[2] Celebrations of Lope (also known for centuries as the *fénix de los ingenios* [phoenix of geniuses]) organized by the Spanish state and its public academic institutions to commemorate anniversaries, birthdays and other such milestones have remained constant as far back as the Golden Age itself, when three days of national mourning were declared to commemorate his death in 1635. This kind of public adulation is not unique to Lope, as evidenced by similar celebrations of other prominent cultural figures from the period like Cervantes, Velázquez, and Calderón.

Valdés and Di Pinto express surprise at the spontaneous nature of this flurry of performances and celebrations of all things Lope in 2014, as Spanish cultural programming was expected to be fully engaged with preparing for important anniversaries related to Cervantes in 2015 (the 400th anniversary of the publication of *Don Quixote*'s second volume) and 2016 (the 400th anniversary of his death). An important element in the unexpected "year of Lope" was the publication (by Alejandro García Reidy) and performance (by the Fundación Siglo de Oro, under the auspices of the Biblioteca Nacional) of the lost play *Mujeres y criados* [*Women and Servants*], the first of several Lope-centered events that year. A number of other high-profile productions of other Lope plays by both Spanish and foreign theater troupes continued throughout the year, both during the summer theater festivals and in other urban venues by various theater troupes, including the CNTC.

This *año Lope de Vega* included a special exhibition at the Casa-Museo Lope de Vega, located at the house in Madrid's *barrio de letras* [neighborhood of letters] where Lope had lived for decades. The exhibition was titled "Es Lope," which its curators from the RAE describe as a play on the old expression,

---

2 https://www.elmundo.es/cultura/2015/01/08/54ae3f4522601d21278b456c.html

es de Lope, used since Lope's own lifetime to denote high quality and cultural prestige.[3] And while the average *madrileño* may not use that phrase in the twenty-first century with the same regularity, the name "Lope de Vega" still circulates in contemporary Spanish culture in a similar vein, to communicate quality and high cultural prestige.

But unlike its use during his own lifetime, Lope's name now communicates something much more powerful and complex. According to those who invoke it, the cultural capital invoked with his name represents cultural authenticity, national pride, and even the essence of Spanishness. However, any such invocation of Lope also bears with it considerable ideological and political baggage, for this association of his name with Spanish identity is not new. Appeals to the cultural capital of the "Lope brand" made by previous generations of Spaniards, including those made during the Franco regime, are inevitably awoken with each new revival. The very meaning of Lope's name is a site of contest, where different understandings of Spanish identity and history compete. If we can study the uses of Lope and his works according to this pluralistic dynamic, and if we can situate the development of that dynamic historically, we can arrive at a better understanding of the many mixed messages for which his name is used to communicate in the current century.

To be sure, contemporary usage of the name "Lope de Vega" is considerably varied, sometimes in explicit acknowledgment of him and other times not. The more banal, incidental, or casual uses occur as contemporary Spain's inheritance of a proper name grafted into the very DNA of the state's infrastructure long ago, as with addresses, buildings, and businesses that bear the name of the *fénix* because at some point *since* the Golden Age itself, someone stood to gain something from using his name in this way. But regardless of how deliberately one names him, and regardless of how directly one thought of the man behind the phrase *es de Lope* in earlier centuries, the currency of Lope's name and image in contemporary Spain serves as an excellent case in point of the ever-evolving, enduring legacy of the Spanish Golden Age. In many ways, this legacy mirrors the phenomenon in other developed Western nations that Michael Billig has termed "banal nationalism," the effect of subtle reminders in everyday life of national identity, but it also points to how Billig's term needs to be updated in order to account for the often contradictory uses and interpretations of Lope and the Golden Age itself in contemporary Spain.

A Google image search of the name "Lope de Vega" will yield a stream of images that at first glance appears incoherent and random: digital renderings

---

3 http://www.rae.es/la-institucion/iii-centenario/es-lope

of traditional portraits of the poet are intermingled with PowerPoint slides of student projects, merchandise for sale, covers of published editions of his works... and with images of schools, theaters, small businesses in Spain and Argentina, buildings, statues, and street signs. Google does not discriminate between what we might consider "valid" and "invalid" search results, and as such it affords an unfiltered view of all of the ways in which Lope's name circulates. As with other important Golden Age figures and names from other bygone eras, like Cervantes and Cisneros, Teresa de Ávila, and Isabel la Católica, some images simply appear because they refer to places that happen to be located on a street or plaza bearing the name Lope de Vega. The fact that Lope's name floats through cyberspace in such incidental ways reflects the fact that Spain has regularly chosen to name its urban spaces after cultural figures who refer to an earlier era of cultural splendor, the memory of which is invoked to remind its citizens that they are Spanish, much as Billig describes. However, because nationalism of this "banal" kind prescribes a certain implicit narrative of what the word "Spanish" means, any interruption of that narrative or change in narrator can shatter the illusion of its ordinariness or banality.

Cultural narratives of Spanish identity have certainly evolved over the centuries, and the political tumult suffered by Spain in the twentieth century led to dramatic developments in that evolution with consequences that are still felt today. But amid these cultural-narrative twists and turns, references to the Spanish Golden Age remain a reliable constant. And while that fact might speak to the enduring power of the *Siglo de oro*, in other words while the incidental presence of Lope's name in contemporary Spain might prompt us to read his works with an eye to better understanding that presence, it can also be a useful barometer of contemporary Spain itself in all its complexity. When decades or even centuries have passed since commemorating Lope by engraving his name on a public plaque, and the people involved in that naming have passed as well, what remains is more than just his name in a street address: all of the cultural baggage that informed that naming, all of the cultural value ascribed to that name when it was chosen and since it was chosen remains as well.[4]

As Billig explains, banal nationalism tends to hide in plain sight, for example when one sees a national flag above a public building or square, and that "visible invisibility" itself constitutes a powerful but subtle means of reinforcing national identity. Undoubtedly, a beer served at the *Restaurante Lope de Vega* will taste the same as it would at the bar next door; in fact, this

---

4 Marc Gil Garrusta and Jaime Subirana examine the naming of public spaces in Barcelona from a more political perspective.

casual dropping of Lope's name is no more conscious than is connecting the word "America" to its original namesake, Amerigo Vespucci, when "God Bless America" is sung during a baseball game in the U.S. However, while one does not enter *Frenos Lope de Vega* looking to replace her car's brake pads by technicians who speak in verse, and homebuyers do not choose a property on the *Calle Lope de Vega* because they expect their lives to be more filled with amorous intrigue or because they think it will make their posted mail appear more culturally sophisticated, the effects of repeatedly reading and hearing these "banal" utterances of Lope's name (as part of a wider grid of Golden Age references of similarly "banal" circulation) do contribute to the often unconscious ways in which daily life in Spain reinforces its citizens' cultural identities through references to intangible cultural patrimony. Important cultural "work" is done by the continual utterance of his name in such incidental and subconscious ways, which Billig would describe as "flagging": "Daily, the nation is indicated, or 'flagged', in the lives of its citizenry. Nationalism, far from being an intermittent mood in established nations, is the endemic condition" (6).

Billig's argument works against the trend of scholarship in recent decades to treat nationalism as a peripheral phenomenon, in other words as a movement used to establish emerging national identities or to inspire peripheral nationalist movements within established nations. Research on contemporary Spanish culture has certainly seen its fair share of this kind of analysis, from Jaine Beswick's study of Galician language policy and politics to a recently published volume of essays edited by Richard Gillespie and Caroline Gray entitled *Contesting Spain? The Dynamics of Nationalist Movements in Catalonia and the Basque Country*. While the reasons for such a peripheral focus are clear as Spain continues to redefine itself as a modern democracy after four decades of anti-periphery dictatorship, Billig's work reminds us that the notion of "Spanish nationalism" did not die with Franco:

> [N]ationhood provides a continual background for their political discourses, for cultural products, and even for the structuring of newspapers. In so many little ways, the citizenry are daily reminded of their national place in a world of nations. However, this reminding is so familiar, so continual, that it is not consciously registered as reminding. The metonymic image of banal nationalism is not a flag which is being consciously waved with fervent passion; it is the flag hanging unnoticed on the public building. (*Banal Nationalism*, 6)

Treating the Lope brand as a kind of "flag" makes sense from a synchronic perspective, and during extended periods of political stability and ideological continuity (for example, in Spain during the 1950s and 1960s), the uses of his name and works likely acquired a degree of orthodox predictability that would be described very well by Billig's definition.

Because Billig associates banal nationalism with established Western nations, however, it can also be seen as a mode of culture-as-resource (as George Yúdice would describe it) reserved for the exercise of hegemonic nationalism, without allowing for contested uses of the would-be banal. The "metonymic image" of the flag "hanging unnoticed on the public building" assumes the exercise of the flag's symbolic capital by corporate and institutional forces that can ultimately be traced to the State itself. But when the State's government is overturned or replaced, as was the case various times during the twentieth century in Spain, the national flag itself—and more to the point, the Lope brand—will take on multiple and contradictory meanings, as when during the post-dictatorship *transición* Spaniards debated whether to keep, revise, or scrap the national flag that had hung unnoticed on public buildings for so long, and indeed now as the flag's use by the far right political party Vox has made the most elementary national symbol a divisive and polarizing one. Several decades earlier, the flag of the Second Republic would have perhaps flown unnoticed for a few years before the outbreak of civil war, but the Nationalist victory converted that once banal image into a prohibited symbol of resistance. In contemporary Spain, even before Vox the national flag was no less contested, and thus no more "banal," as evidenced by its highly politicized use in communities with significant peripheral nationalistic movements like Barcelona, where the Catalonian national flag (a symbol of Catalonian autonomy and nationalism) is far more commonly displayed than is the Spanish flag. To be sure, the Spanish flag is still displayed in public spaces where legally prescribed and also by private citizens with clear pro-Spain or anti-independence political allegiances, but in such instances its presence is a kind of "marked" banal nationalism—marked because it stands in contrast to (and perhaps in protest of) the more commonly and enthusiastically displayed flag of Catalonia. Even beyond the autonomous regions in which Castilian hegemony is challenged by peripheral nationalist movements, the Spanish flag has come to be a polarizing symbol across the nation, as Javier Moreno Luzón and Xosé M. Núñez Seixas explain.

These cultural symbols, in other words, lose their banality and attract considerable notice when their political context changes. Lope de Vega and indeed the Spanish Golden Age are no different: the extent to which the classics are associated with the hegemony will certainly influence their meaning (and thus their usage) after that hegemonic power is replaced. In this way, Spain's so-called *pacto de olvido* or implicit agreement to heal the wounds of the civil war and dictatorship by focusing on the future (as opposed to prosecuting the past) does inform how we should understand the cautious and tentative use of Lope and the Spanish Golden Age during the transition to democracy and into the current century. Indeed, it would not be until the establishment of the CNTC in 1986 that concrete steps would be taken by the new democracy to support an appreciation for Golden Age theater and to return it to the arena of banal political symbolism.

The value of Lope de Vega as a brand name in the twenty-first century is actually the end of a long process that begins with, to borrow a term from Pierre Bourdieu, the *consecration* of his name by public institutions to denote high cultural achievement. While national and nationalistic celebrations of Lope in Spain date back to his own lifetime (or at least his death), their politicization and nationalistic deployment would accelerate considerably in subsequent centuries, from the eighteenth-century "culture wars" of the theater industry (in which the orthodoxy of French neoclassical theory would be embraced by some while denounced by others as Lope's "heterodox" works continued to be performed), to the nineteenth-century debates of *casticismo* and campaigns to support the *refundición* of plays by Lope and his contemporaries over more fashionable foreign plays,[5] through the early twentieth-century Socialist/Nationalist divide and beyond. In all of these conflictive historical moments, Lope and other Golden Age artists were continually held as models of an autochthonous and authentic national spirit whose deployment was meant to correct the corruption of Spanish identity by foreign cultural and political influence. While today's politics and media landscape are very different in comparison to those of the previous century, this tradition of associating the Spanish Golden Age with authentic Spanishness continues to inform its public reception as it filters through popular culture to become part of a faithful repository of prestigious names (again, like Cervantes, Calderón, Velázquez) that Spaniards invoke when they want their street, business, or building to plug in to an underlying sense of Spanish identity associated with the name. Lope de Vega is, in a word, monumental.

This monumentality becomes more strategically important when the name is used more deliberately than accidentally, especially when used to denote high culture in the Arts, as in the numerous *teatros Lope de Vega* throughout the Spanish-speaking world or even the numerous schools named after him, such as Madrid's Instituto Lope de Vega. It is logical, for example, that a school would use Lope's name to connote higher learning

---

5 See Charles Ganelin for a deeper dive into nineteenth-century *refundiciones* of the *comedia*.

and academic achievement: Lope was a famously gifted man of letters who claimed to have written his first play as a young child. As we will see, however, the saturation of his name during periods of political turmoil can have its own negative consequences, according to the political fate of those political parties or movements that deploy it.

The most straightforward use of Lope de Vega's brand of monumentality consists of the public spaces that have been dedicated to his name and memory. By placing Lope's portrait alongside his name in a public square, park, or street, the municipal, regional, or national governments in Spain make an explicit connection between that location and the cultural capital associated with the Lope brand. While there is much to be said about this connection in and of itself, and Cultural Studies have produced ample tools to do so—Bourdieu's notions of consecration and symbolic cultural capital, Robert Harbinson's notion of monumentality and Billig's banal nationalism, to name a few—what is often less attended to about these Lope-branded statues, plaques, and plazas is how, in their more deliberate efforts to plug into Spanishness via the Golden Age, they reinforce and are reinforced by the more incidental uses of his name. State consecration of the name leads to its "banal" deployment, which in turn leads to Spaniards seeing or hearing it in their everyday lives. In this way, each time a child walking by *Frenos Lope de Vega* asks an adult "Who is Lope de Vega?," a perfect teachable moment is presented: *Lope de Vega is one of Spain's greatest poets. He was a famous playwright from the Golden Age. The Golden Age was hundreds of years ago, when Spain was the world's great superpower and its cultural achievements were without equal.* This kind of cultural education is literally institutionalized in standards dictating the curricula of the nation's primary and secondary schools, just as no Spaniard escapes his *colegio* without having read or watched some version of *Don Quixote*. And so goes the self-fulfilling prophecy of cultural programming, that Lope's name is everywhere, because it is important; Lope must be important, because his name is everywhere.

While the Lope brand is most ubiquitous in Madrid, the city where he lived (when not in exile) and where he oversaw the reinvention of the early modern Spanish theater industry, it is instructive to step outside of the capital to see how Lope's brand works in more peripheral communities in Spain. To a certain extent, Lope's name appears with less frequency according to how far from the center of the peninsula one looks. There are a number of reasons for this phenomenon, but one is that Lope wrote more plays about Castile than about anywhere else. Hence a number of local communities featured in *comedias* written by Lope have embraced his legacy to support their own economies and identities. (We will see below that Olmedo is a perfect example of this phenomenon.) On the flip side of this question of proximity, communities farther from Madrid are more likely to choose Golden Age figures tied more closely to their own communities, such as Guillén de Castro in Valencia.

In many ways Billig's notion of banal nationalism aligns well with the ways in which Spaniards are subtly reminded of their national identity, even if that identity finds itself continually debated and even if it means very different things to different people. What is decidedly different about Spain, however, is that in the autonomous regions with strong peripheral nationalist movements like Catalonia and the Basque region, even the banal can stimulate resistance and controversy. The 2010 World Cup is a case in point: the victory of the *selección española* (the term used to describe the team of Spaniards assembled to represent their country) appeared to offer a point of cohesion and unity for a nation in turmoil and economic crisis, as upwards of 75,000 citizens watched the final game in the streets of Barcelona, the city with the most intense peripheral-nationalist tensions at the time and from whose professional soccer franchise the majority of the *selección* were drafted into (Spanish) national service. Multiple news outlets, both foreign and domestic, quoted elderly Barcelona residents observing that they had not seen so many Spanish national flags since the Nationalist victory there at the end of the Civil War in 1939. Controversy did arise when in a postgame press conference the Catalonian defender Carles Puyol choose to answer a question, asked in Catalonian, in that other "Spanish" language—a political choice that was met with immediate pushback from some of his Castilian teammates, especially the Real Madrid star Sergio Ramos. These tensions were later satirized in the film *Fe de etarras* [Bomb Scared] (2017), a dark comedy in which four Basque would-be terrorists witness the national solidarity of the World Cup victory and ultimately abandon the attack they had been planning.

The use of Lope and other staples of the Spanish Golden Age could ostensibly be similarly charged in such contexts, as those cultural symbols of "Spanishness" run the risk of representing Castilian hegemony in environments where that hegemony was once imposed at the expense of more local identities. If we accept Luisa Elena Delgado's premise that Spain's political and media industries project a fantasy of a singular Spanish nation by way of an assumed "culture of consensus" that excludes the "non-consenting" members of its communities (in other words, voices contesting the hegemony for economic or political reasons), the symbols and artifacts of the Spanish Golden Age might be perceived as tools of Castilian cultural hegemony and thus be met with dissention by communities who reject or resist that hegemony. But while Lope is staged and commemorated more in Madrid than outside of Castile—he is a "hometown hero," after all—his plays are still staged regularly in Barcelona and throughout the peripheries of Spain, and my research yields no evidence of any peripheral nationalist movement protesting or boycotting a production of a Golden Age play. To be sure, occasional lighthearted spoofs of the classics appear in Spanish media. José Mota's satirical pieces for Spanish national television (RTVE), in which Mota assumes the character of Francisco de Quevedo as a pompous buffoon, play off of the same cultural trope of the so-called *código de honor* [honor code] that is frequently associated with traditional Spanish values; the carnivalesque stage production *Siglo de Oro, Siglo de Ahora* by the company Ron Lalá connects the political and economic crises of early modern Spain with those of the twenty-first century; and the parody of Golden Age theater by the Galician comedians "Mofe e Befa," which highlights centuries-old stereotypes of Galicians as an inherently submissive people, made its debut outside of Galicia at the 2015 Almagro festival. But beyond these benign parodic satires, non-Castilian Spain remains far more interested in the Spanish-Castilian Golden Age than it is in promoting the Spanish national flag.

El valenciano Lope de Vega

A good case in point of this dynamic is Valencia, where we see efforts to link the local community to its own native contributors to the Spanish Golden Age. Without a doubt the favorite Golden Age son of the city is Guillén de Castro, whose name is infused in the city infrastructure in many ways that are similar to how Madrid brands Lope's name: major city streets (a *carrer* or street and an *avenida*), parks and gardens, schools, health care centers, and small businesses adopt the name "Guillén de Castro" in an effort to commemorate Valencia's contribution to Spanish Golden Age theater, and to make the locale more explicitly grounded in the history of its community. These efforts do not stop with such local celebrities, however, as the names Cervantes and Lope de Vega also appear on the city grid—Cervantes as a street name and Lope as a Plaza.

Indeed, Lope de Vega has a special connection to the Valencian community, as he resided there for a number of years while exiled from Castile. Because this cosmopolitan Mediterranean city enjoyed a thriving theater community at the time of Lope's residence, and because his theatrical output increased in both quantity and quality after his stay there, it is presumed that Lope was inspired by the Valencian theatrical scene and its creative blend of influences from throughout the Mediterranean world. The fact that Lope wrote at least two famous *comedias* set there, *Los locos de Valencia* and *La viuda valenciana*, does not simply reflect his fondness for the city: it also has become a staple of local efforts in Valencia to stage Golden Age *comedias* and has served as direct evidence of Valencia's value to Lope and all of the cultural capital his name conveys. In Valencian cultural programming and in the local press, then, Lope would not be Lope were it not for his connections with Valencia; by extension, Spanish Golden Age theater (if not the Golden Age itself) would not have been possible were it not for Valencia's contribution to it. Celebrating the national Spanish cultural legacy of the Golden Age becomes an opportunity to highlight its local Valencian components. Taking a step back, we can say that Lope's Valencian presence is but one compelling example of a local community's contribution to the mosaic of people and cultural products spanning the diverse cultural and linguistic communities across the Iberian Peninsula that collectively construct the Spanish Golden Age. It is also a telling example of how, because of this cultural and linguistic diversity, the conceptual grid built around the Golden Age will invariably engender local customizations and variations according to the publics for whom it is curated.[6]

A closer look at this Valencian appreciation of Lope is worthwhile, because it allows us to move past the standard theater industry data from the two major metropolitan areas of Barcelona and Madrid that are often taken to represent Spain as a whole, an important point when trying to understand how questions of Spanish nationalism and national identity have become increasingly complex in the era of autonomous regions and constitutional democracy, and especially when trying to understand the experience of contemporary Spaniards on the local level. The problem of disproportionate emphasis on Madrid and Barcelona has been recognized by Duncan Wheeler[7] and is true of most twentieth-century Spanish theater studies working through the lens of Cultural Studies, but the complexity of contemporary Spanish national identities is especially true of theatrical activity during the democratic period following the Franco dictatorship.

It is only by "thinking locally" in understudied places like Almagro and Fuente Obejuna that we can move beyond these thornier questions: if each region of Spain experiences its own unique cultural dynamic between regional and national self-identification, as Sebastian Balfour and Alejandro Quiroga have argued, a more localized focus on a particular region would presumably provide insight into the specifics of how its people understand

---

6 See, for example, Alejandro Martí's article for the Valencian edition of the newspaper *Las Provincias*, "La huella del Siglo de Oro en las calles de Valencia." https://www.lasprovincias.es/planes/huella-siglo-20190820171802-nt.html

7 This point is discussed in detail in the first chapter of Wheeler's book *Golden Age Drama in Contemporary Spain*.

themselves as both a part of and as distinct from the traditional concept of the Spanish Nation. Valencia's unique connections to the *Comedia*, as the home to Lope de Vega during his exile in the late 1580s and early 1590s and the site of a thriving local theater industry preceding him, can provide important insight for our inquiry, as a community with a language and cultural identity that is clearly not Castilian, but that also has not experienced the same extreme politicization of the field of cultural production as one finds in regions with stronger peripheral nationalistic movements, like Catalonia.[8]

During his stay there, Lope witnessed emerging modes of theatrical activity that had not yet reached Madrid, often from Italy. Valencia's cultural activity has always been impacted by its function as a major international port with close ties to Italy, as has its political relationship with Castile at least since the eleventh century, when the Cid famously participated in its *Reconquista*. Despite its implicitly essentializing understanding of history, Valencian historians and tour guides will invariably note that Valencia is in fact older than Spain (it was founded by the ancient Greeks, before the Roman colonization of *Hispania*). This dynamic is both central to its more recent local revivals of Golden Age theater and indicative of how Valencian identity is inherently fluid, a question under constant cultural negotiation.

To be sure, Valencia has its own history of political nationalism and even separatism, but such elements have never translated into the kind of majority popular support for political or cultural autonomy that characterizes other regions. A number of surveys and polls conducted in recent years consistently find that by and large, Valencians are more likely to understand their identity as both *valenciano* and *español*, and especially among younger citizens they are more likely to choose *español* over *valenciano* if forced to do so (Balfour and Quiroga, 198). These questions of identity predictably extend to the realm of language, as *valenciano* and *castellano* are interwoven in cultural and educational programming in a way that is far less contentious than is the case to the north in Catalonia. Indeed, since *valenciano* is often classified as a southern dialect of *catalán*, efforts to distinguish a discreet cultural identity in Valencia as separate from Catalonia often appeal to a *lack* of the tensions with Castilian hegemony that have characterized Catalonian nationalism, at least in terms of popular support. In other words, in an effort

---

8 Alfons Cucó explains that while Valencian nationalism has existed for centuries, it has never generated sufficient public support like in Catalonia. In fact, tensions with Catalonia may help explain the disparity: because of Catalonia's own attempts to have *valenciano* be classified as a dialect of *catalán*, Valencian nationalism has asserted its right to autonomy against both Spain and Catalonia.

to resist the emerging cultural gravitational pull of *catalanismo*, Valencia is less resistant to the gravitational pull of Castilian cultural hegemony. This dynamic directly informs how public and private cultural programming in the city of Valencia approaches the *Siglo de oro*, especially as it relates to its most famous temporary resident from that era, Lope de Vega.

When Lope arrived in Valencia in the late 1580s while in exile from Castile, he encountered a thriving local theater industry at a time when his own career as a dramatist had only recently begun. While there is little disagreement that *comedias* like *La viuda valenciana* and *Los locos de Valencia* reflect Lope's fondness for and intimate knowledge of the city, there is less of a consensus as to the nature of his relationship with its burgeoning theatrical scene. Did Lope and his prolific talents come to Valencia and inexorably change its theatrical landscape, or did Valencian dramatists offer Lope a model that he could bring back to Madrid and for which he would claim credit as the inventor of an *arte nuevo*?

Answers to such chicken-and-egg questions regarding the flow of influence between Lope and Valencia depend on whom you ask. Rinaldo Froldi's seminal study from the 1960s, *Lope de Vega y la formación de la comedia: en torno a la tradición dramática valenciana y al primer teatro de Lope* [Lope de Vega and the Formation of the *Comedia*: Valencian Dramatic Tradition and the First Theater of Lope], makes a thorough and compelling philological case for reading Lope's experience in Valencia as pivotal in his own dramaturgical development, for both formal and cultural reasons. Froldi's scholarship reveals that in the decades preceding Lope's arrival, the Valencian theatrical scene had developed its own *corrales*, had begun shifting its performances linguistically from *valenciano* to *castellano*, and most importantly, it had already made the transition from a more private and elite *teatro cortesano* [court theater] to the kind of spectacles for a socioeconomically diverse public that we now associate with the (Castilian) Golden Age *Comedia*. Revisiting Froldi's argument in light of today's cultural circumstances in Valencia is instructive: for example, his philological approach effectively demonstrates that the same Valencian linguistic pluralism noted above (that the Valencian people move between *castellano* and *valenciano* without the same political acrimony that often characterizes language policy in Catalonia) was true in the sixteenth century as well, when Joan Timoneda and his contemporaries began composing plays in *castellano* for the Valencian *corrales*, not to mention Timoneda's printing of books in *castellano* destined for a wider Iberian audience. Melveena McKendrick takes a more nuanced approach to the chicken-and-egg, Lope-Valencia question but recognizes the validity of both perspectives.

Like McKendrick, I would argue that the lack of clear and documented evidence ultimately makes this question unanswerable, but I would add that it also creates room for interpretation by interested parties in either direction—and that process of deploying Lope to articulate twentieth- and twenty-first-century identities, whether Spanish or Valencian, is precisely where we can see the benefits of "thinking locally" about the *Comedia* and contemporary Spain. The national and even international *culto del fénix* [cult of the phoenix] that credits Lope for inventing the *Comedia nueva*, in other words the tendency to read the Spanish Golden Age through the lens of Castilian cultural hegemony, would have us believe that Lope's exile allowed him to experiment and hone his craft in observance of a peripheral and more primitive theatrical scene before rebooting his career in Madrid at the turn of the century. He watched and learned from the Valencian theater and then reformulated that information into his own work, which was being sent back to be performed in Madrid for a commission. This Castile-centered narrative of the *comedia*'s development would thus consider Lope's contemporary Valencian dramatists to have been capable but not-so-original artists who were fortunate enough to have been inspired by the *fénix*, a fact that probably resonates with standard Hispanist narratives about the history of Spanish Golden Age theater. We would do well to remind ourselves, however, that the classification of such dramatists as Guillén de Castro and Cristobal de Virués as members of a "school of Lope" was made neither by those playwrights nor by Lope himself. Like the very notion of the Spanish Golden Age, this subordination of Lope's Valencian contemporaries was a narrative forged retroactively by scholars from subsequent centuries eager to present a coherent vision of a Spanish national theatrical tradition in which all regional variants stem from the *metrópoli* of Madrid, Lope's hometown.

While it is tempting to read against the grain of this Spanish nationalistic narrative and construct an alternative local Valencian narrative, I find even more revealing the fact that Valencian scholars and government officials involved in cultural programming have *not* chosen to do so. At the regional branch of the Centro de Documentación Teatral in Valencia and in the municipal archives of the city, my search for evidence of resistance to Castilian cultural hegemony by Valencian nationalists, or indeed any voices that would contradict the subordination of its local classical theatrical traditions to those of Castile, was continually frustrated by what I read as instead a very comfortable identification with this subordinate relationship. In other words, rather than reject the appropriation of Valencian artists and culture into a narrative constructed at the service of Castilian cultural hegemony, all evidence points to *valencianos* highlighting their local early modern theater as an essential ingredient of the Spanish Golden Age, as if the saffron to the paella of Spanish culture. The city's place in Lope's biography is in this way a natural point of local pride because of his trans-Iberian and global importance.

As in many places throughout Spain, the name "Lope de Vega" functions as a powerful brand for marketing a wide array of products, goods, and services in Valencia. The location where Lope is supposed to have lived during his time there is now named the Plaza Lope de Vega, and just as is true in many places throughout Spain, his name is used to sell hotel rooms, language classes, and countless other goods and services. But more focused attention on the recent theatrical scene shows an interest in promoting both native Valencian dramatists, especially Castro and Virués, and Lope himself. Productions of *comedias* composed by native Valencians are clearly advertised as points of local pride, or as homegrown contributors to the Spanish Golden Age, but these locally born and raised playwrights receive less attention than Lope himself. Even when public money from the Valencian municipal government is at stake, Lope's national prominence trumps any local celebrities, as in this example posted in a local newspaper:

> Sabéis que siempre estamos pendientes de publicar opciones que nos permitan disfrutar de nuestro tiempo de ocio a buen precio, y en esta ocasión lo hacemos para los valencianos y amantes del teatro. Este año se festeja el doble aniversario de Lope de Vega (de su nacimiento y de su obra "La dama boba") y la Conselleria de Educación, Cultura y Deporte, y el Consorcio de Museos de la Comunitat Valenciana lo van a celebrar con dos representaciones gratuitas.[9]

> [You know that we are always looking to publish opportunities to enjoy our free time at a good price, and on this occasion we do it for Valencians and lovers of the theater. This year marks the double anniversary of Lope de Vega (of his birth and of his play "Lady Nitwit") and the regional Ministry of Education, Culture, and Athletics, and the Consortium of Museums of the Community of Valencia will celebrate with two productions free to the public.]

It is not surprising that *Los locos de Valencia* and *La viuda valenciana* have been staged with the greatest frequency in Valencia; these productions are normally presented in press releases and publicity with titles such as *Lope de Vega regresa a Valencia* [Lope de Vega Returns to Valencia], *Vuelve Lope de Vega a la ciudad del Turia* [Lope de Vega Returns to the city of the River Turia], and

---

9 https://www.compradiccion.com/otros/valencia-celebra-el-doble-aniversario-de-lope-de-vega-con-representaciones-teatrales-gratuitas

so forth, with the understanding that any Lope production is to be seen as a kind of homecoming. Both plays were written within five years of Lope's time there, but probably from Castile.

Celebrating productions of *Los locos de Valencia* is especially attractive because the play allows us to be reminded that the mental asylum in which the action takes place, founded in 1409, was the first of its kind in Europe and for centuries a model for those that followed it. And while the plot of *La viuda valenciana* may not seem as culturally specific, a case can be made for reading its erotic content as a fond recollection of the playwright's own alleged escapades in Valencia: the title character (a widow) has a strapping young *galán* repeatedly delivered to her chambers blindfolded, so that she can have her way with him without revealing her identity. The Ayuntamiento de Valencia found such content to be absolutely appropriate to celebrate, as evidenced by its own publicity for a 2008 production:

> ¿Has hecho el amor alguna vez con los ojos vendados y sin saber con quién?, ¿Te han rondado tres hombres al mismo tiempo?, ¿Has gozado un carnaval lleno de romances enmascarados, enredos eróticos y lances arriesgados con enigmáticos contendientes?
>
> Lope de Vega vuelve a su casa valenciana 400 años después. A principios del XVII la primera sala teatral de Valencia "el corral de la olivera" estrenó, en vida del propio Lope, esta comedia llena de sensualidad ambientada en Valencia. La obra es un canto a los sentidos, un grito feminista, un susurro de palabras bellísimas. En definitiva, cultura con letras mayúsculas, teatro grande. Una cita ineludible con nuestra historia.
>
> La Compañía de Teatro Clásico El Corral de la Olivera (primera Compañía de Teatro Clásico valenciana) se presenta en nuestra ciudad con este sugerente y encantador espectáculo que hará llegar al gran público los grandes clásicos del Siglo de Oro.
>
> ¡¿Quién ha dicho que los clásicos son aburridos?![10]

[Have you ever made love blindfolded and without knowing to whom? Have three men ever surrounded you at the same time? Have you ever enjoyed a Carnival full of masked romances, erotic intrigues, and dangerous duels with mysterious rivals?

Lope de Vega returns to his Valencian home 400 years later. At the beginning of the seventeenth century the first Valencian theater "the corral of the olive tree" debuted, during Lope's own lifetime, this comedy

---

10 https://documentacionescenica.com/banco/archivos/Prensa_La_Viuda_Valenciana.doc

full of sensuality set in Valencia. The play is an enchantment of the senses, a feminist calling, a whispering of beautiful words. Definitively, culture in capital letters, great theater. A date with our history that can't be missed. The Classical Theater Company "The Corral of the Olive Tree" (the first Valencian classical theater company) presents itself to our city with this suggestive and enchanting spectacle that will bring the great classics of the Golden Age to the broader public.

Who said that the classics are boring?]

El Corral de la Olivera is the first "locally sourced" Valencian theater troupe to dedicate itself exclusively to *teatro clásico*, so named after what was allegedly the city's first permanent *corral*, established in the early sixteenth century.

Rather than imply that Valencians remain willfully subordinate to Castilian hegemony more than 40 years after the end of the dictatorship, I would argue that Valencia and especially its municipal government and local media have instead tried to call attention to the fact that their culture is an essential ingredient of a national Spanish culture. This attitude seems to be the most common among print and online media sources, as exemplified by the following bit of literary history provided by journalist Carmen Velasco for *Las Provincias*:

Aquí [Lope] aprendió a desobedecer la unidad de acción narrando dos historias en vez de una en la misma obra, el llamado embrollo italiano. Dos años después se marchó a Toledo con lecciones aprendidas y ya lejos de Valencia recordó los años en la calle Comedias, donde acudía a los corrales de teatro, y su etapa valenciana le inspiró en su madurez obras como "La viuda valenciana" o "Los locos de Valencia."[11]

[Here Lope learned to disobey the unity of action narrating two stories instead of one within the same play, the so-called Italian *embroglio*. Two years later he departed for Toledo with lessons learned and then far from Valencia he remembered his years on Comedy Street, where he attended the theater *corrales*, and his Valencian phase inspired in his matured career plays like "The Widow of Valencia" or "The Crazy Valencians."]

Without Valencia, the story goes, there would be no model to inspire Lope and therefore no Golden Age dramatic tradition to speak of. The culture of this port city has always identified itself as a Mediterranean crossroads

---

11 http://www.lasprovincias.es/v/20131105/culturas/lope-vega-regresa-valencia-20131105.html

with particularly strong ties to Italy. Scholars like McKendrick and Froldi have established that it was in Valencia where Lope was likely to have first encountered the elements of Italian theatrical practice and literary traditions that so informed his body of work, and today Valencia seems to embrace its pluralistic cultural identity with pride. Unlike the more polarized and popular Catalonian nationalist movement, Valencians generally see their identity as not an either/or proposition, and they are happy to hold up the example of Lope de Vega as a case in point. Thus, while the Catalonian nationalists' 2018 campaign for secession from Spain featured the slogan "Catalonia is not Spain," Valencian cultural programming seems to be more interested in reminding us that Spain would not be Spain without Valencia.

Thinking (even more) Locally, Situating Historically: *Fuenteovejuna*

While theaters across Spain are named after Lope de Vega and his Golden Age contemporaries, there are other specific locales that speak to the cultural and economic power of the Lope brand. Ocaña, for example, has leveraged its own name recognition via the literary canon, as the titular setting of Lope's famous play *Peribáñez y el comendador de Ocaña*, to promote the arts and especially to generate tourism revenue. Ocaña's Teatro Lope de Vega, located on the Calle Lope de Vega [Lope de Vega Street], is the center of cultural activity in this village near Toledo, and their centuries-old association with theater has resulted in its being the site of an annual *Festival de Teatro Universitario* [Festival of University Theater]. Moving north to Castilla-León we see similar Golden Age and especially Lope de Vega branding. In Valladolid there is another Teatro Lope de Vega, first opened in 1861 and recently renovated. Nearby, the much smaller village of Olmedo seems to have embraced its own association with Lope to the extreme. Beyond adding a classical theater festival to the summer circuit discussed above, Olmedo's infrastructure has embraced Lope's brand perhaps more extensively than anywhere, with a wide array of buildings (including the Palacio Caballero de Olmedo) and small businesses making reference to the play that put the town on the proverbial map. These businesses include restaurants making reference to the play's cast of characters like *Los Caballeros*, *El Caballero de Olmedo*, and *La Cueva de Fabia*, hotels like the *Hostal Don Alonso*, retail venues like *La Tienda Lope de Vega*, the retirement community *Residencia El Caballero*, and the florist *La flor de Olmedo*, the last of which echoes the famous *coplas* [couplets] that foreshadow the protagonist's death in Lope's play.

As noted at the beginning of this chapter, Fuente Obejuna is another small community that has leveraged its place in the legacy of Lope's theatrical output, and thus the literary and cultural canon, for rallying its citizens to a common local identity. In the last two decades the village has staged the play in its town square with funding provided by the municipal government and featuring local residents in all aspects of production. The municipal government website (fuenteobejuna.es) even features links to information about Lope and the play, both to inform residents of their local cultural legacy and to inform prospective visitors that yes, this place is *that* Fuenteovejuna, despite an alternate spelling of its name. In a series of articles and in her more recent monograph, Elena García Martín has analyzed this phenomenon during the twentieth century in Fuente Obejuna, Zalamea, and the region of Soria (location of the ruins of Numancia, the inspiration for what is perhaps Cervantes's most famous drama). A clear pattern emerges: while we know that the brand name of Lope and his Golden Age contemporaries like Cervantes has served as a powerful political and ideological tool on the national level, these local uses point to the complexity of such branding, and how they ultimately contribute—again, as pieces of a larger national mosaic—to the larger narrative of the Spanish Golden Age in Spain today.

Fuenteovejuna dramatizes the medieval uprising of a rural village against its tyrannical and sexually predatory *comendador*. Synchronic archival research has revealed some fascinating data on the historical events informing the play, as well as on Lope's manipulation of those events to suit his own early seventeenth-century political agenda. The play is structured to alternate between two ongoing narratives: while the *pueblo* suffers the abuse of its ruler, the monarchs Ferdinand and Isabel negotiate a Civil War in which interests from Portugal attempt to dissolve the recently formed union of medieval kingdoms made possible by their marriage. Robert Lauer has revealed the historical inaccuracies of this arrangement, in effect demonstrating that Lope manipulated his historical sources so as to make an isolated local incident take on proto-nationalistic implications. Anthony Cascardi has read the play as a dramatization of Spain becoming Spain, of the formation of the modern nation-state through the defeat of medieval institutions like the military *Orden de Calatrava* [Order of Calatrava], all of which allows Lope to entertain his seventeenth-century audience while solidifying the public theater's allegiance to the early modern state, especially in light of how the play was written and performed during the reign of King Phillip III, a descendant of the *Reyes Católicos* [Catholic monarchs]. William R. Blue has further elucidated Lope's motives behind writing the play as he did: the *maestre de Calatrava*, who fought against the monarchy during the civil conflict, is ancestor to the Duque de Osuna, a high-profile patron for much of Lope's literary career. The *maestre* is portrayed in the play as a young and inexperienced leader manipulated by the evil *comendador* into joining the war, until at the end of the play he begs for forgiveness at the feet of the merciful monarchs, thus putting the ancestor of Lope's patron on the right side of history.

Beyond these contextual dynamics specific to the historical material explicitly treated in *Fuenteovejuna*, scholars since the 1980s have established more broadly that the nature of Lope's theatrical output overall (and indeed that of his contemporary *comediantes* as well) reflects a cultural context far more complicated than had been previously thought. Through most of the twentieth century, scholars took his famous treatise *Arte nuevo de hacer comedias en este tiempo* at its word, at least in terms of the rather straightforward playwright-to-public transactional formula that he offers to explain his success—the famous phrase "Porque como las paga el vulgo, es justo / hablarle en necio para darle gusto" [Because the crowd pays for it, it is fair to speak to them simply to please them] (87). As more historically nuanced analyses like Donald Gilbert-Santamaría's *Writers on the Market* have shown, Lope's arrival coincides with the emergence of what might be called Spain's first consumer-centered marketplace for cultural production. While theatrical production had for some time depended on popular success, in this period the industry exploded, not coincidentally as economic and social forces combined to provide a public whose demand and expendable capital had stimulated that explosion. Indeed, the *Arte nuevo* itself can be read, as it is by Gilbert-Santamaría, as a creative commentary on this same seismic shift: Lope at once nods to a traditional model of cultural funding—noble patronage—while explaining the dynamics of an emerging mass market that would render that model increasingly irrelevant. At the same time, cultural production faced unprecedented institutional scrutiny, both secular and religious. Thanks to such scholarship, we now understand more clearly how being a successful playwright in early modern Spain meant knowing how to walk a very thin line from which multiple "publics" or constituencies, often with conflicting demands, could all be satisfied.

A synchronic analysis therefore shows that, just as we know to be true of all cultural production, *Fuenteovejuna* is a play whose cultural and historical context can yield information that is very useful for its interpretation. What such scholarship has done for our understanding of this and other *comedias* is to question the older, *a priori* historical "master narratives" that have traditionally framed their study, to examine the archives for the faultlines of such narratives, and to re-cast the text as a site of negotiation for cultural and ideological tensions that can be corroborated by the so-called "thick description" of early modern Spanish culture via any number of textual and discursive sources. Thanks to this work, we can now offer a more nuanced vision of the play's implicit politics than that of previous generations of scholars. For example, while Meléndez y Pelayo could assert in 1949 that compared to *Fuenteovejuna*, "no hay obra más democrática en el teatro castellano" [there is no play that is more democratic in Castilian theater] (Lauer, 175), we now can see a more complicated balancing act: between populism and the kind of advocacy of authoritarian rule that motivates early modern political discourses such as the theory of *razón de estado* [reason of state], between medieval and emergent absolutist modes of governance and institutional control (best explained by Cascardi), and even between competing early modern models of agrarian policy (Gasta). Understanding this delicate discursive context can help us better understand how eminently adaptable *Fuenteovejuna* is to new interpretations, new contexts, and contradictory cultural deployments.

Getting our hands dirty with a thick description of *Fuenteovejuna*'s original context is of obvious value to early modern scholarship, but the field has been slow to recognize how it also can better inform our analyses of more contemporary reproductions of the play. Ample scholarship dedicated to contemporary Spanish cultural production in which the dialogic study of literary and non-literary discourses can reveal the political and ideological tensions in which cultural production is engaged resonates in principle and method with the synchronic scholarship described above. What remains to be done is to connect these dots: given the political nuance of Lope's play, as well as the broader scope of the censorship regime under which he wrote his plays for diverse and competing constituencies,[12] it stands to reason that these circumstances might help explain the contradictory causes for which *Fuenteovejuna* was deployed in subsequent centuries, or at least why the play might lend itself to being "spun" in so many ways and for so many causes. In other words, the fact that *Fuenteovejuna* dramatizes a creative rearrangement of historical data in order to align itself with the Spanish monarchy and to associate the State with a populistic and transhistorical conception of justice can perhaps clarify what otherwise might be a confusing performance history since the early modern period.

Fuenteovejuna, Diachronically Historicized

In early twentieth-century Spain, *Fuenteovejuna* proved to be a powerful propagandistic instrument for both sides of the Civil War that would end with the establishment of the Franco dictatorship. While the Falange would

---

12 Elizabeth R. Wright examines these competing claims in far greater detail than the context of this chapter allows. In her monograph *Pilgrimage to Patronage*, she sees this same tension between seeking the favor and support of the powerful and appealing to the masses. Wright argues that Lope's success brought with it "a necessary subjugation to patrons and censors" (23).

stage the play both before and after the war so as to associate itself with the inheritance of those same transcendental populist values that Lope attributes to Ferdinand and Isabel, the regime's use of the name *Fuenteovejuna* extended beyond the numerous stage productions of the play, which span across each decade of the regime. A state-sponsored film version in 1947 and for-television remake in 1974 would keep the association between the regime and Lope's play alive for decades, as would the popular and populist expression ¡*Todos a una, Fuenteovejuna!* [All as one, Fuenteovejuna!], even if that phrase was never actually uttered in Lope's original playscript. Kessel Schwartz has characterized the play's importance to the Falange as its functioning as a "symbol of their ideology" (207), while more recently Jason Parker has teased out the ways in which the play's ostensible political message lends itself to a fascist reading. The traditional values with which Lope aligns the villagers in the play (a harmonious relationship with nature, Christianity, and above all, honor), along with the perverse elitism of the despotic *comendador* and his foreign allies, constituted a perfect analogy for the Falange, which cast itself as the guardians of traditional nationalist values against the leftist elites of the second republic. In short, *Fuenteovejuna* helped the regime cast itself as standing on the right side of Spain's national history, effectively linking a work of historical fiction to the regime as co-participants in a longstanding struggle to defend true Spanishness against the contagion of foreign (and anti-Catholic) leftist influence.

How, then, do we explain the fact that this "symbol" of fascist ideology and Francoist nationalism was deployed by those same liberal intellectuals during the Second Republic, the very same political and ideological movement that Franco would overthrow? Perhaps the most convincing explanation has to do with the nature of the ideological polarity itself informing the Civil War. As Enrique García Santo-Tomás has argued, a conservative-nationalist approach was derived from the intense national self-reflection among Spanish intellectuals after the *fin de siècle*'s so-called "Crisis de 1898," in which the Golden Age was seen as a mythic repository of essentialist national values that had somehow been lost. (It should be noted that Christopher Britt-Arredondo makes a similar assessment of the period's obsession with Don Quixote, which he reads as having unwittingly laid the foundations of Spanish fascism, as we will see in the next chapter.) This reverence for the Golden Age would translate into a conservative-nationalist approach to staging Golden Age theater guided by the conviction that only through a return to the past could Spain reconnect with the transcendent essence of *hispanidad* denied to the people by the Second Republic, and through this connection face its contemporary problems.

On the opposite end of the ideological spectrum is a liberal approach through which Golden Age artifacts were seen as raw material to be honed according to the needs of the present. The most famous example is the performance by La Barraca, the theater group founded by a group of liberal university students and directed by Federico García Lorca. Lorca's production is based upon a more populist interpretation of the play, no doubt influenced by pre-Civil War cultural and political circumstances that in turn influenced his directorial decisions regarding how to stage it. These decisions, particularly the elimination of all scenes involving the Catholic monarchs and the Maestre de Calatrava, which constitute one third of Lope's original script, and with them the political (and according to Lorca, the secondary) plot interwoven with the village drama, fit neatly within Lorca's agenda for using Golden Age theater to forge national identity during the short-lived Second Republic (1931–1936). La Barraca was founded by Lorca in order to reinvigorate what was commonly considered an anemic Spanish theatrical scene in the 1930s. By recruiting promising young university actors and touring rural Spain, Lorca hoped to breathe new life into that scene. The plays selected for adaptation by La Barraca were by and large the classics of the Golden Age—including a calderonian *auto sacramental*, some cervantine *entremeses*, and of course Lope's *Fuenteovejuna*—because, as Lorca and many of his Barraca colleagues would explain in a number of interviews and essays, these classics spoke to an atemporal and transcendental national character in a unique way.[13]

Lorca's agenda to ground *Fuenteovejuna* in an anachronistic notion of Spanish nationhood would require some deft audiovisual supplementation to the abridged original playscript, which Lorca provides by dressing his actors in "rural" or "rustic" costumes that resembled conventional working-class garb of the early twentieth century, and by seamlessly weaving into the play a number of newly composed and choreographed Spanish songs and dances from a number of different "local" folkloric traditions, including those of Aragón and especially Andalucía (no doubt due to Lorca's life-long obsession with Andalusian folk culture). Suzanne Byrd explains these supplements as follows: "El propósito de llevar al pueblo más humilde, a las aldeas más aisladas, un vivo retrato del baile y la música folklóricos de España, en conjunción con la obra clásica de teatro, comunicó a la escena de esa época un nuevo sentido de valores artísticos y a la vez populares" [The goal of taking a live portrait of folkloric Spanish dance and music along with the classical play to the humblest people, to the most isolated villages, communicated to the era's theatrical scene a new sense of artistic and popular values] (15).

Lorca's political engagement, in an echo of Unamuno's *intrahistoria*, implies an interpretation of the text that is less concerned with its original historical specificity and more concerned with connecting the play's action

---

13 Suzanne Byrd's *La Fueneteovejuna de García Lorca* compiles these interviews.

to the ideological struggles of his contemporaries.[14] Of particular concern, according to studies by Byrd and Teresa Huerta of the La Barraca production, was simplifying Lope's multilayered plot so as to not distract the largely rural audience from the play's applicability to the here-and-now. The play thus opens with the third scene of Lope's original, as Laurencia and Pascuala discuss the sexually predatory *comendador*, and with the ensuing action to remain exclusively in the village throughout the performance (all scenes involving the Catholic monarchs, the Maestre de Calatrava, or the battles at Ciudad Real are excluded). Both Byrd and Huerta see the production as an "actualization" or "updating" of Lope's original message, and liberating the plot from its secondary and historically specific level is taken by both scholars as essential to that aim. According to Byrd, "no se tomó Lorca ninguna libertad con el texto de Lope de Vega, sino que lo sintetizó para lograr una unidad más clara del desarrollo" [Lorca did not take any liberties with Lope de Vega's text, but rather synthesized it to realize a clearer unity of its development] (16). Streamlining the action for a modern audience is a production strategy that one finds frequently in performance studies of Spanish classical theater, but in this case the editorial work assumes that eliminating the political context of the play's action can somehow liberate its universality: again Byrd explains that "De ningún modo la supresión del argumento secundario perturba el objetivo primordial de la pieza lopesca" [In no way does the suppression of the secondary plot disturb Lope's primordial objective] (16). The suggestion, it would seem, is that Lorca knew what Lope meant to say better than Lope himself, that 300 years later he could resuscitate the primordial *duende* of Lope's work and somehow improve upon its exposition.

The lion's share of recent scholarship on the play, however, calls into question the extent to which Lope would have agreed that the political dimension of his play was superfluous, especially those scholars (particularly Lauer, Blue, and Wright) engaged in the synchronic "thick description" outlined above. Lorca's work during the first third of the twentieth century, of course, could not benefit from synchronic research realized several decades after his death; more to the point, the deployment of Lope's play in the political arena is inherently shaped by dynamics specific to that twentieth-century context. Nowhere is the impact of Lorca's edits more obvious than at the end of the play: La Barraca's performance closes with the celebration of the *comendador*'s death and the wedding of his last female victim, in effect with the realization of the pueblo's dream of self-determination. What is eliminated is the process through which the Catholic monarchs had

---

14 While more focused on Lorca's lyric poetry, Jonathan Mayhew connects Lorca and a number of his contemporaries to Unamuno's notion of *intrahistoria*.

attempted to identify the assassin of their local ruler, their unsuccessful torture of the villagers, and their reluctant decision to pardon the town as a whole when "enhanced interrogation" yielded no individual who could be charged. Lorca's version effectively reduces Lope's oscillation between the exercise of power on a micro/local or macro/national level, and in so doing, it avoids aligning the "spirit of Lope" with the violent exercise of fascistic power, including the same techniques of forced interrogation and torture that Lorca's Nationalist enemies would soon practice on those opposed to their ideology. Lorca's ability to erase that authoritarian violence from Lope's play, unfortunately, stands in ironic contrast to his inability to avoid it in his own tragic death at the hands of the Nationalists.

During the Franco dictatorship, a regime of censorship would make it impossible for artists like Lorca (had he survived) to appropriate the Spanish Golden Age in any way that could be seen as antithetical to the policies or ideology of the censors, even though the Civil War itself and its immediate aftermath had largely purged Spain of the artists and intellectuals that would have voiced such opposition—whether through imprisonment, assassination (the fate of Lorca himself) or exile—and established an ideological state apparatus that would repress and silence any remaining or emerging contesting voices during the early years of the regime. It is therefore difficult to assess the extent to which early modern cultural artifacts would have continued to be appropriated in conflicting ways for much of the twentieth century, although anti-*franquista* appropriations did emerge from political exiles abroad, as Henry Kamen describes in his book *The Disinherited* and as Helena Buffery's edited volume *Stages of Exile* explores. These diasporic adaptations include a number of performances by the famous Catalán Republican actress Margarita Xirgu, who would bring plays by Lope (including *Fuenteovejuna*) and Tirso de Molina to audiences in Uruguay during the 1950s and lead cultural programming there to celebrate the anniversary of Lope's birth in 1962. Luis Savslasky's 1945 film adaptation of Calderón's *La dama duende*, made in Argentina with an almost exclusively Spanish cast and based on a screenplay by Rafael Alberti, also fits with this pattern of deploying the Spanish Golden Age in contraposition to the regime. So too does Pablo Picasso's famous sketch of Don Quixote and Sancho, drawn in France to support that nation's communist party. Within postwar Spain's national borders, however, the conceptual grid of the Golden Age was carefully curated to serve the fascist state.

Tradition and Transition

It should be no surprise, then, that the early modern *Comedia* and other forms of Golden Age cultural production would gradually acquire an association with the regime—an association with lasting effects even today, nearly half a century after Franco's death, in many ways due to the steps taken by Spanish cultural institutions during the first decade of Spanish democracy. The Falange inherited a longstanding tradition of using Lope and his Golden Age counterparts to represent traditional Spanish values in the previous century, and the dictatorship would eventually privilege Golden Age classics by granting their adaptations special "national interest" status, such as was given to Antonio Román's 1947 version of *Fuenteovejuna*, and by allowing unaltered *comedias* to pass almost automatically through the censorship process before being staged. Declaring the dissemination of Golden Age cultural production to be of national interest conferred upon it both eligibility for state subvention and ideological pre-approval from an otherwise time-consuming and cumbersome censorship process, all of which incentivized the production of adaptations (both for stage and screen) of this patrimony for public consumption. Indeed, as Duncan Wheeler reports, Franco's official declaration of victory at the end of the Civil War included the boast that the Nationalists won with the Cid's sword, Don Quixote's lance and the mayor of Zalamea's cane (the latter reference is made to *El alcalde de Zalamea*, a play originally written by Lope and famously adapted decades later by Calderón). Lope was among the most frequently revived cultural figures in this process of appropriation, from the very beginning of the dictatorship. Even the first annual celebration of the Nationalist victory in 1940 featured a theatrical spectacle organized by the Valencian and pro-Nationalist Felipe Lluch Garin, titled *España, Una, Grande y Libre* [Spain: One, Big, and Free]. This early example of Golden Age-themed propagandistic cultural production included a pastiche of scenes from Lope's most canonical works and an original *auto sacramental* meant to allegorize the new regime as the ultimate destiny of the Spanish people.

Franco's death would usher in a transformative period of rethinking Spanish national identity and nationalism in the late 1970s, and the new democracy would approach the cultural authority of the Golden Age with ambivalence—if not outright resentment—as it defined itself while resisting the use of any symbols that would invoke memories of the old regime. This is precisely why the fate of the Golden Age in the popular Spanish imaginary— an imaginary haunted by "spectres" (188) of Francoism, as Wheeler describes it—is so inextricably linked to the fate of Spanish nationalism itself: while under different circumstances the cultural pluralism that continues to thrive among many of Spain's autonomous regions would normally be deflected by conservative appeals to traditional national Spanish symbols as a culturally centripetal force, the political mainstream and relevant cultural institutions were understandably hesitant to be associated with similar appeals made continually during the dictatorship. For progressives, then, *teatro clásico* represented conservative orthodoxy; for conservatives such as those constituting the Partido Popular, the need to articulate many ideals with which Franco would have sympathized without overtly referencing the dictatorship itself implied the need to find new cultural symbols that had been left unexploited by the dictatorship. If the Golden Age represented Spanish nationalism under the old regime, it would have to be treated with caution during a transition period in which the wounds of civil war and despotism were still healing. At the risk of neglecting the cultural narrative of the Golden Age that Franco had appropriated, cultural institutions and producers were eager to move beyond Spain's troubled recent history.

An example of the close association between the ideology and politics of Franco regime and the cultural symbols that it appropriated can be found in a newspaper editorial written by the novelist Juan Goytisolo, whose Communist sympathies led him to leave Spain in exile during the dictatorship. The piece appeared in the May 5, 2000, edition of the Spanish newspaper *El País* under the title "*Fuenteovejuna, señor.*" Goytisolo's use of the play's title is seasoned with a healthy dose of postmodern irony and cynicism, as he applies it to the case of a local uproar in 1999 over the arrest of two young Castilians for shooting and permanently disabling a young man of Romani (gypsy) descent. He admonishes Spain's complacency about the racism of this and other acts of discriminatory violence by associating it with Lope's play, in which the instigators of the popular uprising against the *comendador* are protected by the village: as the royal "forced interrogators" asked each citizen to name those responsible for the rebellion, the unanimous answer (even from children being tortured) was simply *Fuenteovejuna*. In effect Goytisolo associates the cultural vestiges of Francoism with *Fuenteovejuna* in order to align his own politics with progress and with Spain's claims to membership in a modernized European Union, regardless of how radically different his implied reading of the play may be from more mainstream interpretations of it. What many twentieth-century studies of the play characterize as a dramatic representation of social and moral justice, or more recently as an ideological manipulation of history supportive of the absolutist monarchy, is for Goytisolo a symbol of a culturally primitive tribalism of the masses, a stand-in for *lo castizo* [authenticity] meant to remind his readers of Spain's barbaric and intolerant past.

The fact that the symbols of the Spanish Golden Age can be used to denounce the cultural vestiges of Francoism has not made it impossible to use the early modern classics to express a more positive vision of Spanish national identity, but it has made it more complicated. In the realm of the public theater, for example, the Franco regime had nationalized the major theatrical venues shortly after the Civil War, and as the political situation stabilized the production of Golden Age drama became an increasingly highbrow affair during the 1950s and 1960s, as the regime hoped to promote a vision of an elite cultural patrimony comparable to that of its European neighbors. By the 1970s, theatrical activity related to the *Siglo de oro* had waned considerably, and with the fall of the regime came an increased emphasis on new Spanish playwrights and those formerly repressed by the regime's censors, such as plays by Lauro Olmo, Martín Recuerda, and others involved in Madrid's so-called underground theatrical scene during the second half of the dictatorship. With a strong cultural impetus to celebrate newly recovered artistic liberties, and with the enduring impression that the *teatro clásico* had been affiliated with the old regime, efforts to revive enthusiasm for Golden Age drama would require time, and some innovative thinking.

The Return of the Golden Age in Democratic Spain

The Ministerio de Cultura of the Socialist government of the 1980s would attempt to revive interest in Golden Age theater by founding the CNTC, an institution meant to guarantee regular offerings of classical Spanish theater by a stable core of actors and producers trained specifically for the task, not unlike England's Royal Shakespeare Company. The CNCT's efforts would dovetail with the Festival de Teatro Clásico in Almagro, as Luciano García Lorenzo explains, and it continues to lead the way in high-profile revivals of Spanish Golden Age artifacts. These determined efforts ultimately speak to the power of governmental cultural programming to influence public appreciation and demand for the classics, despite the cultural headwinds that during the early years of the transition to democracy suggested that *teatro clásico* might not overcome the cultural baggage it had acquired during the dictatorship. While enthusiasm in Spain for Golden Age theater has been sustained for decades by these efforts, others have attempted more radical approaches in order to make the Golden Age accessible to a broader public, to make *teatro clásico* and *teatro popular* no longer mutually exclusive concepts.

One noteworthy approach involves appropriating the Golden Age *through* its previous pre-Franco or anti-Franco appropriators. For obvious reasons, these more contemporary cultural figures do not bear the same cultural baggage as the Golden Age figures who had come to be associated with the regime. Quite the opposite, in fact: seeing Lope through the eyes of the Second Republic is an excellent strategy for divesting the *fénix* of that ideological baggage. Most recently, Spanish National Radio sponsored a radio broadcast, called *Fuenteovejuna en frente* [Fuenteovejuna on the Front Lines], in which actors performed the role of Second Republic actors performing

Lope's play during the Civil War.[15] Two other efforts adopting this strategy draw upon the famous Federico García Lorca troupe La Barraca, which as we have seen defined its mission of reviving Spanish theater by bringing the classics to the *pueblo*. The first of these Lorca-framed "Golden Age revival-revivals" is a private theater company that has adopted the name Los Barracos. By framing each performance with the arrival and preparations of Lorca's group, a clear distinction is made between the cultural baggage that the Golden Age *Comedia* may have acquired during the dictatorship, and the supposedly ideologically divested, "no spin zone" vision of the Golden Age embraced by Lorca. Los Barracos define their mission as to "desarrollar y resucitar de una forma profesional el espíritu de la mítica compañía La Barraca que fundara Federico García Lorca" [develop and revive professionally the spirit of the mythical company La Barraca that Federico García Lorca founded]. The company's website includes an *historial* that notes the socioeconomic factors informing this mission:

> Si ciertamente vivimos tiempos de crisis, no tenemos más remedio que adaptarnos, y este proyecto nace de la necesidad de mantener vivo un elenco y una compañía con espectáculos que, por sus características especiales, se podrán desarrollar con unos cachés absolutamente accesibles a muchos presupuestos. Muy adecuados para campañas escolares y siempre acordes con el espíritu de La Barraca de Federico en cuanto a su desarrollo y funcionamiento.[16]

> [If we certainly live in a time of crisis, we have no choice but to adapt, and this project is born of the need to keep alive a cast and company with performances which, because of their special character, could be developed with materials that are absolutely accessible for many budgets. Very adequate for programming at schools and always in keeping with the spirit of Lorca's La Barraca in terms of its development and function.]

This statement reflects a common populist mission shared between La Barraca and Los Barracos to wrest control of the public theater from established urban governmental institutions, which is to say that both respond to institutional practices and attempt to provide public access to the *Siglo de oro* in a new way.

Another invocation of Lorca's Golden Age is more closely associated with governmental institutions, specifically the Ministerio de Cultura. In 2006

---

15 https://www.rtve.es/play/audios/ficcion-sonora/fuenteovejuna-frente-1936/6738657/
16 https://www.redescena.net/compania/31800/los-barracos/

the Sociedad Estatal de Conmemoraciones Culturales (which is overseen by the Ministerio de Cultura) began a program of cultural outreach under the title *Las rutas de la Barraca* [The Routes of La Barraca] in which university theater repertoires are chosen to perform the same Golden Age *comedias*, *entremeses*, and *autos sacramentales* that Lorca had selected, and to travel to the same rural areas that had originally been visited by La Barraca. The organizers of this cultural initiative explain that "Este proyecto trata, por un lado, de que el ejemplo de La Barraca perdure, y, por otro, de abrir la posibilidad a una empresa colectiva que represente comedias y entremeses por toda la geografía española, en condiciones que la profesión escénica actual no tiene oportunidades de realizar" [This project seeks on the one hand to keep alive the example set by La Barraca, and on the other hand to open the possibility of a collective company that stages *comedias* and *entremeses* across all of Spain's geography, in conditions for which the current theatrical profession does not allow].[17]

The reference to a *profesión escénica* implies the contemporary Spanish theater industry, which is necessarily more concerned with the production of new and living Spanish playwrights, and with maintaining economic viability in an increasingly tenuous national and global economy. The suggestion seems to be that the government does not do enough to preserve the cultural patrimony of Golden Age theater, which is a curious charge coming from an agency promoted and subsidized by the Spanish government. More to our point here, this and similar efforts reflect an appetite for "reclaiming the classics," despite its misuse by the dictatorship, as an inherent element of the Spanish national narrative.

Given the longstanding association between classical theater and "high" culture that had been perpetuated by the Franco regime, the desire to break from the past is understandable. Even the CNTC attempted to reinvent itself in 2004, not coincidentally as the PSOE—the same socialist party that had founded the CNTC in the first place—regained control of the Spanish government for the first time in more than a decade. Beyond its resident director and theater troupe, the Compañía created a more experimental arm of its institution, the Joven Compañía [Young Company], and it now invites foreign acting companies to stage classical Spanish plays. As we will see in greater detail in the conclusion of this book, the CNTC's international turn gathered steam in 2011 when Helena Pimenta was named its director. Pimenta, whose long dossier as a theatrical director was heavily weighted towards productions of foreign playwrights like Shakespeare, Molière, Ionesco, and Beckett, extended

17 https://www.culturaydeporte.gob.es/va/dam/jcr:7fb8b4ce-fe9a-4e9a-8067-5b41c858c628/barraca2.pdf

the institution's foreign entanglements to include workshops, programs, and CNTC performances across Europe and Latin America.

At the same time, this renovated CNTC also began a sustained engagement with the various ministries of culture of Spain's semi-autonomous regions to promote Golden Age theater as an essential ingredient of Spain's cultural heritage and patrimony. Its resources were leveraged to foster local interest in its own national tours with professional multimedia publicity campaigns, but their sponsorship of regional public institutions like the Teatre Nacional de Catalunya (TNC) allowed them to enjoy the benefits of those resources for its own production of *Fuenteovejuna* in 2005–2006. As what could be considered a return on the CNTC's investment, a Jove Companyia [Young Company] was launched by the TNC in 2013 with a mission like that of the CNTC's Joven Compañía: to develop young talent to "volver a tener una manera propia de representar a nuestros clásicos" [have an authentic way of representing our classics], but with a peripheral twist: the company's mission statement clarifies that by "nuestros clásicos" it actually means "el patrimonio cultural catalán" [Catalonian cultural patrimony].[18] Its productions of *Tirant lo Blanc* and *El Cantador* are at best peripheral to the Spanish Golden Age (*Tirant* was among the books burned by Don Quixote's friends in an effort to cure him of his madness), but its 2019 adaptation of Calderón's *El gran mercado del mundo* (directed by Xavier Albertí) reflects an inclusion of Castilian patrimony that surely did align with the CNTC mission. This engagement with public institutions across Spain's semi-autonomous regions, I would argue, is strategic: the CNTC performs a valuable service for the federal ministerial authorities that fund it by fostering the kind of local identification with the Spanish Golden Age that was shown above in Valencia, but in this case in Catalonia only two years after a constitutional confrontation between Catalan and Spanish administrations that left the former in legal jeopardy, if not exile.

Beyond such collaborations, the CNTC and its sponsoring cultural ministry have taken full advantage of digital and social media to attract more Spaniards to their performance venues. The dissemination of trailers and visually stimulating poster images reflects a concerted marketing strategy that suggests two things: first, that the Spanish government's promotion of Golden Age patrimony is becoming increasingly active, aggressive, and media-savvy, perhaps because it is no longer "too soon" to invest in cultural artifacts that had previously been tainted by association with the dictatorship; and second, that further research into the nature of contemporary deployments of the Spanish Golden Age must consider more directly the visual and digital media

---

18 https://www.tnc.cat/es/la-jove-companyia-del-teatre-nacional-itnc

through which they are deployed. The postmodern promotion of the classics, it seems, is closely connected to the postmodern media through which they are promoted and adapted, and the industries within which they must compete. As we will see in the third chapter of this book, this connection involves a globalized media marketplace that has only complicated the ways in which the Spanish classics are now experienced by contemporary Spaniards, especially children. But before that chapter's "zooming out" to the global dimensions of Golden Age artifact deployments, it is important in the present chapter to understand the impact of this democratic-era national reclaiming of the classics on the contemporary local experience of patrimonial figures like Lope de Vega. It is only with an awareness of the efforts of national cultural figures like Pilar Miró and directors of the CNTC that the emergence of these local experiences can be fully understood.

Situating the Local in the National

Throughout all of these developments in how Spanish Golden Age theater now circulates in contemporary Spain, Lope de Vega has remained its most prominent brand name, even if that brand has meant different things to different constituencies. In general terms we may say that the basic contours of this narrative are as follows: after the dictatorship had left Lope and his contemporaries with the taint of association, the cultural production of the so-called *destape* [opening or uncovering] era tended to move forward by leaving such tainted cultural artifacts aside, before slowly and cautiously returning to them as the transition progressed; during the latter part of the 1980s, the PSOE government began to pursue this reconnection more aggressively in what might best called a "preservationist" spirit exemplified by the CNTC's initial, philologically conservative approach to staging that would endure through the 1990s; finally, by the turn of the twenty-first century, that spirit had gradually been replaced by more "liberal" and creative attempts to make the classics appeal more broadly to contemporary cultural sensibilities, including those public and private efforts (noted above) to reconnect with Lope through reconnecting with Lorca (La Barraca). These national dynamics are indispensable for a comprehensive account of how Lope is appreciated and experienced on the local level.

Pilar Miró represents a key figure in this transition from adapting Lope only with "high culture" reverence to more flexible standards that allow for greater synchrony with more contemporary cultural production. Her work with the PSOE government (as director of the government's cinema ministry) brings that preservationist spirit to her 1996 adaptation of Lope's *El perro del hortelano*, which was both critically acclaimed and moderately profitable.

This earlier trend, to which we might add Manuel Gutiérrez-Aragón's *El Quijote* miniseries (1991), consisted of high-budget efforts to treat prized cultural artifacts with the greatest possible reverence, and to faithfully recreate the cultural context of early modern Spain, at least as that context was understood by the adaptors. As Duncan Wheeler explains, what proved to be truly groundbreaking about Miró's film is that it demonstrated the viability of Lope and the Spanish Golden Age artifacts in the contemporary cinema industry.

Miró's cultural deference to the classics was consonant with her original vision for Spanish Cinema and television when she assumed her posts during the Felipe González presidency in the 1980s. The implicit mandate of her appointment was to remedy the perceived aesthetic and artistic decadence of the *destape* period immediately following Franco's death—a period characterized by an explosion of low-budget productions in which more attention was paid to exploring the previously forbidden fruit of sexually explicit material than to the production of a national cinema worthy of comparison to Spain's European neighbors. When Miró would eventually leave her government service and direct *El perro del hortelano*, she made minimal changes to Lope's original script and privileged an extravagant baroque visual spectacle, complete with an elaborately choreographed musical epilogue meant to capture the traditional festive atmosphere of the early modern public theater. Along similar lines, *El Quijote*'s five-hour miniseries format—five hours that adapt only the first half of the novel—is indicative of the production's attention to detail and reluctance to cut anything from Cervantes's elaborate and voluminous masterpiece. While both Miró and Gutiérrez-Aragón would seek to raise the prestige with which contemporary Spaniards associate the *Siglo de oro*, one could also argue that their "high culture" vision of the classics is in many ways an inheritance of the Franco regime, which had worked in a similar spirit with the Spanish Golden Age, especially when treating the early modern *Comedia*.

The more recent adaptations of Spanish Golden Age theater, whether the more experimental approach of the revitalized CNTC (featuring, for example, transgressive casting such as Blanca Portillo's turn as Segismundo in *La vida es sueño*, aggressive digital and social media publicity efforts, and modernized settings) or Manuel Iborra's film adaptation of *La dama boba*, indicate a changing sensibility that allows Golden Age classics to provide opportunities for more creative interpretation, even if such creativity is not necessarily a guarantee for popular or critical acclaim. Iborra's film, a failure relative to the commercial success and critical acclaim that Miró's *El perro del hortelano* had earned, creatively filters Lope's original *comedia* through the codes of contemporary romantic comedy films. If *La dama boba* is in its most basic sense a play about the transformative power of love, Iborra's adaptation explicitly characterizes such love in sexual terms. The sisters' sexuality thus features prominently in the film, including in numerous scenes without dialogue that show each with her respective lover that we can be sure that the Counterreformation censorship regime would not have permitted. Iborra further ups the erotic ante in numerous ways, including a series of erotic encounters between the servants Pedro and Clara and a curious scene in which the sisters Nise and Finea discuss their prospective suitors while sharing a bath.

But eroticizing Lope's play is not the only way in which Iborra's film alters the sexual dynamics, presumably to adjust Lope's original playscript to the aesthetic sensibilities and preferences of a twenty-first-century Spanish cineplex audience. The most striking instance is the conversion of Otavio to Otavia, father to mother, in a role played by the actress (and the director's wife) Verónica Forqué. Critical readings of *La dama boba* as an intergenerational battle of the sexes—overbearing conservative father vs. young daughters who would satisfy their desire on their own terms—are flipped on their heads by this change. Otavio's efforts to protect Finea from the male predator Laurencio take on new meaning when played by a woman, as do his (or her) conservative diatribes regarding proper female behavior. And finally, when the truth about Laurencio's betrothal and secret rendezvous in the *desván* is revealed, Otavia's attempt to do him violence by the sword are rendered pathetic and futile, due not to her age but to a stereotypical representation of her gender as physically frail. Laurencio's skills with the sword are highlighted throughout the film, and in this climactic scene he literally knocks Otavia down on her rump, at which point she begrudgingly accepts the marriage, as imposed upon her and her family by the virile young man.

Regardless of how one might interpret or appreciate how Iborra's film rethinks the gender dynamics of Lope's play, it is safe to say that Spain continues to grapple with issues of gender equality in ways that are uniquely inflected by the nation's history. After four decades of Francoism, which placed legal limits on women's rights and access to power that stood in stark contrast to the rest of Western Europe (especially since the 1960s), not even the dramatic legal and social reforms of the new democracy could immediately erase the deeply ingrained problems associated with gender inequality. Modernized and progressive laws to combat domestic abuse and other vestiges of misogyny, primarily realized after the election in 2004 of José Luis Rodríguez Zapatero—who would declare himself to be Spain's first feminist president and require fully equal gender representation in his cabinet—have not erased this cultural inequality entirely, but they have made gender a key issue in the political arena and in the Spanish cultural imaginary.

Returning to the geographical place from which this chapter began, the village of Fuente Obejuna allows us to see the local ramifications of these national cultural dynamics—in this case, with particular regard to the longstanding problem of sexual violence. The municipality's productions of the eponymously titled play are uniquely useful to our understanding of how a *comedia*'s significance is a diachronically evolving process, to the extent that each new community production both reauthenticates local identity and responds to community productions mounted in previous years. Javier Osorio, director of the 2004 production, for example, emphasized to Manuel J. Albert of *El País* that in that year they wanted to emphasize the pivotal role of women in the drama, especially Laurencia's call to arms at the beginning of the third act, in an effort to raise public awareness of the persistent national problems of sexual violence and domestic abuse: "Uno de los temas centrales de la obra de Lope es el de la violencia contra la mujer. En lo que llevamos de año han sido 72 las mujeres asesinadas en España. Quizás al ver la obra, la gente se sensibilice algo más al respecto" [One of the play's central themes is violence against women. So far this year 72 women have been murdered in Spain. Maybe when they see this play, people will be more sensitive to the issue].[19] A current issue in Spanish social and political discourse thus dictates the director's interpretation of Lope's play so as to renew its cultural relevance, and it demonstrates how the broader cultural circumstances surrounding a twenty-first-century production of a *comedia* will condition both its performance and its interpretation. These circumstances include the ways in which information is now circulated globally—a point illustrated in this case by the marketing and commemoration of previous community productions in the village of Fuente Obejuna that can be conveniently accessed at https://www.fuenteobejuna.es—as well as the messages carried by those media.

The political and civic discourse through which domestic abuse and violence against women are confronted in contemporary Spain are similarly produced in a globalized context and influenced by the discourse of contemporary feminism, a political movement largely repressed in Spain by the Franco regime as it spread widely throughout the Western world in the 1960s and 1970s. Beyond the clear synchrony between the village's refreshed interpretation of the play and the progressivism of the Zapatero government (including legislative initiatives meant to guarantee gender equality among elected officials and even in the division of domestic responsibilities among

---

19 https://elpais.com/diario/2004/08/27/andalucia/1093558930_850215.html

private citizens), it should be noted that this synchrony also affects the way that scholars read the classics in the academy.[20] As twenty-first-century audiences consume productions that treat the gender dynamics in an "actualized" manner like Ossorio's 2004 production in Fuente Obejuna, twenty-first-century scholars will read and analyze those same dynamics in ways that are not necessarily identical, but that do resonate with broader patterns of cultural consumption.

Fuenteovejuna, to be sure, does lend itself to a gender-focused reading that would privilege the same monologue by Laurencia that is cited by Ossorio in his interview for *El País*. As the third act begins, she takes the men of her town to task for their failure to protect her from the tyrannical and sexually predatory *comendador* Fernán Gómez. Her speech, the catalyst for the climactic village uprising that would culminate with the parading of the tyrant's head on a stake, is an unequivocal attack on their masculinity:

> Liebres cobardes nacistes;
> bárbaros sois, no españoles.
> Gallinas, ¡vuestras mujeres
> sufrís que otros hombres gocen!
> Poneos ruecas en la cinta.
> ¿Para qué os ceñís estoques?
> ¡Vive Dios, que he de trazar
> que solas mujeres cobren
> la honra de estos tiranos,
> la sangre de estos traidores,
> y que os han de tirar piedras,
> hilanderas, maricones,
> amujerados, cobardes... (*Fuenteovejuna*, 1776–82)

[You were all born cowards; you are barbarians, not Spaniards. Cowards, you allow your women to be taken by other men! Tie a knot in your belts. Why carry swords? I swear that I will plot for us women alone to recover our honor from these tyrants, to spill the blood of these traitors, and to throw stones at you—spinsters, sissies, girly-men, cowards...][21]

The entire text of Laurencia's tirade is full of such references to the male villagers' emasculation, as she calls them among other things "medio-hombres" [half-men] and "ovejas" [sheep] and poses to them

---

20 See Molly Moore's article in *The Washington Post*, October 7, 2006.
21 All translations from Lope de Vega are mine.

similarly pointed rhetorical questions: "¿Vosotros sois hombres nobles? / ¿Vosotros padres y deudos?" (1755–56) [Are you noblemen? Are you fathers and kinsmen?]. Furthermore, Laurencia treats the villagers' failure to live up to the standards of masculinity as an affront to Spanish national character ("bárbaros sois, no españoles" [You are barbarians, not Spaniards]). Donald Gilbert-Santamaría reads Laurencia's invocation of gender as a "rhetorical goad" (78) meant to catalyze the male citizenry of the village, and its effectiveness stems from tapping into the profound cultural anxiety about gender in seventeenth-century Spain that is the subject of a number of recent publications in the fields of history and literary studies, including Sidney Donnell's *Feminizing the Enemy*. If we accept Teresa Kirschner's conception of the Fuenteovejuna villagers as a *protagonista colectivo* [collective protagonist] reflective of the collective identity of the play's seventeenth-century audience, we can assume that Laurencia's linkage of "effeminacy" with Spanish national identity would have resonated loudly in the early seventeenth-century *corral*.

The fact that it continues to resonate onstage well into the present century, despite obvious contextual differences, is illustrative of how Spanish Golden Age cultural patrimony can speak to Spaniards and scholars today. While this chapter's insistence on referring to Lope de Vega as a "brand name" engages the jargon of capitalism, the reasons for this terminological choice should be clear: the local linkages to Lope explored in the pages above have a very real economic dimension to them. In the kind of economic climate in which Spain finds itself today, where the effects of the 2008 economic crisis and budget austerity affect federal, regional, and municipal government budgets alike, it makes sense to think of this cultural activity in such terms, insofar as we see economic interests collide with cultural patrimony. David Morley and Kevin Robins make this economic-cultural matrix explicit in their discussion of what they call the "heritage and enterprise cultures" (117): because globalization involves a re-visioning of local communities in an international context, local communities see their cultural heritage as a distinguishing feature to be promoted in their quest for growth and investment. It is not my intention to suggest that the celebration of Spanish Golden Age cultural patrimony is only driven by economic motives, but rather to posit that such motives are indeed relevant when seeking a full understanding of the circulation of Golden Age cultural artifacts.

What is missing from this global-local nexus as described by Morley and Robins, however, is the fact that Spain's history has already "flagged" these artifacts for nationalistic purposes since long before anything resembling a global economic system existed. This national(ist) dimension, as will be shown in the next chapter, does not reach its greatest intensity with Lope, but with Miguel de Cervantes, a would-be playwright from the Golden Age who also happened to write several works of prose fiction. We will see that the unparalleled cultural profile enjoyed by Don Quixote does translate to similar local cultural experiences (in the small villages El Toboso and Esquivias, for example), but also that his figure has been deployed even more often at the service of the Spanish state itself. Like the "Lope brand," the continued cultural ubiquity of Cervantes and his literary creation reflect a kind of cultural alchemy revealing a fascinating and persistent belief that there is still gold to be mined from the Spanish Golden Age.

CHAPTER TWO

Don Quixote de la Mancha, "Made in Spain"

The kind of local economic activity described in the previous chapter—leveraging performances of *El caballero de Olmedo* in Olmedo, *Fuenteovejuna* in Fuente Obejuna, and so forth in order to sell flowers, fill hotels, or enhance real estate value—reflect more than cultural resourcefulness in austere times. This kind of activity would not be possible were Spain not invested in Lope and his Golden Age contemporaries on a national scale, and were it not for a tradition of associating such cultural artifacts with the very idea of Spain since the modern nation emerged. By cultivating the cultural capital of the Spanish Golden Age through institutional cultural programming, Spain and its autonomous communities promote social and economic causes as a function of national identity—which in turn motivates Spaniards from all autonomous regions to visit and invest in local communities like Almagro, Olmedo, and areas of rural Castilla-La Mancha like El Toboso. At first glance, the economic dimension of this cultural activity is easy to identify with other, more dystopic symptoms of late-stage capitalism, from financial crises due to speculative corporate finance to widening income inequality. But the economic currency of Golden Age cultural patrimony is also tied to a longer process of economic development that began during the Franco regime, and that is ultimately tied to earlier nationalistic uses of this patrimony stretching back to the turn of the twentieth century.

Spain's emergence in the 1950s from the geopolitical and economic isolationism of the dictatorship's first decade depended on its presentation of the nation for foreign consumption. The projected image of Spain as its own kind of brand or commodity, "open for business" and no longer isolated on the international stage, took advantage of earlier nationalistic and identitarian uses of the Golden Age to solidify national cohesion. Romantic-era mythologization of this patrimony yielded a *fin-de-siècle* embrace of it to navigate national existential calamity through cultural nostalgia. As Christopher Brett-Arredondo has argued, the enhanced symbolic potency of the Spanish Golden Age gained from this nostalgic engagement with its patrimony would in turn open a pathway for a Franco's more ideologically driven mode of domestic nationalism to engage the Golden Age as a repository of symbols and messages apt for reinforcing and underscoring the regime's own cultural narrative. As the midcentury economic opening developed, that cultural repository would be leveraged in an international context to attract tourism revenue and foreign investment. This additional dimension of Golden Age currency meant that Golden Age patrimony would become a product for both foreign and domestic consumption.

As the complicated process of globalization gathered steam during the second half of the twentieth century, so too did the disappearance of a clear distinction between the idea of Spain in the context of national identity and in the context of a national image projected outward to the world, a turn in the history of Spanish identities that Justin Crumbaugh associates with "the spectacle of Spanish tourism" (4) spearheaded in the 1960s by Manuel Fraga Iribarne, the regime's Minister of Culture and Tourism. Beyond the establishment of the now infamous "Spain Is Different" international marketing campaign, *fraguismo* and related strategic initiatives would impact the discourses used to curate a domestic, homogenized "consensus" vision of Spanish identity for the duration of the dictatorship and beyond. The Spanish Golden Age, in short, became an instrument through which Spain both reflected its own identity and projected itself for the sake of foreign investment, tourism and the sale of cultural artifacts and their simulacra. Long after the Franco regime faded into history, the association that it had made between the Spanish Golden Age and the modern nation's self-branding for the sake of tourist appeal continues to resonate, in ways not unlike Nicola MacLeod's observations regarding postmodern tourism, insofar as "the virtual, highly mediated and staged image becomes part of our lived experience and part of our contemporary authenticity" (222–23). The local economic strategies described in the previous chapter constitute a twenty-first-century "glocal" version of this conversion of cultural to economic capital,[1] but this chapter will focus on the earlier efforts to leverage the Golden Age's cultural capital on a national scale (and often for the sake of nationalist causes) that would provide the template for

---

1 This allusion to the "glocal" needs qualification, insofar as it reflects the inverse of the term's normal usage. Since Robert Livingston's thought piece on the place of the "glocal" as a counterweight to notions of globalization in literary studies, published in *PMLA* in 2001, critics have engaged the term as borrowed from the Japanese notion of *dokacucha*, a strategic term used by businesses to describe appeals to the cultural sensibilities of local markets so as to make their goods more likely to appeal to those markets. Here we are discussing the inverse—the locality itself is the product being "sold."

such instances of "glocalization." Across Spain, the cultural authenticity embodied in the Spanish Golden Age was and continues to be leveraged to promote domestic policy related to cultural production, for example the celebration and promotion of the arts, theater, and, as we will see in this chapter, reading and literacy.

The best example of this nationalized packaging of the Golden Age is Miguel de Cervantes's *Don Quixote*. After its immediate best-seller status during the seventeenth century, the novel's reception developed into a more diverse and complicated array of readings (ranging from burlesque satire to sublime heroic epic), the explanation for which will require revisiting the original text itself and the discursive context in which it was written. Beyond that original context, we will see that later developments in how the novel came to be understood were due to a fascinating mix of foreign and domestic readings, all of which increased the frequency with which Don Quixote would come to be considered a national symbol, if not a national hero. In post-Franco Spain, the commodification of Don Quixote and his author would evolve in dialogue with their institutionalization by public cultural institutions for a variety of purposes. Regardless of one's understanding or judgment of this intriguing "public-private venture," there can be little doubt as to the resulting ubiquity of Don Quixote and Miguel de Cervantes in contemporary Spain.

This high cultural profile renders Sancho's words in Part 2 of the novel eerily prescient: "—Yo apostaré—dijo Sancho—que antes de mucho tiempo no ha de haber bodegón, venta ni mesón, o tienda de barbero, donde no ande pintada la historia de nuestras hazañas" ["I would bet," said Sancho, "that before long there won't be a bodega, inn, or barber's shop without paintings of our deeds"] (*Don Quixote* II, 71). The illiterate squire's emphasis on graphic (rather than verbal) representation proves to be an accurate descriptor not only of his (and his master's) prominence in touristic merchandise—and, more importantly, of the countless televisual and graphic adaptations of *Don Quixote* that maintain their celebrity in contemporary Spain. Ironically, the nation's cultural programming has leveraged this graphic and iconographic presence to promote literacy, the capacity beyond Sancho's grasp: *Don Quixote* is now embraced as a symbol of the power of imaginative literature and high idealism, and Miguel de Cervantes is celebrated as a founding father of the modern Spanish language and its literary traditions. A book about books that is rarely read in its entirety anymore is now featured in annual celebrations of the *Día del Libro* on April 23, the anniversary of the death of that bookish book's once obscure but now famous author.

Don Quixote, Discursive Palimpsest

A first step to understanding this unique cultural presence is to consider how, as was argued of the *Comedia* in the previous chapter, the discursive composition of Cervantes's novel might contribute to it. The fact that *Don Quixote* lends itself to diverse readings is a common point of departure for scholars, but little consensus has been reached to explain how or why Cervantes was able to write such an open-ended book.[2] Our understanding of Cervantes's biography has developed through the intense efforts of *cervantistas*, particularly in the last several decades, to better understand the man behind the first modern novel. While his relative obscurity until the final years of his life has made such work painstaking and inconclusive, it does seem clear that the man whose statue sits above those of Don Quixote and Sancho Panza in Madrid's Plaza de España only came to write his masterpiece after a relatively long life of frustrated attempts to be recognized by and incorporated into the upper echelons of the emerging nation's imperial administration and cultural pantheon. Beyond making especially ironic his current status as the patron saint of Spanish literature, culture, and language, his pre-*Quixote* obscurity has also made efforts to recover information about his life all the more difficult. This ironic struggle reached a climax when, a year before the 400th anniversary of his death, the municipal government of Madrid verified via forensic testing that his remains were finally recovered after their unmarked burial beneath a convent in the city in 1617. The Real Academia Española organized a public dedication of a new, marked tomb for Cervantes in the Church of the Trinity, and despite the efforts of Mayor Ana Botella's dedication speech to frame the event as a correction of past injustice, one cannot fail to note the convenient consequence of a new tourist destination added to the city's cultural pantheon.

Such ironic circumstances might also be a productive point of departure for understanding why *Don Quixote* has proven to be so interpretively malleable. Cervantes was clearly equipped to be a famous author, but prior to his waning years he had not achieved the kind of transcendent fame that he enjoys posthumously. While scholars now frequently resist the kind of biographical approach that would consider the author's life as an interpretive key capable of unlocking the meaning of his text, there is considerable

---

2 My own understanding of the *Quixote*'s facility for diverse readings, as these pages will show, tends to align with what Cascardi (2002) describes less as an utterly new discursive phenomenon than as an innovative reconfiguration of inherited discursive models.

consensus that some events of his life—the most frequently cited examples are his captivity in Algiers and his work as a traveling representative of the monarchy's financial interests—undoubtedly inform the novel in some way. Certainly, the kind of linguistic and discursive diversity represented in the text are the result of such personal experiences, of the wide variety of people (and linguistic communities) he must have encountered on the road in Spain and as a soldier and prisoner of war abroad. It stands to reason that the way in which (and to what end) that diversity is arranged and combined would also be informed by that experience. To my knowledge, no better theory exists as to why *Don Quixote* eludes a fixed, facile, or exclusive reading than the fact that, amid the same cultural circumstances informing Lope de Vega's ability to write eternally adaptable plays, Cervantes also viewed his society from the critical distance of an aging man whose efforts to be embraced by the budding Spanish state were repeatedly frustrated. Because he wrote the *Quixote* after failing to be recognized by a monarchy for which he had risked and sacrificed his entire adult life (and for which he literally gave his left arm),[3] the posthumously canonized genius manipulated discursive models, both canonical (chivalric and pastoral romance, classical epic) and hegemonic (historical narrative, autobiography, biblical scripture, political theory), emanating from a system by which his efforts to be recognized were repeatedly thwarted.

Regardless of how closely we associate his text with his life, the discursive games played throughout the *Quixote* clearly impact the presentation—and more importantly, the interpretation—of its title character. Scholars have been intrigued by this ludic discursivity since at least the 1930s, when Mikhail Bakhtin examined the text's decisive influence on Dostoevsky, and the terminology and theoretical grounding of similar approaches have only increased in sophistication since (from Leo Spitzer's "linguistic perspectivism" [1948] to Cascardi's "orphic fiction" [2010] and all points in between). From the very front matter presenting the book—a series of mock-dedicatory poems meant to ape the conventions of literary tradition, for example by having the Cid's horse Babieca dedicate an elegy to Don Quixote's horse, Rocinante—through the 1605 metaprologue and indeed throughout all 126 chapters of the novel's two installments, the discursively subversive games of parody and satire constantly demand that the reader navigate ideologically slippery waters. The ironic juxtaposition of discursive models—for example,

---

3 Cervantes's many biographers invariably note at least two failed attempts to solicit positions in Spain and the American colonies as a functionary of Castile, of which Cervantes felt deserving due to his service, disabling war injuries, and captivity as a soldier in the Castilian King's military.

the chivalric discourse of Don Quixote with the picaresque discourse of the galley slaves in Part 1, Chapter 22—reveal and undermine the ideological orientation of each such model. The dizzying framing and re-framing of narratives, the use of narrators of questionable reliability, and of course the frequent recurrence of metafictional elements all contribute to a reading experience in which an authorial voice—let alone the author's clear intent—cannot be pinned down. Scores of articles and monographs, including Carroll B. Johnson's *Don Quixote: The Quest for Modern Fiction*, have attempted to account for the novel's elusive meaning; Johnson's book, for example, isolates Cervantes's masterful use of irony as a lesson learned from Erasmus in the context of writing under theocratic scrutiny in early modern Spain. James Parr's pivotal study *Don Quixote: Anatomy of a Subversive Discourse* is one of the more sophisticated narratological attempts to treat the issue, and with clearly different methodology Parr arrives at conclusions that echo those of Johnson and many other late twentieth-century scholars: *Don Quixote* is deliberately open to interpretation, by design.

It is therefore not surprising that the novel's eponymous protagonist has come to mean different things to different people. John Jay Allen's seminal question of "Don Quixote: Hero or Fool?" reflects how those who study the novel must invariably come to the question of how readers experience the protagonist; it echoes our desire to understand the text via a false binary from which any argument for "hero" can be easily answered with equally persuasive evidence for "fool." A middle-ground position is now often taken by critics, in effect that Don Quixote is both heroic and foolish—a foolish hero or a heroic fool, according to by whom, when, and how the text is read.

Between a "Soft" and a "Hard" Place: A Critical Reception History

What makes Cervantes's text truly exceptional, however, is the passion with which both poles of this binary have been argued. As scholars established during the second half of the twentieth century,[4] the cacophony of critical interpretations can be synthesized into the basic contours of the novel's reception history: the so-called "funny book" (Russell) or "hard" (Close) reading, in which Don Quixote is understood as a foolish object of ridicule, appears to have dominated its initial popular success through the seventeenth century and into the eighteenth. As Eduardo Urbina, Ana Laguna, José Manuel Lucía Megías, and Rachel Schmidt have effectively demonstrated through the

---

4 See Russell and Close for arguably the most influential efforts in this regard during the twentieth century. An excellent and more recent tracing of the novel's reception history is offered by Howard Mancing.

study of illustrated editions of the novel over the centuries, the satirical focus of early readers would eventually spread throughout Europe as the novel continued to be translated into new languages for new readerships. By the closing decades of the eighteenth century, Don Quixote was a world-renowned mock-hero inspiring laughter across Europe and the Americas.

The earliest significant effort in Spain to present Don Quixote as more than a "fool" was the RAE-commissioned 1780 edition published by Joaquín Ibarra, the production of which was enthusiastically supported by King Carlos III himself. As the first institutionally directed effort to control the novel's reception, this edition featured a biographical sketch of Cervantes, a critical introduction and textual analysis by Vicente de los Rios, extensive illustrations commissioned by the Real Academia from a number of high-profile artists, and even a map of Don Quixote's alleged route drawn by Spain's official royal cartographer, Tomás López. This edition of the novel, then, communicates a degree of monumentality that reflects how seriously Spaniards were meant to take it as a cultural artifact (from the perspective of the Real Academia), with the appended map suggesting even a presentation of Don Quixote as a quasi-historical figure. Such considerable institutional muscle suggests that by 1780, Spanish cultural and political institutions had come to see the *Quixote* as a collective treasure, an artifact of cultural patrimony whose image and reception should be managed according to proto-national interests. Among those interests would be that of promoting an understanding of the text that acknowledged its sophistication and complexity, or that it was more than "just a funny book" and therefore a source of pride for the Spanish people.

The problem with this early strategy of "nationalizing" the *Quixote*, however, was that the text itself stubbornly resists a homogenized consensus reading. Even prior to the publication of the 1615 sequel the text and protagonist's meaning were subject to debate, a point featured by Cervantes in the opening chapters of the sequel during Sancho's metafictional description of Part 1's reception. (Sancho reports that the opinions of Part 1's readers are divided: some think Don Quixote heroic, others foolish.) Cervantes's opening prologue declares an authorial distance from his text (he is Don Quixote's "stepfather," not his father) that frees his "idle readers" to say whatever they want about it without offending him. And while the case can be made that the conclusion to Part 2 ("for me alone was Don Quixote made, and I for him") attempts to reclaim authorial control of his subject, a reversal no doubt stimulated by Avellaneda's spurious (and to Cervantes, offensive) false sequel published in 1614, this final chapter could not reverse the openness to interpretation of the previous 125 chapters—as evinced by the novel's diverse reception history.

Beyond the fact that Cervantes problematizes existing discursive models and their interpretation throughout his novel, its presentation by the publishing industry for the bulk of the early modern period contributed to the interpretive instability. The episodic nature of the text lends itself to fragmentary reading of adventures or chapters isolated from the context of the novel's broader narrative trajectory, and its publication in cheaply produced smaller and more portable installments (most commonly four volumes) during the eighteenth century, as both Rachel Schmidt and Enrique Rodríguez Cepeda explain, only furthered the tendency to read the text in fragments without concern for the longer narrative within which his episodic adventures originally appeared. As early as 1605, Don Quixote began appearing outside the pages of Cervantes's novel—first in public festivities and spectacles, later in the public theaters, and ultimately as a ubiquitous point of cultural reference in countless writings about Spain. As we will see, this phenomenon of "taking Don Quixote out of context" (i.e., treating the hero but not the text through which he was created) would become an enduring practice that can still be observed today, particularly in digital media and touristic merchandise. It is an understandable practice, given the interpretational challenges and the often contradictory presentations made of the protagonist by Cervantes throughout the novel; more to the point, the practice of "liberating" Don Quixote from the complex narrative design of his original author has undoubtedly contributed and continues to contribute to his propensity for being enlisted for diverse and often contradictory causes.

Don Quixote and the Nation

Two major developments in Western thought relevant to the fate of *Don Quixote* converge in the nineteenth century: the modern concept of "nation" and the aesthetic sensibility of Romanticism. Their combined impact on how *Don Quixote* and its eponymous protagonist would be interpreted cannot be overstated. While the emergence of modern nation-states in this century is integral to the process through which the Spanish Empire unraveled, Spain's own efforts to achieve the kind of modernized nation-state undertaken by its European neighbors were slow and fraught with complications. Economic, legal, and infrastructural measures were slow to develop as Spain concerned itself with maintaining its waning empire and negotiating its own political instability. As Eric Storm has explained, this delay is in large measure due to the emergence in the nineteenth century of peripheral regional nationalist movements (in Catalonia and the Basque Country), which gathered further steam and momentum as Spain's colonies were lost (145–47). An underfunded and outdated system of public education resulted in literacy rates significantly below that of its neighbors, as it still remained below 50% in the year 1900. Given the inextricable links between nation-building and language policy, not to mention the linkage between language policy and the peripheral nationalist movements that impeded Spain's efforts to organize itself into a modern nation-state in line with the rest of Europe, the low rates of literacy were particularly problematic.

As this fraught process of modernization continued in the nineteenth century, readers of *Don Quixote* outside of Spain began to treat the novel in ways that departed radically from the burlesque-satire tradition that dominated the seventeenth and eighteenth centuries. Anthony Close's seminal book *The Romantic Approach to Don Quixote* details both the considerable number of writers and scholars associated with Romanticism and their common cause of linking nation and national identity with cultural production, thereby rendering national identity and cultural traditions so as to allow for the latter to evince the character of the former. It was then, as the aesthetics of Romanticism inspired a more general nostalgia for the historical (and national) past, that earlier literary achievements became directly implicated in the articulation of more contemporary political concerns, including such notions as national literary traditions and canons. If scholarship on the *Quixote* during the Enlightenment worked to establish for Cervantes a place among the great writers of Classical Antiquity, that cultural prestige would be leveraged by Romantic scholars to argue for his pre-eminence in the Spanish national pantheon, and in turn for the pre-eminence of that national pantheon itself in the grander scheme of Western literature.

While Close explains in detail how nineteenth-century Romantic writers and thinkers, especially in Germany and England, provided the initial impetus behind what would become the "soft" or Romantic reading of the novel (in particular highlighting the work of the Schlegel brothers, Schelling, and Tieck), in Spain this approach acquired new resonance and urgency as the nation faced an existential crisis in 1898. That year provided definitive closure to Spain's imperial past, as the nation's remaining major colonies of Cuba, Puerto Rico, and the Philippines were surrendered to the U.S. at the close of the Spanish–American War. The sense of cultural calamity was felt no more acutely than among the nation's intellectual elites, and a group of diverse thinkers who explicitly addressed the crisis (including Miguel de Unamumo, José Martínez Ruiz or "Azorín," Antonio Machado, and Pío Baroja) became known as the "Generation of 1898." In the group's varied efforts to address the *fin-de-siècle* problem and define a post-imperial national identity, no cultural figure was more prominently invoked than that of Don Quixote.

The most celebrated figure of the Generation of 1898, especially in terms of his use of Don Quixote to argue for Spain's need to forge a new sense of common national identity, is Miguel de Unamuno, whose *Vida de Don Quijote y Sancho* (1905) consists of an extended, chapter-by-chapter gloss of Cervantes's entire novel. This gloss is atypical, insofar as it does not attempt to clarify for the reader of Cervantes his ostensibly intended meaning, but rather to retrain the *fin-de-siècle* Spanish reader so that he may take the text as a map for navigating his nation's current existential crisis. In many instances, in fact, Unamuno often pauses to question or belittle the way in which Cervantes characterizes what his protagonist does, or what happens to him. Paradoxically, Cervantes is not worthy of his own literary creation—a notion upon which Unamuno would further elaborate in his prologue to the book's second edition: his task in writing *Vida de Don Quijote y Sancho* was to "liberate" Don Quixote from Cervantes himself (*Prólogo a la segunda edición*, 134). For Unamuno, the actions of Don Quixote require re-interpretation so as to more clearly demonstrate the hero's invariable utility to twentieth-century Spain.

Along similar lines, José Ortega y Gasset's *Meditaciones del Quijote* (1914) engages Don Quixote as a cultural figure from whom Spain can take inspiration as it works to clarify its modern national identity. For our purposes here, more important than his articulation of a post-Cartesian philosophical model to account both for individual subjectivity and an engagement with one's external circumstances is his appropriation of Don Quixote for philosophical purposes with ultimately nationalistic implications, not unlike Unamuno. In both cases, philosophical meditations inspired by reading and glossing Cervantes's novel are not aimed at explicating or better understanding *Don Quixote*, but rather at deploying its protagonist for more contemporary concerns.

The list of philosophers and other intellectuals who would continue to invoke the figure of Don Quixote over the course of the twentieth century to address contemporary national concerns is both impressive and long. Indeed, as Christopher Britt-Arredondo explains, the messianic nature of the "Quixotism" of the Generation of 1898 unwittingly laid the ideological groundwork for the Franco regime's vision of an essentialist, homogenous Spanish national identity:

> As a form of cultural nationalism, Quixotism did generate new imaginary ways in which Spaniards could represent to themselves their real relationship to the modern world. Insofar as these imaginary representations served to nationalize the modern nation, Quixotism helped to lay the conceptual groundwork for the political nationalism that became a permanent feature of fascist Spain. (*Quixotism*, 173)

To validate such a claim, one need look no further than Ramiro de Maeztu, a nationalist thinker whose writings worked synchronously with the dictatorships of both Primo de Rivera and Franco. Maeztu's *Don Quijote, Don Juan y la Celestina. Ensayos de simpatía* (1926) mines decades of Romantic praise for the genius of Cervantes and his work, but more importantly he takes the title character himself as point of departure for elaborating a nationalist archetypal myth, with emphasis placed on Don Quixote's persistent references to his Catholic faith and argumentation grounded in a platonic notion of essences and appearances. Don Quixote, in other words, re-casts the platonic orientation of reality in a quintessentially Spanish way. What is striking about Maeztu's analysis is its dependence on the "soft" or Romantic treatment of the character as a serious and inspirational voice for the Spanish people, which stands in stark contrast to the pre-Romantic treatment of him as a buffoonish object of ridicule.

Britt-Arredondo's book analyzes the consequences of such "Quixotism" to show that they would continue to reverberate in the Spanish political system over the course of the dictatorship and beyond. *Don Quixote* would be similarly invoked with each national crisis and indeed with each politically exploitable opportunity, including the commemorations in 1992 of Columbus's "discovery" of the New World and in 1998 of the Spanish–American War, not to mention the 2005 and 2015 celebrations of the 400th anniversary of the publication of the novel and the 2016 anniversary of Cervantes's death. In order to understand these most recent instances of *Quixote*-related cultural programming, however, it is important to understand the ways in which twentieth-century Spanish intellectuals developed ideas inherited from Romantic criticism into a sophisticated philological tradition—even if, as we shall see, that intellectual tradition evolved independently of more popular invocations of *Don Quixote* in Spanish culture over the course of the twentieth century.

Don Quixote and the Philological Tradition

It is difficult to achieve a clean separation of many twentieth-century Spanish philological *Quixote* studies and the political and cultural functions they are implicitly meant to serve. This is especially true during the Franco regime, when the exodus of the Falange's political opponents featured a number of heterogeneous and heterodox philologists and intellectuals, leaving behind a more homogenous national university system to be monitored and controlled by the state. One can, however, detect a gradual shift in Spanish *Quixote* studies over the course of the twentieth century from studies linking Cervantes's biography to his literary achievement (the *vida y obras* or "life and works" approach, which can be linked to Romantic notions of artistic genius and national canon formation) to philological studies, especially since Franco's death, focused synchronically on better explicating and contextualizing Cervantes's novel. The former tendency, exemplified by such celebrated studies as Américo Castro's *El pensamiento de Cervantes* (1925, republished in 1972), Luis Astrana Marín's *Vida ejemplar y heroica de Miguel de Cervantes Saavedra* (published in seven volumes between 1948 and 1958), and Juan Bautista Avalle-Arce's *Deslindes cervantinos* (1961) and *Don Quijote como forma de vida* (1976), is characterized by philological admiration for Cervantes, the Spanish nation's seminal man of letters, and for his greatest masterpiece.[5] This is the same nationalist-heroic projection of Cervantes, we should note, that inspired the Primo de Rivera regime to erect his statue (along with Don Quixote and Sancho) in Madrid's Plaza de España, and that would increasingly become the focus of philological study over the course of the twentieth century.

As the field of philology became influenced by the emergent (at least in Spain) discipline of Linguistics, Spanish *Quixote* studies focused their attention on questions of language and stylistics, as in Joaquín Casalduero's *Sentido y forma del Quijote* (1970) and Ángel Rosenblat's *La lengua del Quijote* (1971). More recent philological inquiry, including such notable studies as José Montero Reguera's *El Quijote y la crítica contemporánea* (1997) and José Manuel Lucía Megías's *De los libros de caballerías manuscritos al Quijote* (2004), has narrowed its focus to questions of the literary and linguistic traditions that informed Cervantes's writing and to which Cervantes himself contributed.[6]

Not coincidentally, this narrowed focus on sources and influences coincides with the surge of "hard" readings of the novel across the Atlantic initiated by Anthony Close's seminal book. Spanish philology found itself in the awkward position of being best equipped to access archival materials that would confirm the anachronistic nature of the Romantic approach—evidence of the *Quixote*'s original reception in Spain—but working from a tradition that through the 1970s (the waning years of the dictatorship and its immediate aftermath) continued to embrace that approach, as is apparent in such titles as Avalle-Arce's *Don Quijote como forma de vida* [Don Quixote as a Way of Life]. Over the course of the 1980s and 1990s, however, Spanish *cervantistas* would gradually transition away from nationalist

---

5 While Avalle-Arce is not a Spaniard, I include him here because his work did resonate with and participate in this current of Spanish philology.

6 See Jauralde Pou for a more detailed assessment of the Spanish philological tradition and its "linguistic turn."

impulses and join the Anglo-American academy's "historical turn," which included studies reliant upon a narrowed and more synchronic Spanish philological enterprise in order better to understand the original literary and historical contexts within which their objects of study originated. It should also be noted that since the 1980s, Spanish *Quixote* studies have more explicitly extricated themselves from the political and ideological baggage that often inflected the work of earlier generations of *cervantistas* such as José Antonio Maravall—a tendency that holds true of Spanish philological studies more generally.

The move away from the political and ideological and toward a more dispassionate "return to history" has brought with it unintended consequences. If the Spanish academy's treatment of *Don Quixote* has become less political and more disinterested, it has also become less engaged with the very political nature of Spain's broader cultural reverence for Cervantes, his masterpiece and his protagonist. To be sure, admiration for Cervantes among philologists is as strong as ever, as one can easily perceive when these experts are asked in non-academic venues to contribute to cultural programming that celebrates the author and his work. But in academic publications, the inherent public appeal of what may be called the "hero worship" of previous generations of Cervantes scholars was replaced with a mode of philological inquiry that, as with humanistic studies in North America, found its engagement with the broader public waning as its focus became increasingly archaeological and formalist in nature. This fading public engagement has been placed in stark relief by Europe's recent economic crises, which have gravely impacted the Spanish economy and left its university system vulnerable to the budgetary chopping block of "austerity." Calls for drastic measures to restructure and downsize the system have placed the field of philology itself in a precarious position at the same time as *Quixote* studies find themselves more distanced from the public, popular figure of Don Quixote in cultural programming and popular culture than ever before.

Don Quixote, Commodified and Institutionalized

Beyond the proverbial academic tower, the sustained ideological appropriation of *Don Quixote* as filtered through its "soft" or Romantic tradition—Don Quixote is Spain, Spain is quixotic—runs parallel to a broader cultural embrace of the hero that is readily visible in the nation's tourism industry. As Bernabéu-López and Rocamora-Abellán explain, a series of efforts by various Spanish governments to promote tourism in the country began in 1928, eventually featuring the most famous national slogan, first launched in 1948: "Spain is different" (94). The tourism industry's emphasis on "difference" as Spain emerged from a decade of post-Civil War isolationism and began an intensive effort to modernize (known as the *etapa de desarrollo* or "period of development") was a creative attempt to put a positive spin on the consequences of the Franco regime's economically and culturally disastrous retrograde policies, not unlike the quixotic spin applied to the aftermath of 1898. This effort to sell Spain to the world inevitably enlisted Don Quixote and in the process raised his global profile: while "different" is a relatively non-descriptive adjective, the implicit modifier "quixotic"—implicitly reinforced with every monument erected and souvenir sold bearing the image of Don Quixote or making reference to Cervantes—makes clear how that adjective is meant to be understood: Spain is idealistic, romantic, delightfully impractical.

During the final years of the dictatorship, Don Quixote's cultural profile continued to thrive in an international context. Film adaptations from Hollywood, France, Yugoslavia, Finland, and Russia (among other places) were produced in the 1960s, and by 1972 a film adaptation of the Broadway musical *Man of La Mancha* had furthered the "soft," romanticized reading of the text and titular protagonist as an emblem of heroic idealism. While Franco himself did not explicitly identify with Don Quixote—his preferred Golden Age object of identification was the Cid—nor cast his regime as explicitly "quixotic," the international association made between Cervantes's protagonist and high idealism was no less evident in Spanish cultural references to and adaptations of the novel. Within the context of a dictatorship that floundered in its waning years amid broader social and cultural upheaval, Don Quixote's anachronistic quest to apply values and codes of conduct from a bygone era would resonate in a culture where fascistic notions of cultural homogeny and spiritual devotion were confronted by the complicated emerging realities of postmodernity and globalization. *Una, Grande y Libre* had been a running domestic political narrative of the regime since the 1930s, but its erosion over the decades was in many ways precipitated by social, cultural, and political movements across the Western world that largely contradicted it—again, not unlike the medieval narratives informing Don Quixote's chivalric values and mission when applied to the social realities of early modern Spain. Like Don Quixote, the waning regime insisted on values that had become anachronistic. For better or for worse, the Romantic approach to *Don Quixote* that had become a global phenomenon by the 1970s had also penetrated the Spanish cultural zeitgeist.

Writers would continue to link Spain to quixotic heroism well into the post-Franco democracy: Alejandro Quiroga would write in 2010, for example, that only Spain's dramatic success in international football competitions culminating in their 2010 World Cup victory allowed for the "strange death" of Don Quixote. For Quiroga, Don Quixote is a metonym for the Spanish nation, with a full century of frustrated attempts to win the World Cup standing for so many windmills knocking them to the ground. Their world dominance in the sport during the years surrounding their 2010 victory, which has often been cited as inspiring a level of cultural solidarity across Spain not seen since the dictatorship, effectively allowed the nation to claim the kind of victory that Don Quixote had always hoped to achieve, but which for him had never materialized. The rewritten conclusion of *Man of La Mancha*, in which Alonso Quijano rises from his deathbed to embrace his chivalric identity for a final song, is more in keeping with Quiroga's narrative than are the closing pages of Cervantes's novel.

This post-Franco heroic treatment of Don Quixote would present something of a dilemma for Spanish academics, for whom the enthusiasm with which he circulated in the national cultural imaginary presented both an opportunity and a threat. The opportunity, of course, was to raise awareness of Spanish Golden Age literature in popular culture, and to celebrate it as a source of national pride while enhancing the standing of the tradition's scholars through demonstrating their expertise. The threat, however, stemmed from how disconnected their own understanding of the novel was from the commodified and "soft" reading that had led to his popularity as an inspirational figure. Notwithstanding Anthony Close's impact on how scholars read *Don Quixote*, popular and touristic enthusiasm for the figure of Don Quixote remained far removed from any "hard" or burlesque line of interpretation. Scholarship among Spanish philologists, as we will see below, has generally been less engaged with *Don Quixote* than it was during the dictatorship, and has focused its efforts on subjects that avoid an open challenge to the popular "soft" readings driving the novel's cultural reception outside of the academy (identifying texts that inspired Cervantes, establishing criteria for new critical editions, connecting the text to its early modern cultural, discursive, and linguistic context, etc.).

If the "commodified" Don Quixote has been a "soft" idealist, the "institutionalized" Spanish scholarship since the end of the dictatorship has instead focused less on the ostensible heroic idealism of the character than on the genius of its author and the complexity of the first modern novel. In his *El Quijote y la crítica contemporánea* (1997), for example, José Montero Reguera organizes the "greatest hits" of *Quixote* studies published between 1975 and 1990 according to several categories relating to the novel's structure, context, and reception—with no mention of the symbolic value of the novel's protagonist that so dominates his presence in popular culture. It is worth noting that Montero Reguera's book, published in Alcalá de Henares and awarded the Premio Fernández Abril by the RAE, features more non-Spanish than Spanish scholars. Pablo Jauralde Pou notes that the methodology of Spanish philology has limited the impact of its practitioners on current *Quixote* studies, leaving the bulk of innovative scholarship on the novel to scholars based (and trained) outside of Spain. Jauralde Pou also attributes the problem to Spanish scholars' lack of "aesthetic distance" (110) from the novel, a concept that I would relate to the kind of tension described above between popular and academic understandings of the text and its protagonist. Rather than openly confront the popular embrace of quixotic heroism in order to offer a more historically nuanced interpretation of the novel, Spanish philology has for the most part preferred to focus on issues that do not openly contest the protagonist's popular "soft" symbolic capital.

There are, of course, other institutions beyond university philology departments that have made more concerted efforts to work synergistically with popular understandings of Don Quixote (the character) and *Don Quixote* (the text). The global and universal acclaim as a literary classic assigned to *Don Quixote* explains the cultural authority of its author, whose name in turn has proven a powerful cultural signifier for a wide array of governmental and academic institutions—most notably the RAE, the Instituto Cervantes, and local and regional governments like that of Castilla-La Mancha. The bulk of these institutional efforts to harness the popular cultural capital of *Don Quixote* are more amenable to the romantic-idealist understanding of its protagonist, and are leveraged to promote economic development, tourism, and (especially in the case of the Real Academia and the Instituto Cervantes) literacy and reading. The focus on literacy is especially striking, given that the afterlife of the *Quixote* is fundamentally different from that of other Golden Age texts. The repackaging and adaptation of other "classics" of the *Siglo de oro* must, like the *Quixote*, depend on the interpretive lens of its adaptors, but the *Quixote* has become such a fixture in the popular imaginary both within and outside of Spain that its afterlife has taken on a life of its own, so to speak—and one largely independent of the bulk of critical attention the novel has received. The continuing cultural pertinence of *Don Quixote* depends increasingly less on the work of academic *cervantistas* and more on the meanings attached to it by a broader constituency of *desocupados lectores* and, for better or worse, non-readers.

This is of course the great irony of the *Quixote*'s perpetual celebrity, brought clearly into focus with the 400th anniversary fanfare of 2005: the novel's celebration would on the surface suggest avid readership, but with the *Quixote*, cultural ubiquity is not necessarily a function of how many people have actually read the text. Indeed, one would normally equate increased sales of copies of the text with increased readership, but

Francisco Rico, Martín de Riquer, and other Spanish scholars associated with the Real Academia regularly lament—and actively work to correct, via cultural programming—the Spanish people's general disconnect with the novel that produced their beloved character. The fashionable Christmas gift of the fourth centennial anniversary of the publication of the novel's first installment (2005), for example, was one of several luxury, leather-bound editions of the novel produced for the anniversary, but not so much as a book to be read as an object to display, a symbol of cultural prestige and status that did not require actual readership. The most noteworthy edition, published by the Real Academia Española, sold half a million copies within a month of its release. And yet the dirty little secret of Spain's embrace of *Don Quixote* is that, as Andrés Trapiello and many others often note, the spine of the book remains pristine. Extrapolating from the most recent survey available online (2015, from the Centro de Investigaciones Sociológicas and later reported by the newspaper *La vanguardia*), the spine remains pristine for approximately 400,000 of those half-million copies sold. As E. C. Riley notes, the most surprising detail of Don Quixote's fame is that it extends to those who have never read *Don Quixote* (106).

Don Quixote, Mediated

The reason why *Don Quixote* can be so well known by non-readers is that it has been so institutionalized as to present itself more easily and more accessibly through the various filters of Spanish national cultural and educational programming: graded readers, abridgements, modern adaptations (novelistic, theatrical, and filmic), and even graphic novels. These simulacra render the original novel seemingly unnecessary, and better left upon the bookshelf to be admired with its unbroken spine, in order to participate in Spanish national celebrations of it. If we limit the discussion to printed texts alone, countless versions bearing the name *Mi primer Quijote* have been used in elementary schools throughout the Spanish-speaking world to promote both reading and, particularly in Spain, the cultural patrimony of the original text. A popular Spanish television animated series and interactive books based on those animations have also helped to literally institutionalize the novel, to graft it inseparably to the programs for reading and literacy in the Spanish elementary educational system. More recently, interactive websites and digital editions are amplifying this institutionalization in sync with the habits of cultural consumption by millennials and other twenty-first-century "readers." Add to this the number of film and television adaptations of the *Quixote* in Spain and beyond, including the six-hour miniseries produced by Televisión Española in the 1990s and the very romantic and liberal approach to the text taken in the Broadway musical *Man of La Mancha*, which was itself translated in the late 1990s and appeared on Madrid's Gran Vía (in the Teatro Lope de Vega) as *El hombre de la Mancha*. In 2007, the Spanish animation company Filmax produced a film, *Donkey Xote*, for young audiences who are even less likely to have read the novel than their older compatriots; in this adaptation, Sancho's donkey assumes the role of protagonist and self-consciously identifies its narrative style as an extension of Hollywood Pixar films like *Shrek*. Baudrillard's notion of the postmodern simulacrum seems to more aptly describe what the *Quixote* means today than it does any other classical text. With all of these more accessible and user-friendly packages available to us, the reasoning seems to be, who needs to read Cervantes anymore?

Spain's academics, of course, would promote readership of Cervantes's novel over viewership of his simulacra—which is precisely what their role has been in state-sponsored institutions beyond the academic contexts of peer-reviewed journals, books, and scholarly debate. That role is increasingly complicated by the growing disparity between the enthusiastic embrace of all things Quixote in popular culture and current research driven by philological textual analysis. *Don Quixote*'s high cultural profile is a good thing, most scholars would agree, but at the same time there is considerable frustration that this profile rarely matches the novel as understood through an academic lens. The same is true of the insights and messages currently assigned to Cervantes more generally, and philologists like Rico who inform Spanish cultural programming find themselves celebrating the text in a nation that is increasingly less likely to read it. This double-bind consists of the dual role of scholars as enthusiasts and as respectful guardians of literary tradition, of an ambassadorial desire to provide students and readers with fuller access to Cervantes and his work and a hesitancy to recognize that such access is irrevocably tied to the historically and culturally contingent vantage point from which Spaniards now access it. In the quest to have the *Quixote* be more widely read and enjoyed, Spanish philology is increasingly resigned to recognize that its own academically informed, synchronic understanding of the novel might necessarily be pushed aside.

This dilemma has not been treated by scholars, despite its importance for understanding the ways in which *Quixote* scholarship has developed since the late-twentieth century explosion of commoditized and visually mediated versions of the novel. I would argue that it explains why, as noted above by Montero Reguera and Jaiuralde Pou, the most innovative *Quixote* scholarship since that period has been generated outside of Spain. Anthony Close's *The Romantic Approach to Don Quixote* (1978) in a sense completes the work begun ten years earlier with the publication of P. E. Russell's seminal article "*Don*

Quixote as a Funny Book" by identifying and naming a line of interpretation that had systematically become mainstream since the nineteenth century, often with the encouragement of governmental cultural programming, but that is disconnected from what subsequent historicist scholarship has taught us about the novel's original reception. By signaling a history of diverse readings, this period of critical activity during the late 1960s and 1970s constituted a kind of interpretive *desengaño* for the field outside of Spain, insofar as it marked the recognition of a dominant mode of reading the *Quixote* as only one of many ways in which it could be interpreted.

It is worth noting, moreover, that the terminological shift in the broader field of North American Hispanism that has replaced "Golden Age literature" with "early modern Spanish literature" is not unrelated to this academic *desengaño*: the term "early modern studies" divests the field of the implicit valorization and cultural nostalgia of "Golden Age" and instead maps it onto a continuum that is synchronized with the broader currents of European literary and cultural studies. But if the Golden Age to early modern shift outside of Spain reflects an effort to distance the field critically from the cultural nostalgia implicit in the notion of a Spanish Golden Age, current terminological practice in the Spanish Academy has not followed suit: philology departments across Spain continue to refer to the field as *Siglo de oro*, the spinoff term *literatura áurea*, or, with no less cultural nostalgia, the self-affirming label *literatura clásica*. The recognition of a Romantic approach to the *Quixote* by British and American Hispanists ushered in a similar critical distance that reflects a broader theoretical and methodological shift in Hispanism (and in literary studies more generally) heading into the 1980s, when a variety of developments in critical theory worked their way into the field. But while Spanish philology has been influenced by these developments, the impetus to divest academic institutions of such nationalist terminology has taken root more firmly outside of Spain's borders and institutions than within them. The New Historicism, for example, developed first in the field of Shakespeare Studies in the United States. Its methodology of rigorous early modern textual historicization, which would by the end of the twentieth century find itself implicitly absorbed by most Hispanists outside of Spain, would bring lasting disciplinary consequences. Indeed, Close's and especially Russell's work may be seen as a prelude to neohistorical research, in that they urged scholars to not assume that any dominant reading of the *Quixote*, romantic or otherwise, runs parallel to the novel's seventeenth-century reception. It is a *desengaño*, in other words, of the illusion that any scholar can access early modern Spanish cultural production from a critical position of ahistorical omniscience.

Therefore, current scholarship outside of Spain has been especially keen to link the *Quixote* with more contemporary cultural concerns, for example by examining Cervantes's engagement with the *morisco* expulsion, representations of gender and race, political philosophy and shifting economic conditions, the ideological pressures of Church and State in early modern Spain, and similar problems informed by current events and contemporary social movements. In this spirit, scholars work to access Cervantes's early modern culture and society so as to better understand him, while also reading him to better understand his world in terms that resonate with our subject positions today.[7] While there is a healthy diversity of approaches and areas of focus in global Cervantes studies today, and while Spanish philology is itself diversifying, it does seem fair to consider the end of the last century and the first decades of the present century to be an era in which historically oriented research has played a major role, while "Romantic" readings of the *Quixote* have become less prominent.

Due to this academic disconnect from the popular "Romantic" afterlife that *Don Quixote* now enjoys in Spain (and beyond), there are effectively two novels called *Don Quixote*: an academic one that is elusive, discursively complex, and ideologically slippery, and a popular one that is intellectually stimulating, sentimentally appealing, spiritually inspiring, and politically valuable. This latter *Quixote* is the one evoked by José María Aznar and José Luis Rodríguez Zapatero at the turn of the twenty-first century just as it was by Miguel de Unamuno and his fellow *noventaiochistas* at the last turn of the century.[8] The problem for academic champions of the text is that this decontextualized, romanticized *Quixote* has carried the day in the realm of popular cultural production—the filters of simulacra that have largely replaced readership of the novel in Spain and beyond. To the same extent that *Quixote*-related Spanish cultural programming relies on the authority of academic "experts" in its messaging, it also requires respect for its cultural and political currency. Thus what began as philosophical and academic romanticization in the nineteenth century became a nationalistic political phenomenon that ultimately spilled over into *refundiciones*, re-creations, and references in popular culture to Don Quixote de la Mancha, romantic hero and paradigmatic idealist. It is a post-cervantine master narrative that, for the time being, appears to be here to stay. If philologists in Spain wish

---

[7] Recent examples of such historically oriented research, even if not overtly bearing the theoretical label of "neohistorical," include Carroll Johnson's book *Cervantes and the Material World*, William Childers's *Transnational Cervantes*, and William Eggington's *The Theater of Truth*.

[8] Internationally, Don Quixote's name has been invoked across the Hispanic world, from Subcomandante Marcos to Fidel Castro and Hugo Chavez.

to leverage popular enthusiasm for *Don Quixote* to promote contemporary causes, including literacy and the funding of humanistic fields of study in an era of fiscal austerity, they must pragmatically avoid dismissing or openly questioning that new master narrative.

Outside of Spain, of course, academics work from a vantage point that is (by comparison at least) free of such political and cultural entanglements. Hispanism has begun to turn its attention to the ripe field of popular and romantic deployments of *Don Quixote* since the German Romantics. As noted above, Christopher Britt-Arredondo's *Quixotism* reveals how Spanish thinkers beginning with the Generation of 1898 persistently invoked the figure of Don Quixote to reinvigorate a nation in crisis, a nationalist campaign to which Britt-Arredondo assigns blame for sowing the ideological seeds of the twentieth-century fascist movement. A more global approach to studying the *Quixote* as it is deployed today is taken by Julio Vélez-Sainz and Nieves Romero-Díaz, whose edited volume *Cervantes in/ and/on the New World* includes a number of essays focused on contemporary Latin American appropriations of the hero. Bruce Burningham has shown us that the Baroque aesthetics at work in the *Quixote* and other Golden Age texts resonate in postmodern culture in fascinating ways, all the while maintaining a healthy critical self-awareness and with full acknowledgment that such comparative studies always work as a function of the scholar's personal, subjective, and necessarily limited vantage point. In a recent review of Burningham's book *Tilting Cervantes*, William Childers explains very well why such exploration into the deep affinities between Cervantes's seventeenth-century literary production and our twenty-first-century postmodern culture is important: "The literature of the past means insofar as it continues to have meaning for people, people of flesh and blood who are alive now" (239).

Childers's statement reflects his own interest in engaging Cervantes with contemporary cultural circumstances. His book *Transnational Cervantes* includes the following statement: "I affirm the relevance of his seventeenth-century texts to pressing concerns of the twenty-first century by establishing analogies between the historical period during which the nation-state began to emerge and its current crisis" (ix). One example of Childers's method is the connections he draws between Cervantes's treatment of the Muslim world and the Spanish *morisco* expulsion in the *Quixote* and Spain's current immigration crisis in the wake of the Madrid Atocha terrorist attack in 2004. And yet, as compelling as this analogy is, it underscores how we must tread lightly when drawing such connections. Beyond the problematic lumping together of foreign Muslims like Zoraida and Spanish *moriscos*— two discrete communities and political problems, to be sure—is the fact that the analogy is made in a way as to suggest that Spain was devoid of *morisco* and immigrant north African communities between 1610 and the death of Franco. Such analogies, like adaptations, are always made through an interpretive lens deserving of critical scrutiny.

This last point does not diminish Childers's efforts to bring Cervantes to bear on contemporary cultural problems, nor does it prevent him from striking a balance between historicizing Cervantes and engaging him with today's world. A similar balance can also guide the study of how Cervantes is being engaged, adapted, and appropriated today, by elucidating the material conditions that stimulated his writing while also exploring the extent to which his continual re-interpretation is a function of similar or analogous circumstances in subsequent historical periods. Philological studies aimed at better understanding *Don Quixote*'s discursive complexity can be brought to bear on how he has proven to be interpretable in so many (often contradictory) ways. In this sense, to the extent that the figure of Don Quixote continues to be deployed, and to the extent that all such acts of deployment involve an interpretation of him (or of his multimedia simulacra), the novel *Don Quixote* continues to be written, notwithstanding Cervantes's efforts to bury him at the end of *his* version of the story. The *Quixote* holds a mirror up to Spanish society with each instance in which he is revived, a function that will endure as long as he continues to stimulate cultural production and reproduction.

Don Quixote, Cervantes, and the Written Word

Ironically, the popular and "Romantic" *Don Quixote* (transmitted by the simulacra of so many televisual adaptations and touristic items for sale) has been re-enlisted by the academy and the Spanish government to promote reading—the written word itself. The *Día del Libro* [Day of the Book] is celebrated in Spain annually on April 23, the date of Cervantes's death in 1616. It features the continuous reading of the novel aloud by various celebrated cultural figures. For the 2016 holiday, cultural institutions like the autonomous regional government of Castilla-La Mancha amped up their cultural profile by tweeting the entire novel. More recently, the Madrid metro system has decorated several stations with statues, murals, and even long passages of the novel's text for commuters to observe or read while they wait for the next train. *Don Quixote*, it seems, has come full circle as an object of consumption: the originally best-selling novel, subsequently canonized by scholars as a "classic," would become so potent a symbol of national identity and so powerful a brand name for popular consumption that it could finally serve as ambassador for literature itself, and for a Spanish philological establishment desperate to revive its cultural relevance and to restore the mode of consumption for which the knight had originally been created, and ironically to which he owes his insanity: reading.

Upon examining Spanish cultural programming surrounding the 400th anniversary of the publication of Part 2 of *Don Quixote*, a pattern emerges in comparison to the cultural response to the 2005 commemoration of Part 1's publication. While to some extent the differences between the 2005 and 2015 anniversaries reflect the differences between the two installments of the novel, I would argue that they have more to do with the very different circumstances in which the anniversary celebrants found themselves in Spain, where in 2005 there was little worry about an impending economic collapse. The recently elected PSOE government led by President José Luis Rodríguez Zapatero promised to shift gears and stimulate prosperity, but the global economic crisis of the intervening years led instead to unprecedented unemployment, brutal policies of economic austerity (made worse by the policies of the subsequent Partido Popular government) and indeed a general existential crisis in Spanish society, particularly among the millennial generation. In other words, in 2015 Spain celebrated the second anniversary differently than it did ten years beforehand, because in many ways it was a different country that thus enlisted *Don Quixote* to tilt at fundamentally different windmills.

What is especially ironic is that in this case, context seems to reflect text, at least in the sense that Spain's pre- and post-economic crisis periods seem reminiscent of how the 1615 sequel departs from the 1605 first part of the *Quixote*. While Part 1 is a kind of Renaissance reader or sampler plate, through which the reader may taste the diverse modes of literary representation at Cervantes's disposal, Part 2 is a dissertation on the Baroque that traces a slow spiral of disillusion. The insane optimism of Part 1 is gradually replaced by disenchantment (of Dulcinea, of Don Quixote himself) and a depressing return to self-awareness—what a Shakespearean scholar might call more *Hamlet* and less *Twelfth Night*. The discursive games continue, of course, but their scope widens beyond the sphere of literary genres to include political theory, philosophy, and the material practices of cultural production like bookmaking and puppeteering. Characters are inserted and their narratives are interpolated less as stand-ins for literary genres, and more as reflections of current events and debates that had occurred in the years between 1605 and 1615, including the expulsion of *moriscos* from Spain. To manage this "breaking news coverage," Cervantes also includes far more chapters in the 1615 sequel in which Don Quixote himself is not present, especially when Sancho parts ways to try his hand at governance. But the single greatest difference between the two volumes is that while

Part 1 leveraged humor from the relationship between Don Quixote and his books, in Part 2 the intertext is replaced: from the opening of the sequel, Don Quixote dialogues not with chivalric romance but with Part 1 of *Don Quixote*. By the end of the sequel, that intertextual dialogue is expanded to include Avellaneda's apocryphal continuation of the novel, published just as Cervantes wrote the final chapters of his own sequel.

This difference between the two parts may help explain why the 2015 celebrations seem to focus more on *Don Quixote* the novel and on Cervantes the author, whereas 2005 celebrations focused more on the character and hero Don Quixote. While in the U.S. and Latin America there seems to have been less difference between the two anniversaries, the pattern in Spain was that while 2005 featured a heavier load of *Quixote*-related commerce (new critical and vanity editions of the novel for sale, heavy marketing of DVD copies of the many televisual adaptations of the text, and a wide variety of Quixotic paraphernalia and memorabilia), 2015 appeared to be less about profit and more about institutional and community-based cultural programming.

Among the most interesting institutional efforts are those by the autonomous and eponymous region of Castilla-La Mancha, whose culture and tourism ministry launched Qvixote2015, a website and social media presence for disseminating its own programming during the year, which might also be described cynically as an opportunistic attempt to generate tourism for the region on the back of its most famous icon. From poster competitions and all kinds of educational events aimed at children to museums and other artistic exhibits, film screenings and theatrical performances, and especially literary events like public lectures and readings (including an ambitious effort to arrange the entire novel in eight-line fragments read individually and uploaded to a designated YouTube channel by readers across the globe), this campaign has leveraged twenty-first-century technology to call attention to a region whose tourism industry, like Don Quixote himself, has always been defined anachronistically; visiting rural La Mancha is billed as a return to tradition and to the cultural past. At the same time, Castilla-La Mancha has sponsored *QuijoteTeam*, a crowd-funded effort to aid global charities and to call attention to climate change. Two Subaru four-wheel drive trucks, named Don Quixote and Sancho, traveled across Europe that summer to deliver humanitarian aid and educational materials to Mongolia, with stops along the way in Germany, Kazakhstan, and Moscow to promote awareness of Don Quixote's "impossible dream" and to take lots of selfies. At the end of the trip, the carbon emissions required for the drive were offset by planting pine trees in Mongolia. Beyond *QuijoteTeam*, the Qvixote2015 campaign included a prolific presence on Twitter to promote all *Quixote*-related cultural programming across the globe—especially those activities that might also promote the exporting of Manchegan goods, such as the wines whose storage in skins Don Quixote mistook for bleeding giants and the cheeses that Sancho would keep in his saddlebags. This point is driven home by the regional government's launch of https://quijote2015.blogspot.com/, Castilla-La Mancha's website organizing the celebration of the 400th anniversary of the publication of Part 2 of the *Quixote*:

> Todo ello con el firme propósito de convertir a Castilla-La Mancha, región que lleva con orgullo el nombre del ingenioso hidalgo Don Quijote, en el epicentro cultural y turístico nacional e internacional, con lo que esto último tiene de beneficioso para el fomento la actividad económica regional, cuyos sectores más pujantes aprovechan estas emblemáticas citas para atraer el mayor número de visitantes.[9]
>
> [All of which has the firm purpose of converting Castilla-La Mancha, the region that carries with pride the name of the ingenious gentleman Don Quixote, into the cultural and tourist epicenter nationally and internationally, which is beneficial to fostering regional economic activity, of which the most dynamic sectors take advantage of these emblematic quotations to attract the largest number of visitors.]

In sum, the 2005 celebrations of the novel were dominated by capitalistic opportunism, while 2015 activities instead focused on philanthropy and cultural awareness, which suggests that the novel's commercial value is now being leveraged for local and regional economic growth rather than private enterprise. As noted above, the difference between 2005's use of *Don Quixote* as a product for sale and 2015's use of *El Quijote*—the monumentality of the novel and its author more than the character himself—may be partially explained by how the novel's 1605 installment presented a more coherent optimism resonant with Renaissance Humanism, while the 1615 sequel presents a more baroque hall-of-narrative mirrors that engages contemporary problems and decenters the mock-hero's role. But another compelling explanation, especially in Spain, would be the very different cultural and economic climate in Spain today in comparison to ten years ago. This cultural change, occasioned by a post-2005 economic collapse and numerous political scandals, seems to parallel the trajectory of the novel itself from Renaissance optimism to Baroque pessimism. Millions of copies, often in deluxe leather binding, were sold in 2005. During the following ten

---

9 https://e00-elmundo.uecdn.es/documentos/2015/01/23/quijote.pdf

years, as staggering unemployment, recession, and economic austerity took their toll, surveys revealed that despite these record sales of the novel, only one in five Spaniards has actually read it.[10] Franciso Rico argues that this ignorance of the text itself is not due its inaccessibility to modern audiences so much as it is due to Spanish culture and society today, which has chosen smart phones over book reading and is generally too lazy to pay the kind of sustained attention that reading the novel requires. While the novel and its hero remain unimpeachable classics, their society and culture have declined so as to leave Rico wondering if Spain really deserves its national hero anymore, given its failure to maintain the artistic and cultural standards for which Cervantes has borne the standard for centuries.

While Rico's dismay at the lack of *Quixote* readership is understandable, it is worth noting that his description of a contemporary culture disinclined to read—especially from a printed book—could easily be applied to most contemporary Western cultures. From a broader perspective we can say that what Rico describes is in fact not unlike Brett Levinson's notion of "the end of literature," by which he means that the literary text has descended from it previously enjoyed place of cultural prestige to compete, as one of so many print and digital modes of cultural production, for public attention and consumption. While I hesitate to extend the analogy with Levinson's term for too long, as it describes the very different cultural circumstances of the post-boom neoliberal Latin American marketplace, it is worth noting that Don Quixote may not be the only hero fighting this culture war. But to the extent that Spanish institutions enlist academics like Francisco Rico to preserve the *Quixote*'s cultural privilege, it seems fair to say that Don Quixote's latest battle pits him against his fiercest enemy of all: the "end" of literature itself.

Rico stands among the most prominent and active of the many intellectuals in Spain working through cultural institutions like the Real Academia and the Instituto Cervantes to promote Cervantes and *Don Quixote*, and his lamentations of the current state of Spanish culture suggests that his participation in cultural programming focused on the novel is seen as a kind of public service. Rico's latest efforts include a state-of-the-philological-art critical edition of the novel, published by the Real Academia in 2005, and a national publicity campaign to promote it alongside the quadricentennial celebrations, despite having already published another edition of the text under the auspices of the Instituto Cervantes (an open-access online edition)

---

10 As reported by the Centro de Investigaciones Sociológicas in its 2015 report, "Barómetro de Junio 2015 (3101)." https://www.cis.es/cis/export/sites/default/-Archivos/Marginales/3100_3119/3101/es3101mar.pdf

only seven years earlier. While the publication of two editions within ten years of one another may appear to be redundant, a closer look at the mission of the Instituto Cervantes itself indicates the very different publics served by each version.

Spain's institutional efforts to standardize and disseminate *castellano* at home and abroad date back to the Golden Age itself. Nebrija's *Gramática* (1492) identified the close ties between language and empire in what would reflect the spirit of the monarchy's language policy for centuries, and he offered the Catholic monarchs a definitive argument for privileging *castellano* as the dialect that would eventually also be known as *español*. Dissemination of the Spanish language is baked into the very fabric of empire; if at the height of territorial expansion the sun never set on the Spanish Empire, it also did not set on Spanish linguistic communities. Such linguistic expansion brings with it an acceleration of language variation, and as the number of colonies speaking the language grew so too grew the understanding that an institutional measure of control was needed to regulate the written Castilian word. In 1713 a group of Spanish intellectuals formed the RAE, which was officially embraced by King Phillip V the following year. Spain followed the lead of its European neighbors and colonial competitors, England and France, to found the RAE with the explicit charges of preserving linguistic continuity and celebrating the language's inherent splendor. Among its first initiatives was the publication of the *Diccionario de autoridades* [Authoritative Dictionary].

The RAE's role would naturally change as Spain's colonies gained independence, and its current pursuit of what it calls its *política lingüística panhispánica* [panhispanic linguistic policy] involves coordinating with the 22 national academies of the Spanish-speaking world. Its prescriptive role in preserving linguistic purity and celebrating the language's greatest aesthetic achievements, naturally with Cervantes and *Don Quixote* at the foreground, is reflected in its official emblem and motto, which have not changed since its foundation: a burning torch surrounded by the words "Limpia, fija y da esplendor" [Clean, fixed, and gives splendor]. The classics of Golden Age Spanish literature have been celebrated and promoted in pursuit of this mission, including an impressive list of critical editions of medieval and early modern canonical texts that (in keeping with its motto) offer definitive, "clean" versions of the classics that will stand as monuments of *castellano* as a mode of artistic expression. The most recent renewal of its royal charter, signed in 1993, describes it as "una institución con personalidad jurídica propia que tiene como misión principal velar por que los cambios que experimente la lengua española en su constante adaptación a las necesidades de sus hablantes no quiebren la esencial unidad que mantiene en todo el ámbito hispánico" [an institution with its own juridic personality and a principal mission to be vigilant so that changes experienced by the Spanish language in its continual adaptation to the needs of its speakers do not break the essential unity that it maintains in the entire Hispanic world].[11] The RAE, in other words, identifies its mission to be that of guardian of a linguistic order guaranteeing that former colonies and the *metrópoli* continue to speak the same language. As Clare Mar-Molinero has noted, it is not difficult to re-cast this mission statement to say that while Spain's geopolitical empire did not survive the nineteenth century, the RAE continues to see itself as the guardian of the nation's linguistic empire.

Mar-Molinero's notion of Spanish "linguistic imperialism" (193) extends beyond the RAE, whose mission is preservationist and curatorial, to include other institutional means by which the Spanish state seeks to expand its global linguistic footprint. In 1991, two years before the charter renewal of the RAE cited above, King Juan Carlos founded the Instituto Cervantes to complement the Academy's work by more explicitly and aggressively seeking to disseminate *castellano* globally, presumably to counter the role of the English language as the *lingua franca* of international business, technology, and foreign relations, and to increase the awareness of cultural activity *en español* worldwide. It was originally founded in Alcalá de Henares, birthplace of Cervantes, and now features a central administrative office in Madrid to coordinate the efforts of its 87 centers in 44 different countries to stimulate and regulate the learning of Spanish as a second language.

Victor García de la Concha, director of the Institute from 2012–2017, characterized its mission as one of linguistic "evangelization" when describing its relationship with the RAE to its academic board of directors at his inaugural speech in 2012: "los Académicos somos los padres conciliares y el Cervantes formará y enviará a todo el mundo misioneros que enseñarán el evangelio del español" [We academics are the conciliar fathers and the Cervantes Institute will develop and dispatch throughout the world missionaries to teach the gospel of Spanish].[12] That *el Cervantes* configures its organization in this way, with its leadership board of "academics" regulating the efforts of its "evangelical" centers (missions?) across the globe, reflects an ideological orientation that begs for comparison with that of the original Spanish Empire, whose evangelical mission was to spread the Christian faith in the new world, in turn making Mar-Molinero's label of "linguistic imperialism" all the more apt. The fact that these "academics" generally share comparable advisory roles

11 https://www.rae.es
12 http://www.cervantes.es/sobre_instituto_cervantes/prensa/2012/noticias/nota-discurso-toma-posesion-victor-garcia-de-la-concha.htm

in the RAE, alongside a number of Spanish government officials, furthers Mar-Molinero's argument that the Spanish state is effectively driving a campaign of linguistic imperialism meant to reinforce the same linguistic hierarchies that informed Nebrija's foundational *Gramática*.

With an annual budget in the hundreds of millions of euros, the Instituto Cervantes constitutes a major investment of the Spanish government and its private investors, and its choice of Miguel de Cervantes as the institution's namesake, its main seat in Alcalá de Henares, and its intensive efforts to promote celebrations of *Don Quixote* during its recent quadricentennial anniversaries leave little doubt as to how Spain continues to see *Don Quixote* as the textual lynchpin of its language policy efforts, both foreign and domestic. Part of those efforts is the critical edition of *Don Quixote* noted above, edited by Francisco Rico and published in 1998; it remains available online for free. Other activities included the coordination of a global effort to record the novel being read aloud in a series of hundreds of YouTube posts in 2016. Nor is featuring *Don Quixote* a passing phase in the Institute's cultural programming: a similar effort in 2008, for example, featured readers from across the Spanish-speaking world in order to celebrate the phonological diversity of global Spanish. Just as language policy is baked into the DNA of empire, *Don Quixote* seems similarly inseparable from Spain's ongoing "linguistic imperialism." García de la Concha drives the point home further in his inaugural speech by re-casting the Institute's linguistic evangelism in quixotic discourse: "Puede parecer un sueño. Y lo es. Un sueño cervantino, quijotesco que lleva la marca más auténtica y fecunda de España, la de la España abierta al territorio universal de la Mancha" [It may seem like a dream. And it is. A cervantine, quixotic dream bearing the most authentic and fruitful stamp of Spain, that of a Spain open to the universal territory of La Mancha].

As this chapter concludes, we are now far better positioned to understand how *Don Quixote* and its author have thrived in the age of postmodern simulacra, as the rarely read bookish book used to promote the written word, after examining Spain's institutional responses to the development of what was described at the beginning of this chapter as a cultural blurring between images of the nation projected for foreign consumption and those used to foster domestic understandings of Spanish cultural authenticity and national identity.

Clearly, *Don Quixote* now inhabits a cultural space in Spain where language policy abroad (led by the Instituto Cervantes) and the preservation of Castilian linguistic authority within Spain (led by the RAE) intersect. It is an intersection for which the presence of the figure of Don Quixote bears nationalistic implications, insofar as Spanish national identity is treated as a quixotic dream and a source of pride, and popular "soft" appreciation of the cervantine hero (as opposed to, as John Jay Allen might say, the cervantine fool) is leveraged by the Spanish state as the nation's most compelling political narrative since the fall of the Spanish Empire. The synergy between international linguistic neocolonialism and domestic nationalism is further fostered by the participation of academics who must embrace the political and cultural capital of a popular, Romantic understanding of *Don Quixote* that often conflicts with their own research findings, or at least with the findings of their international colleagues, for the sake of raising the international profile and (it is hoped) domestic readership of the nation's foundational literary text, *Don Quixote*. What remains to be examined, and what will be examined in the pages to follow, is how Spain's Golden Age literary texts like *Don Quixote* interact when deployed into the currents of cultural production and consumption impacted by globalism, in other words how early modern narratives fare against the "globalized" headwinds into which they sail. As we will see, despite how fervently Spain would claim them as cultural patrimony, Golden Age narratives and their diachronic evolution do not respect national borders as they used to. Indeed, as global cultural winds fill the national sails, we will find that the very idea of Spain is no less fluid and resistant to fixed signification than is Cervantes's masterpiece.

CHAPTER THREE

Repatriating the Cid: Spanish Cultural *Reconquista* in the Era of Globalization

> El Cid es el espíritu de España [...] Este ha sido el gran servicio de nuestra Cruzada, la virtud de nuestro Movimiento: el haber despertado en las nuevas generaciones la conciencia de lo que fuimos, de lo que somos y de lo que podemos ser.
>
> [The Cid is the spirit of Spain [...] This has been the great service of our Crusade, the virtue of our Movement: to have awoken in the new generations the consciousness of what we were, of what we are and of what we can be.]
>
> Francisco Franco (cf. McClennen, 87)

In many ways, the cultural dynamics surrounding contemporary uses and understandings of *Don Quixote* point to the limits of what traditional models of literary studies, including Spanish philology, are able to tell us about the hermeneutics of the Spanish Golden Age in contemporary Spain. If, as I have argued, institutionally driven interventions such as the efforts of the Instituto Cervantes and the RAE would leverage non-academic popular understandings of Cervantes's narrative for national cultural programming, it stands to reason that the study of those interventions must step beyond the tried and true methodologies of literary textual analysis to also include the non-literary circulation of Golden Age patrimony, including the adaptation of those narratives into other popular media, so that we can better understand the broader discursive landscape informing those institutional efforts. In other words, these institutional campaigns appear to both resist and ultimately confirm the reality of what Bert Levinson calls "the end of literature," in which the literary text descends from its lofty, privileged place—a privilege that actually consists of a symbiotic relationship between the literary canon and its academic stewards—and instead inhabits a broader cultural space as yet one of so many modes of cultural production informing the popular imaginary.

Put another way, Golden Age classics like *Don Quixote* participate in contemporary Spanish cultural and political contests to promote narratives meant to inform contemporary identities, and those contests—for example, whether Catalonia is or is not "Spanish"—have little to do with the issues to which literary scholars have traditionally been drawn. Golden Age texts, to be sure, bring to these contests the full cultural weight and capital of their "literariness," as traditional pillars of cultural authenticity bearing centuries of institutional deployment, but their participation in contemporary culture is also shaped by economic and political forces informing—and mutually informed by—all forms of cultural expression, including film and television, social media, and journalism. The considerable (and increasingly multinational-corporate) financial investment required to produce entertainment that can be economically viable in an industry whose narrative structures and audience expectations are largely determined by foreign cultural products (such as Hollywood films) requires that they be filtered through the international industry's discursive codes and conventions, lest they fail to appeal to Spanish audiences whose horizons of expectations, tastes, and standards are largely formed by those international codes. In the sector of literary prose fiction, the cultural debates surrounding Andrés Trapiello's modernized adaptation (called by him a "translation") of *Don Quixote*, followed by a like-minded "popular" adaptation realized by the novelist Arturo Pérez-Reverte in conjunction with the RAE, stand as but two salient examples of the inherent complexities of Spanish Golden Age narratives' circulation in what Levinson would call a postliterary field of cultural production.[1]

Putting aside his *edición popular* of the *Quixote*, the commercial success of Pérez-Reverte's *Capitán Alatriste* novels is another example of how the cultural authority of the Spanish Golden Age can both leverage popular interest in Golden Age literature for best-seller status and, in the process of converting that cultural capital into the economic capital that drives the publishing industry, directly impact how Golden Age cultural patrimony is understood and remembered by contemporary consumers. After working as a journalist for RTVE and then becoming a best-selling author of historical fiction set in the Golden Age, Pérez-Reverte has become an active and prominent cultural critic, with regular editorial-page commentaries in high-profile

---

1 These debates, largely fought asynchronously through newspaper editorials, blogs, and other digital and social media, turn on the question of whether the *Quixote* should be treated as a linguistic artifact requiring the contemporary reader to overcome the centuries of historical and linguistic developments separating them from it, or as a living, breathing document whose "translation" is laudable for the sake of making it more accessible to contemporary Spaniards. See Rodríguez-Marcos and Alonso de Santos, https://elpais.com/cultura/2014/11/26/babelia/1417012930_193899.html

serial publications like *El país* and *XLSemanal*. He is also, we should note, a member of the RAE, thus extending his sphere of cultural influence from the popular media marketplace to the academy and presumably leveraging his success in each sphere to impress the other.

The *Alatriste* novels participate in a broader discursive ecosystem tied to the Spanish Golden Age, and which includes a recent wave of contemporary historical fiction set in the early modern period, with televisual miniseries like *Isabel*, *Águila Roja*, and *Inés del alma mía*, as well as several episodes of the hit series *El Ministerio del Tiempo*. This wave also includes the genre in prose fiction first popularized by the *Alatriste* novels, including Andrés Trapiello's post-*Quixote* continuations (*Al morir Don Quijote* and *El final de Sancho Panza y otras suertes*), Olalla García's *El taller de los libros prohibidos*, and Fernando de Villena's *Relox de peregrinos*. This mode of historical fiction, however, is discursively grounded not in early modern but in contemporary Spain, through the discursive forms and generic conventions of fiction that have developed and, in some cases, emerged in the age of globalization. If we accept the premise that cultural production informs cultural memory and identity, a thorough understanding of the diachronic Spanish Golden Age requires an understanding of that production and the discursive forces, whether contained within or extending beyond national borders, that penetrate the conceptual grid constructed around the historical period. Understanding the landscape of globalized digital media as they inform Spanish consumption, in other words, is requisite for understanding how the Spanish Golden Age works and is understood in a contemporary cultural imaginary that is so conditioned by it.

This chapter will explore the tension between nationalist narratives and globalized cultural production through the case study of Rodrigo de Vivar. Although his narrative is based on a life that ended nine centuries ago, the metanarrative of the Cid legend continues into the present day and boasts a broad cultural footprint affecting culturally constructed historical memory, modern medieval philology, historically informed political identities and even contemporary popular culture. The Cid is an especially illuminating case study because it demonstrates how even the most national of Golden Age narratives[2] is inevitably entangled in the media currents of globalization,

---

2 While it can certainly be argued that the legend of the Cid is of medieval origin and therefore not a "Golden Age narrative," these earlier poetic fragments (excluding the *Poema de Mio Cid*, which was unknown to Guillen de Castro and only recovered in the nineteenth century) are only assembled into a coherent narrative by Castro at the beginning of the seventeenth century. More importantly, the basic conflict, plot, and structure of Castro's *comedia* is the point of departure for the narrative developments described in this chapter. In this sense, while *Las mocedades del Cid*

which in turn allow his legend to remain compelling to new generations of Spaniards whose epistemologies and habits of consumption are equally shaped by Spain's post-Franco global cultural turn.³

While the previous chapter established how the appetite to reach global consumers would eventually "wash back" to impact Spain's own national identities—a reversal of the Franco regime's original affinity for isolationism that began during the dictatorship's subsequent midcentury push for economic development through foreign investment—this chapter takes a more explicitly global focus to trace how the literary figure of the Cid, an originally medieval creation that would later be immortalized by Guillén de Castro's Golden Age play *Las mocedades del Cid*, has been transformed in contemporary Spain's globalized media. Castro's *comedia* was the immediate inspiration of Corneille's famous *Le Cid* and a number of other renowned adaptations conceived by and produced for non-Spanish cultures, from Massenet's ballet to Anthony Mann's epic film starring Charlton Heston.⁴ This evolving global narrative of the Cid extracts from the Spanish legend a decontextualized and "universal" representation of heroism, the effects of which would be to present Spain to the world as a nation defined homogenously by the protagonist's heroic values of honor, faith, and patriotism. Most importantly for the context

---

is actually a kind of early modern historical fiction (like *Fuenteovejuna*), it is truly a "Golden Age narrative" in the sense that the consumer demands of seventeenth-century popular theater prompted its narrative structure.

3 The bibliography regarding globalism and media is of course rich and voluminous. In this chapter I use the term "globalism" as a broad descriptor of a cultural and economic environment in which traditional geographic and political boundaries are becoming increasingly porous, if not irrelevant. While scholars such as Marwan M. Kraidy, Scott Lash, and Celia Lury offer more detailed and elaborate conceptualization of globalization that largely support the claims of this chapter, my choice to work with a broader (and admittedly vague) sense of the term is deliberate, as the palpable impact of globalization on Spanish Golden Age cultural artifacts is evident regardless of the specificities of any particular theorization such as Marshall McLuhan's influential but now dated notion of the global village. In broad terms my usage reflects recent developments in the field as articulated by Diana Crane: "It is important to realize that cultural globalization is no longer conceptualized in terms of the emergence of a homogenized global culture corresponding to Marshall McLuhan's global village. Instead, cultural globalization is recognized as a complex and diverse phenomenon consisting of global cultures, originating from many different nations and regions."

4 See Martin Winkler for a more detailed review of Anthony Mann's film and its source material from both within and without Spain. Jancovich analyzes "the process of cultural hybridization through which various myths of the Spanish national hero are stitched together and, in the process, re-interpreted to produce an epic movie for an international market" (79).

of this study, this globalized Cid would later return to its *patria* and inflect late- and post-dictatorship representations of the legend intended for Spanish consumers, not unlike how the "soft" or "romantic" reading of *Don Quixote* would be inflected by Dale Wasserman's *Man of La Mancha*, translated for Spanish consumption as *El hombre de la Mancha* at the end of the twentieth century and far more reflective of popular, Romantic understandings of the Quixote figure than is the historicized, philologically oriented satirical reading of the Academy. When these narratives leave Spain and develop beyond its borders, they acquire new layers of meaning to accommodate foreign circumstances in the process; we may call their return to Spain in the age of globalization—a return as something different, in light of those newly acquired layers of meaning in their travels abroad—a process of "repatriation."

Among the more recent examples of this mediated repatriation of the Cid legend is José Pozo's animated film *El Cid: La leyenda*, which filters the medieval narrative through the discourses and conventions popularized by the Walt Disney corporation. This film invites an examination of how the cultural capital of the Golden Age is converted to economic capital, and to how the industries involved in contemporary cultural production dictate the terms of that conversion. More importantly, this chapter posits the utility of the Spanish Golden Age for understanding the inherent complexity of Spain today as it comes to terms with its fascist past while also simultaneously embracing a transnational European *and* a trans-Hispanic (if not neocolonial) cultural identity, all of which requires a tenuous negotiation of the various pressures of the international community, multiculturalism (as understood in both foreign and domestic contexts), and post-Franco peripheral Spanish nationalisms. The fact that the global film industry has spawned a Spanish production of the Cid (Franco's favorite literary figure for purposes of political appropriation) in which the legend's traditionally (Castilian-Spanish) nationalist narrative is replaced by an innocuously "disnified"[5] adaptation targeting young children is indicative of the extent to which the global marketplace and its implicit strategies for profit have increasingly muddied the waters of Spanish national identity. Beyond engaging the industrial complexities of what is often called "postnational" cinema, where multinational funding and international streams of revenue have inevitably impacted how Spanish Golden Age cultural patrimony is treated, I argue that these very notions of cultural patrimony and identity in Spain are inextricably linked to the discursive currents of globalization.

---

5 I borrow the term "disnified" from Henri Giroux. A similar term, "disneyization," has been used in similar ways by several scholars since the 1990s, including Sharon Zukin and Alan Bryman.

Understanding the currency of the Spanish Golden Age in this environment is no simple task, but examining the redeployment and repatriation of the Cid's narrative and related Golden Age artifacts is a logical place to start.

Franquismo and its Discontents: Transition to Reclaim the Classics

While the literary artifacts of the Spanish Golden Age have long been a mainstay of the tourism industry, it is only fairly recently that their incorporation into mainstream media has gathered cultural steam. Since the 1940s, sporadic efforts to adapt Golden Age theater to film contributed to the carefully controlled development of a Spanish national cinema.[6] The Franco-era state run television apparatus eventually broadcast a long-running series of televisual adaptations of Spanish and European "classical theater" under the title *Estudio 1*, which by the early 1970s had successfully reaffirmed the regime's longstanding project of linking Spanish national identity to a nostalgic, sanitized narrative of its past, largely through the strategic deployment of Golden Age narratives and cultural artifacts. It is not surprising that in the immediate aftermath of Franco's death, Spaniards generally were hesitant to turn to the Golden Age to satisfy the urgent need to rethink and rearticulate Spanishness. In other words, the Golden Age's dormancy during the early years of the transition is a testament to how effective the dictatorship's project of Golden Age cultural appropriation had been after four decades.

By the same token, it can be argued that evidence of political and cultural stability by the mid-1980s can be found in efforts to finally revisit and reclaim the Golden Age classics—a cultural microcosm, we might say, of the broader transition to democracy. The PSOE government under Felipe González during the mid-1980s took important first steps, like the creation of the CNTC, in the direction of "repatriating" Golden Age cultural patrimony. The increasingly complex privatized media industry after the dictatorship, however, would take longer to recognize the Spanish Golden Age as a profitable resource. In the meantime, the Spanish state's presence in the transition towards privatization would continue to probe public appetite for the classics, as when Spanish public television (TVE) adapted the first volume of *Don Quixote* as a screenplay for a televised miniseries. Millions across Spain would watch its broadcast in 1992. As the gradually privatized media landscape stabilized, and as enough distance had accumulated

---

6 See Duncan Wheeler's *Golden Age Drama in Contemporary Spain* for a more detailed narrative of these Franco-era film adaptations, which included *El burlador de Sevilla*, *Fuenteovejuna*, and *El alcalde de Zalamea*.

between democratic Spain and its dictatorial past, the Spanish consuming public's appetite for Golden Age cultural patrimony would return.

The 1992 TVE miniseries project, simply titled *El Quijote*, was the product of years of development begun under the directorship of TVE by Pilar Miró, the former Directora General de Cinematografía [General Director of Cinematography] during the early years of Felipe González's presidency. The screenplay was adapted by Camilo José Cela, among Spain's most celebrated novelists of the twentieth century, and it was directed by Manuel Gutiérrez Aragón in what might be called a "preservationist" spirit typical of how Golden Age classics were approached by the heavily state-subvented television and film industries during the first two decades of the democracy. Pilar Miró's efforts would continue after her departure from state-run media, when in 1996 she directed the film adaptation of Lope de Vega's *comedia, El perro del hortelano*. This film would gain critical acclaim, including seven *premios Goya*, and can now be seen as a catalyst for further cinematic adaptations of the Spanish Golden Age, including one of the anonymous picaresque novel *Lazarillo de Tormes* in 2001 and Lope de Vega's romantic comedy *La dama boba* in 2006.

In all of these cinematic adaptations of Golden Age narratives, to varying degrees, one can discern a pattern wherein the medium's codes and conventions influence their representation in ways no less important than are the ideological footprints left on performances of Golden Age theater in the nineteenth and twentieth centuries (as seen in Chapter One) or the popular Romanticization of *Don Quixote* (as seen in the previous chapter). A telling example of this cinematic re-codification is Fernando Fernán Gómez's re-casting of the *Lazarillo*, the title of which is appropriately changed to *Lázaro de Tormes* so as to reflect its cinematized narrative structure and characterization. The title character's famous exploits as an urchin are narrated by him as an adult, in a series of flashbacks that allow the originally episodic and fragmented text to be woven into a romantic narrative having little to do with the anonymous original picaresque text.

Indeed, the commonly accepted notion that the text of the original *Lazarillo* (1554) concludes ironically—in other words, that the alleged *cumbre de buena fortuna* in which Lázaro finds himself in the seventh *tratado* is in fact an admission of cuckoldry and dishonor—is utterly reversed in the 2001 adaptation's cinematically re-coded "happy ending," according to what is commonly called a classical Hollywood narrative structure. Rather than tenuously accept a sham marriage as part of a package-deal landing Lazarillo his first *oficio real* [royal office], the film's protagonist recounts his "case" before a tribunal in a performance that is so persuasive that it doesn't merely clear him from his legal problems: his previously reluctant wife witnesses his testimony and appears to develop genuine affection for him. The film closes with a liberated Lázaro back at home with his wife, in a wordless bedroom scene in which his courtroom performance is, shall we say, rewarded.

The reconfigured narrative of *Lázaro de Tormes* bears many of the standard features of a Hollywood coming-of-age film, punctuated by the "happy ending" referenced above, but this narrative structure depends on a protagonist-hero at odds with the generically encoded picaresque antiheroic narrative of the sixteenth-century tradition. In order to produce the sympathetic male hero with whom the viewer can identify and in whose fate the viewer is emotionally invested, the ironic presentation of a paranoid and dishonored cuckold in the original is replaced with a relatively honest, hardworking young man whose youthful exploits are told in a series of oral performances, first in public to entertain the town's children (and, conveniently, to attract the attention of the woman who would eventually become his wife) and eventually as testimony in a court proceeding vaguely associated with the mysterious *caso* to which the original *Lazarillo* text alludes in its prologue. These oral performances in the film echo (and often directly copy) fragments lifted from the text of the original first-person narrative, an explicit mode of intertextuality that allows the film to appropriate the cultural capital of the Golden Age artifact while reshaping its protagonist and his story to accommodate the cinematic sensibilities of contemporary Spaniards.

This phenomenon of recent Golden Age adaptations dealing more liberally with their source material while adapting to the codes and conventions of contemporary cinema is even more apparent in a series of films targeting young children. Leaving aside (for the moment) his "disnified" adaptation of the Cid legend, another telling example is Pozo's 2007 adaptation of the *Quixote*, *Donkey Xote*. Before turning our attention to the Cid, a few features of *Donkey Xote* will demonstrate intertextual approach that both films adopt.

From the Producers Who Saw *Shrek*

Like *El Cid*, *Donkey Xote* was produced in collaboration with the Spanish animated film company Filmax and protagonizes Rucio, Sancho Panza's famous *asno*. The savvy consumer of children's entertainment will recognize the character "Donkey" from the American *Shrek* films; posters and DVD cases make the intertextual reference explicit and, for postmodern comic effect, include the byline "de los productores que vieron *Shrek*" [from the producers who saw *Shrek*]. It is Rucio's "impossible dream" to someday be a horse, and he leads a group of anthropomorphically animated animals (Rocinante and a group of farm animals from Don Quixote's village, including a chicken skilled in martial arts) to assist the would-be knight as he searches for Dulcinea. Retelling Cervantes's narrative from the perspective of Sancho's donkey creates considerable separation for Pozo to re-code the story according to the formulae responsible for the American company Pixar's remarkable commercial success, which in turn facilitates the film's target audience (Spanish children) more likely to know *Shrek* and *Toy Story* than the seventeenth-century Golden Age text.

Pozo also leverages the Romantic and popular reading of *Don Quixote*, examined in the previous chapter, in his re-coding of Cervantes. The eponymous knight himself resembles the character Woody from *Toy Story* more than the more typical visualizations of Cervantes's hero: he is young and idealistic, if naïve and gullible (and hence in need of common sense and encouragement from Sancho and Rucio). If *Don Quixote*'s original antagonists are varied and most often either unwitting or imagined, *Donkey Xote* streamlines them into a singular and simplified "bad guy" named Sansón Carrasco, a local mayor whose efforts to thwart the knight are politically and economically motivated. As if these elements in the adaptation were not sufficient evidence of how the Golden Age narrative is reconfigured according to the codes and conventions of the contemporary animated film industry, the point is driven home when Rucio helps Don Quixote confront the Caballero de la Blanca Luna in the film's final climactic joust. After falling in combat and facing the tip of his opponent's sword, Don Quixote proves himself worthy of Dulcinea's love by refusing to renounce his devotion to her to save his own life. As the Caballero de la Blanca Luna removes "his" helmet, we discover that this mysterious opponent is in fact Dulcinea herself, and her jousting tournament an elaborate scheme to determine the sincerity of Don Quixote's intentions. Beyond the obvious revisions to Cervantes's story—for example, that Dulcinea actually exists and identifies herself as such—it is especially noteworthy that the film's "happily ever after" conclusion, including the couple's first kiss, is achieved by Dulcinea's initiative, effectively reversing traditional gender dynamics in classical storytelling.

This discussion of globalized media suggests that *Donkey Xote* inflects the *Quixote* narrative according to the discursive trends of its American models, themselves subject to cultural and political change. Dulcinea's revised role would not be incongruous to the worldview of young Spaniards who have grown up watching Disney's own arguably progressive turn in representing gender in such films as *Mulan*, *Pocahontas*, and *Brave*. But there is another, national dimension to this final plot twist: the repatriated Dulcinea's agency appeared in cineplexes across Spain during the presidency of José Luis Rodríguez Zapatero, the country's self-described first feminist president. While Spanish cultural attitudes regarding gender equality is certainly a complex issue not reducible to a single and universally accepted narrative,

Zapatero's emphasis on reforming Spain's *machista* legal code in areas like domestic violence and labor regulations does suggest that Spaniards of all political persuasions were actively aware of a shifting cultural landscape regarding how women are treated in public and private life. Zapatero's policies surrounding gender equality were foregrounded in his public messaging, which frequently expressed pride in fielding Europe's first majority-female cabinet. For José Colmeiro, both *Donkey Xote* and *El Cid: La leyenda* reflect this environment, as Pozo's re-casting of patriarchal cultural patrimony rendered them "recontextualized as politically correct contemporary visions of intercultural sensitivity and gender awareness" (161).

It should be noted that Colmeiro's perceptible acerbity is due to the context of this citation, from within his book *Peripheral Visions/Global Sounds: From Galicia to the World*, which argues for a "post-peripheral" analysis of Galician cultural production. Galicia is the home to Bren Entertainment, the animation studio feeding the Catalonian Filmax corporation. José Pozo, too, is Catalonian, and Colmeiro's comments reflect a tension between cultural identities in Spain that ultimately are inseparable from the politics and the economics of Iberian peripheral nationalisms. His argument regarding artistic and cultural autochthony reminds us of the simultaneous global, national, and regional tensions at play in the Spanish media industry. *Donkey Xote* is a Galician-crafted, Catalonian-produced and multinationally financed "disnification" of an already Romanticized (in part via the discourses of the Broadway musical) repatriation of a Golden Age narrative.

Indeed, this heavily mediated repatriation of the *Quixote* exposes the complexity of analyzing the cultural function of the Spanish Golden Age in contemporary Spain. One element in this complexity is that *Donkey Xote* is both a single cultural product, and thus subject to its own synchronic analysis, but it is also but one of many products contributing to a broader diachronic process of repatriation, thus rendering a merely synchronic analysis incomplete. In other words, its analysis offers useful information about the moment of its cultural intervention—the shifting cultural perceptions of gender identities in the Zapatero era—and, if one takes a step back to consider this tree in the broader context of its proverbial forest, it also reflects just the latest of so many discursive filters that have inflected its reception since Cervantes's characters were first adapted to other performance contexts in the seventeenth century. What the globalization of media has done to this diachronic process is to have effectively erased the national borders that once separated these discursive filters according to national origin, in other words exposing the autochthonous narrative to global discursive currents and modes of articulation. The impetus behind Golden Age repatriation, in this case the particular cultural and political capital of *Don Quixote* within Spain, is necessarily implicated in this diachronic process, as the national identities of new generations of Spaniards are nurtured and mediated through these targeted repatriated deployments.

If cultural production targeting children bears the potential of performing a powerful mode of banal nationalism, here we see how the cultural capital of the Spanish Golden Age may contribute to cultural narratives regarding contemporary attitudes about gender by reconciling those attitudes to cultural narratives inherited from an historical past that predates them. The example of *Donkey Xote*, then, shows not only that cultural patrimony is reshaped according to the discourses of globally informed media industries, but that such re-coding is hardly immune to local or national politics. Re-coding the classics cannot be analyzed as if they were produced in an ideological vacuum or political "no-spin zone," which is why the re-coding and repatriation of national heroes like the Cid can teach us a great deal about how Spanish identities are understood and negotiated today.

Mocedades para moz@s: Rodrigo de Vivar

Like *Donkey Xote*, *El Cid: La leyenda* (José Pozo/Filmax 2003), which won a Goya award for best animated film, leverages the cultural capital of its protagonist against a globalized marketplace of children's animated film dominated by Disney. The film is framed by an extradiegetic narrator who first sets the scene in the opening minutes by summarizing centuries of medieval Spanish history, reducing it so as to be made accessible to its young target audience. While this opening vignette ostensibly foregrounds the historical importance of the events represented in the film, it also projects a metanarrative of Spanish history that aligns with a twentieth-century narrative of *convivencia* [peaceful coexistence] generally associated with Américo Castro.[7] According to this narrative, we owe the very idea of Spain to a medieval *Reconquista* made necessary by foreign invasion by the Almoravids, a North African political caliphate originally invited by Iberian *taifa* rulers to aid in their defense against the advancing Castilian forces. The Almoravids would eventually take control of the areas of Al-Andalus that they had come to defend, which would effectively put an end to a culturally flourishing pre-national and multicultural Iberia. In the context of this animated film, Castro's narrative is filtered to articulate to whom young viewers should assign the discursively programmed roles of *buenos*

---

7 See Castro's *España en su historia* for the original articulation of his vision of medieval *convivencia*. Darío Fernández-Morera and David Nirenberg are two of many scholars who more recently have questioned Castro's thesis.

y malos [good guys and bad guys]. Peaceful *convivencia* is interrupted by the arrival of a dark and nefarious Muslim Other from Africa, distinguished from the "good" Muslim communities that had inhabited southern Iberia for centuries. This presentation of Iberian history prior to the Cid's life sets the scene for his adventures by framing them as vital to stopping foreign aggression and returning Spain to its peaceful, multicultural essence.

The style of animation during this opening vignette is markedly different from that of the story of the Cid proper, with voiceless and abstract shapes interacting amid pages of ancient manuscripts, all the while dramatizing the historical events being narrated by a disembodied voice.[8] With its conclusion and a visual stylistic shift in animation more reminiscent of Disney films, the narrator is silent until the film closes, when he returns in an epilogue to

---

8 The text of this introductory historical narrative is as follows:

En el año 1064 el rey Fernando I, el grande, rey de Castilla y de León regresó triunfal tras la conquista de Coimbra. La protección de Castilla sobre los reinos de taifas redujo la actividad militar y un período de influencia cultural se abría paso entre musulmanes y cristianos en una época marcada por la convivencia y la tolerancia. Pero la paz no dura eternamente y un gran peligro amenazaba con romperla: Ben Yusuf. Yusuf se empleó a fondo exigiendo la intervención almorávide en los reinos de taifas apresando y eliminando a los reyes que, a su paso, se negaban a luchar junto a él.

Ante la llegada de Ben Yusuf a Zaragoza, el príncipe Al Mutamín decidió huir para evitar ser capturado. El crecimiento del ejército almorávide era imparable e interminables hordas desfilaban rumbo a la conquista de la península ordenando incluso a partir a sus tropas del norte de África. Con la llegada del invierno los días se hacían más cortos y las malas noticias llegaban a la corte de Castilla.

Aunque desterrado, lejos de los suyos y de su hogar, Rodrigo inició una etapa de reconquista. Reyes y reyezuelos se rendían a su implacable avance. Fue en aquel entonces cuando Rodrigo, empezó a ser llamado por los almorávides como "El Cid," el señor. Rodrigo ordenaba a sus hombres que todos los reinos, castillos y cofres fueran puestos a disposición de su único rey, el rey de Castilla, Alfonso VI.

When this narrative voice returns to conclude the film, the text is as follows:

Tras la conquista de Valencia la leyenda de Rodrigo Díaz de Vivar y la de sus hombres aumentaría. Incluso la del conde Ordóñez. Rodrigo moriría tiempo después en el año 1099 manteniendo Valencia bajo su control. Su vida fue una gran aventura, mucho más grande y trascendente de lo que él mismo podría esperar. El Cid no luchaba porriquezas, sino por obtener el perdón de su rey, por recuperar su honor. Lo consiguió. Y ese rey de Castilla, Alfonso VI, el bravo [...] yo [...] aprendí una lección.

remind the viewer of how the story of the Cid made the future of the Spanish nation possible. The narrator's closing remarks also reveal that he is in fact King Alfonso VI, regardless of how many young viewers had any idea who he was. For the roughly 90 minutes in between these two narrated interventions, we see a young Rodrigo make friends, get into trouble, leave the court, and eventually rescue his friend Jimena from the clutches of the evil and militant moor Ben Yussef. All of the staples of Disney classics like *The Little Mermaid*, *Pocahontas*, and *Aladdin* are worked into the mix, including an animal sidekick and a disturbingly androgynous antagonist. Despite its depiction of the invading caliphate, the film is not unequivocally islamophobic: many of Rodrigo's friends are Muslims, and the *convivencia* narrative allows for such nuance by distinguishing between peaceful and tolerant Iberian Muslims and the "bad guys" under the control of Ben Yusuf, freshly arrived from northern Africa.

Indeed, the only historical names that are included in both the framing *convivencia* metanarrative and the main action of the Cid's adventures are those of Spanish monarchs and Ben Yusuf, thus allowing them to appear in both styles of animation. While the abstract Yusuf wears a black cape that eventually transforms into a wave of darkness eclipsing the harmonious coexistence of Christians, Muslims, and Jews in *preconquista* Iberia, his appearance in the Cid's story after this opening vignette reveals more grotesque detail, including deep facial scars, a disfigured eye, and a markedly feminized voice. This non-Spanish antagonist, when not plotting a takeover of Spain as part of a broader agenda to establish a global caliphate, chooses to entertain himself in perverse ways that reflect his troubled masculinity.

While *El Cid: La leyenda* predates the Zapatero presidency and *Donkey Xote*, a clear effort is made in the film to update the legend and especially the role of women in it. After Ben Yusuf kidnaps Jimena and forces her to perform exotic (I would argue a "disnified," sanitized, and euphemistic nod to the erotic) dances in his chambers, Rodrigo breaks into his palace to free her. As if to anticipate the turn towards female agency described above in reference to *Donkey Xote*'s Dulcinea, Rodrigo's climactic rooftop battle with Yussef requires Jimena's intervention: she finds Rodrigo's fallen sword and throws it to him just in time to block the antagonist's blow, knocking Yussef off the rooftop and causing him to fall to his death. As the main action closes, Rodrigo and his friends (both animal and human) jump upon their horses to ride off into the sunset and continue the *Reconquista*. But unsatisfied with her seat on Babieca alongside Rodrigo, Jimena dismounts and reappears riding her own horse.

Even if the film reconciles patriarchal medieval history with contemporary political sensibilities, one would be hard-pressed to argue that it is "feminist." Jimena's role does change, from the passive and objectified damsel of medieval lore to a more assertive collaborator in the Cid's mission, but rendering her a more "useful" accessory does not a feminist historical revision make. Indeed, one could easily argue that such updates of Jimena's agency and action were influenced more by similarly evolving female characterization by Disney (as reflected in the roughly contemporary films *Aladdin, Mulan,* and *Pocahantas*) than by feminist sensibilities in Spain. Those broader developments in the Disney-led industry bear their own problems, as the turn towards stronger female "princesses" butted up against the traditional patriarchal narrative structures on which the Disney brand had built itself. Jimena is perhaps more useful as an ally than earlier versions of the story had suggested (including Sofia Loren's role in Anthony Mann's film), but she remains contained and constrained within a plot that finds her kidnapped and in need of rescue by the male hero and would-be suitor. She is simply a more militant and capable damsel in distress.

This animated rendering of the Cid legend thus updates gender roles along lines similar (if less emphatic) to those described above in reference to *Donkey Xote*, but an additional element of cultural education—understanding the Muslim Other—makes this updating more complicated. It should be noted that the film's release in 2003 came just as Spain had committed its military to U.S. president George W. Bush's "coalition of the willing" during the buildup to its invasion of Iraq, a problematic geopolitical response to the Al Qaeda terrorist attacks of September 11, 2001. Public reaction in Spain to the conservative president José María Aznar's commitment to this coalition was swift, intense, and for the most part negative in Spain. It is a decision commonly considered to have had a causal relationship with Spain's largest foreign terrorist attack in Madrid on March 11, 2004, and the subsequent election of Zapatero and his socialist party.

This context suggests that the film's efforts to distinguish between good, Spanish Muslims (*moriscos*) and an invasive and militant foreign Muslim power is connected to the broader dynamics of cultural production as it relates to young consumers, especially in light of Homi Bhabha's articulation of culture's "pedagogical" dimension in political communities (145). Henri Giroux elaborates on this culturally pedagogical function as it applies to the Disney animated genre that so heavily influences Pozo and Filmax: these films constitute powerful vehicles for transmitting culturally bound and gender-inflected social roles and norms, as well as broader cultural values and ideals. Given the intense cultural reflection on Islamic cultures in the wake of 9/11/2001, this powerful role of children's animated film is clearly relevant to our understanding of how contemporary Spanish media engages the legend of the Cid to articulate contemporary cultural anxieties, especially surrounding the politically contentious issue of immigration. Daniel Ares López notes that, despite the film's immediate reception as harmless entertainment with only loose connections to medieval Spanish history, *El Cid: La leyenda* is clearly informed by "the specific significations of the War on Terror as a media discourse-narrative created and propagated after 9/11" (47) and considers that discursive context as key to understanding the film's treatment of its historical source material. The upshot of how this film might inform debates on immigration from Northern Africa is clear enough: while good, Spanish Muslims contribute to the nation's cultural strength and diversity, the bad foreign Muslim power is an Other whose exclusion should motivate policy reforms.

Ares López also points to the diachronic dimension of the Cid's repatriation in the age of globalization: the plot of Pozo's screenplay is structurally identical to that of Anthony Mann's 1960 Hollywood epic film, *El Cid*. This iconic film (starring Charlton Heston and Sofia Loren) has its own fascinating genealogy,[9] and in the context of this study its most fascinating dimension is that it assembles information from various historical and literary sources according to a binary worldview (protagonist/antagonist, Christian/Muslim, nation/other) inflected by the West's fear of communism in the early years of the Cold War. While largely shot in Spain with permission from the Franco regime and in consultation with the expert advice of the Spanish Academy's leading authority on the legend, Ramón Menéndez Pidal, the Cid's political work in the film pushes back against the same kind of authoritarianism that was associated with the dictatorship. It also situates this binary as a kind of allegory for the Cold War itself, in which the invasive and bellicose Muslim foreigner stands in for Communism and the Cid represents Western democracy and capitalism.[10]

The Cold-War re-coding of the legend according to midcentury Hollywood conventions and political discourses, then, is repatriated by Pozo 40 years later to produce, as Ares López describes it, "neo-Orientalist imaginaries and neo-imperialist views of past, present and future relationships between the West and the Islamic World" (47). Pozo's film, in other words, re-codes an already (geo)politically re-coded narrative, through a discursive re-coding of one midcentury Hollywood genre (Hollywood Epic) through the lens of another (Disney). It should be pointed out that Mann's film was (at the time of its release) only the latest of several narrative refashionings of the Cid,

---

9 There are two excellent studies of this 1960 film in the context of the present discussion, by Martin Winkler and Mark Jancovich.

10 Jancovich elaborates this reading of Mann's film as an allegory of the Cold War—a reading that helps clarify the Franco regime's willingness to permit filming in Spain. As loathsome as Hollywood and American materialism might have been to Franco, the regime's longstanding antipathy toward Communism, which he associated with the Second Republic that he overthrew in the Civil War, was stronger.

most of them carried out outside of Spain, which should remind us of the diachronic nature of "classical" Spanish national narratives, and that the process of global dissemination further complicates the cultural repatriation process for literary heroes like the Cid. We will see that this discursive hall of mirrors depends on a narrative of Spanish cultural patrimony, fostered by late-nineteenth- and early-twentieth-century Spanish Medievalism, that is no less complex and whose examination exposes a diachronic process through which Spanish cultural memory has continually constructed and revised one of its foundational myths.

The Cid and Golden Age Medievalism

While Pozo walked a fine line to both please his young viewers' "disnified" sensibilities and respect the reverence traditionally paid to the cultural capital of the Cid's legend in Spain, his approach blended two distinct textual genealogies through which we have come to know Rodrigo de Vivar. The narrator's opening and closing remarks described above, which prefigure and then recapitulate the Cid's geopolitical importance and military accomplishments, depend on the chronicle and epic tradition of his legend best exemplified by the *Poema de Mio Cid*, while the intervening "disnified" drama drew more directly—through Anthony Mann's 1960 epic film and its more immediate sources, such as from *Las mocedades del Cid*, Guillén de Castro's Golden Age *comedia*. These two genealogies are not completely separable from one another, but their differences are certainly notable. Guillén de Castro's drama would inspire a famous French neoclassical adaptation by Corneille that further strips Rodrigo's story of any geopolitical specificity, to present his troubled relationship with Jimena and his struggles at court as less Spanish and more universal. This approach is echoed in subsequent treatments of the legend outside of Spain, including Massenet's opera and ballet and Mann's epic Hollywood film. On the other hand, the nineteenth-century rediscovery of the more geopolitically engaged *Poema de Mio Cid* (often called the *Cantar de Mio Cid*) allowed scholars and intellectuals in Spain to infuse an emerging sense of nationalism into the history of the *Reconquista*, even if the word *Reconquista* never actually appears in the text. Ramón Menéndez Pidal would build an entire medieval tradition around the text, the so-called *mester de juglaría* [craft of minstrels] through which Spanish history was passed from one generation to the next. It is this second line of textual transmission that would ultimately inspire Francisco Franco to embrace the figure of the Cid as a model for his own role as "Caudillo," and the *Reconquista*-as-manifest-destiny narrative as a blueprint for his own dictatorship in the twentieth century.

These two Cids, the *galán de comedia* and the *caudillo guerrero*, and more importantly the way that the two versions overlap in contemporary Spanish cultural production, make Castro's play an object lesson for what can be learned from studying plays written in the Golden Age about prior historical events. The term normally reserved for such material, "history plays," tends to direct our attention only to how the original practitioners of the *Comedia* engaged with the historical events that preceded them, as when Anthony Cascardi argues that through its representation of medieval history in plays like *Fuenteovejuna* the *Comedia* often acted as a cultural pushback or resistance to ongoing socioeconomic historical change.[11]

What is just as fascinating, if less studied, is how that Golden Age representation of the past in turn shapes our own contemporary understanding of those earlier historical events and personages. When taking up historical material, early modern playwrights reshape legend before handing it off to subsequent generations to stage and adapt, and the ways in which such legends are refracted in the process can have lasting influence on how we understand them, and on how Spaniards consume their own national history. In other words, a traditional reading of a *comedia* like *Las mocedades del Cid* as a "history play" makes a one-way street out of what is actually a more complex, two-way highway of cultural memory transmission. If, as Napoleon Bonaparte once said, history is a myth that men agree to believe, then the historiographer's work must examine the conditions under which such agreements are made, and then consider the implications of our own participation in such inherited agreements as we read and especially as we experience new stagings and adaptations of them.

Guillén de Castro's play constitutes a kind of document or contract of how seventeenth-century Spaniards agreed to believe, as history, the mythology surrounding a man who lived five hundred years before them. That agreement, I would argue, has become permanently infused into our own understanding of the "history" that it claims to represent. It also shows us that, through its cultural capital and continued participation in the cultural repatriation process, all pre-modern narratives in Spanish history— including the narrative of a man who died centuries before the very idea of Spain even existed—lead through the Spanish Golden Age, and that, once incorporated into Golden Age cultural production, the stamp of its cultural articulation is impossible to erase. If the Golden Age is not the origin of the Cid's legend, it is the moment when that legend achieved canonicity, and the moment when the emerging Spanish nation-state would first incorporate this medieval material into a national history.

---

11 See *Ideologies of History in the Spanish Golden Age*.

Many scholars have noted the ways in which Guillén de Castro forges his drama from existing source material ranging from twelfth-century *romances* to fifteenth- and sixteenth-century *crónicas*.[12] If we accept that the now-famous *Poema de Mio Cid* was unknown to Guillén de Castro (as it was only published and disseminated more than a century after he wrote *Las mocedades*), the earliest sources informing his work would be fragments of *romancero* collections and historical chronicles of the military conflicts in which Rodrigo was involved. Guillén de Castro's play coincided at the turn of the seventeenth century with efforts to synthesize and reorganize uncollected and fragmented references to the legend, including Juan de Escobar's *Romancero e historia del Cid*.

While the majority of these texts produced through the sixteenth century emphasize Rodrigo's military and geopolitical accomplishments, an examination of Castro's *comedia* reveals comparatively little about such *hazañas* [heroic deeds]. Scholars have long pointed to a number of plot details in this *comedia* that are altered from the accounts of medieval chroniclers and oral *romances*, for example that the death of Jimena's father comes at the unwitting hand of an adult Rodrigo who is already in love with her.[13] In a play bearing the name of Spain's most famous warrior, it is striking that only roughly one third of its 3,004 verses (1,100) can be characterized as directly related to military or chivalric action. Moreover, the representation of what in a Hollywood context we might call "action" or violent conflict is not distributed evenly across the play's three acts: duels and battles or their negotiation occupy a little more than a third of the first act, approximately one eighth of the second, and then a full half of the final act—roughly the final 20% of the play. The wars that define the warrior, then, are front-loaded and back-ended, with a middle act (spilling into Act 3) primarily focused on the consequences of Rodrigo's first-act duel with Jimena's father and the political intrigues of life at court.

This onstage privileging of speech over violence, of deliberation over doing, of reaction over action, places Guillén de Castro's audience not in the thick of the battle but in the middle of the court as it learns of battles that have happened offstage. In short, we witness not the Cid's brawn, but instead the thinking that informs the *hazañas* of Spain's original action hero. Guillén de Castro presents unsolvable problems and then dramatizes how

---

12 The detailed textual genealogies of the Cid legend and that legend's transmission into the twentieth century is presented in Colin Smith's *The Making of the Poema de mio Cid*.

13 The *romancero* tradition represents a far younger Rodrigo exclusively concerned with addressing the *agravio* committed against his father.

his protagonists grapple with them. How do you maintain loyalty in a royal house divided by sibling rivalries? What to do when the man you love has killed your father? When your would-be father-in-law has dishonored your own father, and thus your family? These circumstances, of course, invite the kind of baroque versification on which the *Comedia* always thrived, informed by the rhetoric of casuistry and the paradoxical dynamics of courtly love. What the practical realities of the *corral* did not invite, however, was the portrayal of military prowess that is the mainstay of epic, oral, and *crónica* versions of his legend, such as the *Poema de Mio Cid*.

As is well known, early modern Spanish history plays often relegated battles and military conflicts to the margins, as offstage occurrences to which onstage actors might refer either after the fact or in real-time. While undoubtedly such decisions regarding dramatic action and the *mise en scène* were driven by practical necessity—it was simply more economical and logistically feasible to focus onstage action on dialogue between a more limited number of actors—I would emphasize that regardless of what motivated this focalization away from what we might call "action scenes" or "battle scenes," the consequence for our understanding of the history being represented is significant. Instead of emphasizing the kind of action that made Rodrigo a legend in the first place, Guillén de Castro embraces *Comedia* convention by focusing on the interpersonal conflicts and on the subjective experiences of desire by his main characters. Guillén de Castro's Rodrigo is a lover, not a fighter—a revision of the historical record that, perhaps unwittingly, made the legend more easily exportable to Corneille in France and beyond.

Generations of scholars have offered explanations for this focus away from the battlefield in the history plays, which again sets Castro's play apart from the bulk of medieval epic representations of the Cid as warrior. Cathy Larson sees *Las mocedades* as an ideal *comedia* to be read through the lens of Speech Act theory, as the primarily courtly setting depends literally on characters "doing things with words," and as a complex negotiation between inherited *romancero* texts and the demands of a fickle early modern public. For Anthony Cascardi, Rodrigo's conflicting demands of duty and desire reflect a struggle between traditional and emerging social orders. Marjorie Ratcliffe sees the shift as one due to Guillén de Castro's interest in representing female subjectivity, while Russell Sebold instead reads the play as a kind of Counterreformation allegory in which Rodrigo is a metonym for Spain, and St. Lazarus's blessing in Act 3 symbolizes the manifest destiny of the Christian Spanish Empire. All of these readings are persuasive, and their variety reflects the complexity of the play—a complexity, I would posit, that is far less often attributed to the epic and more militaristic versions of the legend.

Ample scholarship exists about this phenomenon of subjective focalization in the *Comedia*, for example Thomas O'Connor's seminal book *Love in the "Corral,"* which draws important connections between neohistorical research on the early modern theater industry in Spain and the broader historiographical narrative associating the European Renaissance with the development of a new emphasis on subject formation and self-fashioning, and which links clearly with the so-called "lyric I" of *petrarquismo*. But regardless of how one chooses to situate the *comedia*'s focus on the individual's subjective experience of love and desire, Guillén de Castro's choice to filter the legend of the Cid through such conventions is a pivotal one for how future generations of Spaniards, and the world at large, would come to know and understand the medieval hero, notwithstanding Menéndez Pidal's efforts to repatriate the legend by situating the Cid less in the palace and more in the battlefield.

The Cid legend would continue to reappear both in Spain and abroad in the centuries following Guillén de Castro's *comedia*, such as in 1875 when Manuel Fernández y González produced his *refundición* of the Golden Age play *Cid Rodrigo de Vivar* during a wave of Romantic neomedievalist texts that examined the influence of Arabic culture and literature in Spain's cultural history. That wave of interest in revisiting a medieval cultural past, at least as it pertains to the Cid narrative, had begun to gather steam a century earlier, when Tomás Antonio Sánchez published the first printed edition of the verse epic *Cantar de Mio Cid* in 1779, a full two centuries after the original manuscript had been discovered in Vivar and well after Guillén de Castro's sentimental *comedia* had become the stuff of legend in Spain and beyond.

The Cid and Spanish Cultural Memory

The Romantic period's broader interest in the Cid, the Muslim Other, and the medieval origins of Spanish national history surely informed Ramón Menéndez Pidal, who at the turn of the twentieth century published the first high-profile and academically edited version of the *Poema* and then dedicated decades to its study as a founding text of a new school of Spanish philology. In particular, his book-length study *La España del Cid* argues for the text's historical veracity and for the hero's exemplarity as a founding national myth—just as Spanish intellectuals associated with the so-called Generation of 1898 began an urgent campaign to repatriate any and all available classical narratives in the wake of the disastrous Spanish–American War. As his generation's most influential and innovative literary scholar and as a member of the RAE, this philological champion of the Cid effectively added the more bellicose (and geopolitically consequential) heroism of the *Poema* to the socially virtuous and sentimental character of the *comedia* protagonist, thus further cementing the legend's place in the twentieth-century Spanish cultural imaginary. Just as Britt-Arredondo argues of the Generation of 1898's "Quixotism," Menéndez Pidal's nationalistic repatriation of the Cid can be seen as having unwittingly sown the ideological seeds of the Nationalist movement that would ultimately instigate the Spanish Civil War. With greater certainty we can argue that without the Cid of Menéndez Pidal, it is difficult to imagine the genesis of the cultural narrative of *convivencia* soon to be developed by Américo Castro.

The fact that we see competing narratives of the Cid's legend crossing paths in modern Spain makes it all the more important that we approach the Golden Age's so-called "history plays" like *Las mocedades del Cid*, *Fuenteovejuna*, and *Numancia* critically. Scholars have worked in recent years to situate this kind of drama in an early modern climate that privileged *inventio* in the treatment of historical material so as bridge the Aristotelian divide between "historical" and "poetic" truth and better speak to an emerging paying public. Golden Age playwrights were expected to modify historical or legendary subjects in order to sell out the theater, just as recent films dealing with terrorism in the 1972 Munich Olympic games (*Munich*, 2005) or the 1980 hostage crisis in Iran (*Argo*, 2012) made revisions to the historical record for aesthetic reasons, to tighten up the narrative and thus better meet the sensibilities of an audience nurtured in the digital and global era.

But one cultural moment's aesthetics of *inventio* can be another moment's manipulation of historical data. The skillful insertion of fictional detail into a fragmented, inherited historical narrative may have been seen in Guillén de Castro's day as a means of looking beyond the contingencies of historical specificity in order to speak to a more transcendent plane of truth, just as Corneille and Massenet would later see it in their adaptations, but today it is more likely to earn the ambiguous label of "historical fiction" meant to be taken with a grain of salt. If we define legend as a blending of historical and mythic source materials, Guillén de Castro's *comedia* exemplifies how the Spanish Golden Age has worked as a vehicle for the transmission of inherited legendary material from earlier historical periods and into the future well beyond the early modern period. *Las mocedades del Cid*, in other words, offers neither the first nor the last word on the legend of its protagonist, but it did leave an indelible stamp that resonates throughout all subsequent textual representations of this important national historical figure. This stamp, as I understand it, is to humanize Rodrigo, to show in a very personal way his commitment to an emerging Spanish nation and the values identified with it, including the *código de honor*. Because in Guillén de Castro's palace setting Rodrigo is shown to be a fallible and conflicted young man, the fact that his military heroism helped create what we know today as "Spain" (as legend has it) makes the nationalistic narrative espoused by Menéndez Pidal all the more compelling, as if it were a kind of secular, nationalistic word-made-flesh. Put another way, Guillén de Castro's legacy is to have made the Cid the kind of hero that could be exported abroad as exemplary of a universal principle of the human condition and eventually, with the proper narratological interventions, repatriated by Filmax as a compelling hero for young audiences who would compare him to Aladdin or Mulan.

From History Play to Historical Fiction

A more recent example of this blending of Rodrigo as both lover and fighter can be found in an episode of *El Ministerio del Tiempo* [The Ministry of Time], an immensely popular television series on Spanish national television whose first season aired in 2015. As its title suggests, the show features a government agency with the ability to travel back in time and defend the Spanish nation from threats to its national history. In the show's first season, frequent visits to the *Siglo de oro* were featured, thus allowing its audience to reconnect with prominent cultural figures like Lazarillo de Tormes and Diego de Velázquez. The second season's first episode features Rodrigo de Vivar. Agents from the ministry are dispatched to find out how two sets of the Cid's remains could have been found in different locations. What they learn is that an earlier generation of ministry agents in the 1960s, at the behest of Ramón Menéndez Pidal no less, had been sent back to the eleventh century to capture video footage of the Cid. When the agents' presence unwittingly leads to the Cid's premature death before he had completed his historical destiny, one of the agents chooses to take his place and complete his legacy. By carefully consulting an historical record that was brought from the twentieth century each night in private, the agent meticulously completes the Cid's accomplishments. The text serving as this blueprint, we should note, is the epic *Cantar de Mio Cid*.

This twentieth-century patriot-turned-*caudillo* sacrifices his life for the sake of preserving his nation's history. But while he does not consult a copy of Guillén de Castro's play, what I find noteworthy is that the writers and producers of *El Ministerio del Tiempo* do find it necessary for their story to emphasize his personal life away from the battlefield. Like Castro's Rodrigo, the Ministerio's agent must choose between his honor and his personal life, as he is forced to leave his twentieth-century family behind (or is it ahead?) in order to die as the Cid almost a thousand years earlier. Part of the ruse of assuming Rodrigo's identity is of course that he must become Jimena's husband. While Jimena does not appear to have noticed the switch, she later confesses to the newer generation of ministry agents that of course she knew that the imposter was not her original husband, but also that this imposter was a better man, the husband that she had always wished the original Rodrigo would be. The character within the show, then, performed the emotional work of Castro's Rodrigo unwittingly, while reading his Menéndez Pidal edition of the *Cantar* in order to perform its militaristic version of Rodrigo for the sake of his people—past, present, and future.

The underlying assumption of *El Ministerio del Tiempo* is that the defense of Spain's national history is necessary for the preservation of reality itself. The ministry's charge is to monitor the historical record, to detect anomalies committed by nefarious antagonists that would threaten it, and to deploy its agents to tinker with developments surrounding those anomalies in order to preserve it. To be sure, a significant part of the series' appeal to contemporary Spanish viewers is that allows them to revisit their own national history, but the often literary focus of its episodes set in the early modern period suggests that threats to Golden Age literature are no less existential than revisions to the historical record of the Spanish Empire's military campaigns. Agents are dispatched to the Golden Age to ensure that Lope de Vega completes his military service so that his dramaturgical career can begin; they must save Lazarillo de Tormes from the Inquisition so that he can live on to write his picaresque autobiography; and upon discovering that mysterious, time-traveling British profiteers have bought the unpublished manuscript of *Don Quixote*, they kidnap Cervantes to show him the importance of his novel in the twenty-first century so that he will rewrite it. The underlying ontological importance of the Golden Age, then, allows the series' Spanish audience to be culturally enriched while also being entertained.

In a similar vein, Filmax's *El Cid: La leyenda* strikes a balance between competing versions of the Cid legend by focusing on Castro-like *mocedades*, again directed at young viewers with "disnified" sensibilities, while framing those *mocedades* with the kind of voice-over narrated history that would ring true to those young viewers' parents, not to mention Menéndez Pidal and even Francisco Franco. Guillén de Castro's history play, then, remains inseparable from even the most jingoistic interpretations of the Cid's legend in contemporary Spain, in which the more militaristic content of the *Cantar de Mio Cid* serves as primary intertext.

Mediating Historical Memory

The episodes of *El Ministerio del Tiempo* described above offer but one example of how the global currents of contemporary entertainment industries and the Golden Age artifacts that circulate through them are further complicated by the recent trend of historical fiction set in the Golden Age, including the biopics *Lope* and *El Greco*, the Shakespeare-Cervantes comedy film *Miguel y William*, and popular television series like *Isabel* and *Águila roja*—new fictional narratives composed in today's globalized discursive environment that inflect and refract the nation's cultural memory of their historical setting. Insofar as these fictional engagements tend to reflect popularized narratives of the nation's history that are themselves ripe for critique as anachronistic, positivistic, and simplistic, they also reflect an appetite for the Spanish Golden Age both as an historical period and as a reservoir of classical cultural production.

Lest we forget that the "end of literature" isn't really an end to literature, but rather an end to its uniquely privileged cultural place, we should also note that Golden Age historical fiction received its original impetus in the realm of prose narrative with the best-selling *Capitán Alatriste* novels, notwithstanding the disappointing performance of its adaptation to film. Pérez-Reverte is not the only novelist to tap the well of Golden Age cultural patrimony—another salient example is Juan Carlos Arce's metanarrative of the *Celestina*'s "true" author, *Melibea no quiere ser mujer* [Melibea Doesn't Want to Be a Woman]—but it is the most commercially successful. In light of the previous chapter's observation that only a small minority of Spaniards have actually read the original *Don Quixote* in its entirety, the importance of historical fiction for understanding cultural memory in contemporary Spain cannot be overstated. Apart from *Melibea no quiere ser mujer*, a detective-style narrative describing how a woman author must conceal her identity to evade inquisitorial scrutiny and censorship, he has also published *El matemático del rey*, a mystery set in the court of Philip IV whose plot concerns the Counterreformation Church's efforts to conceal scientific discovery at odds with the narrative of its theology.

Pérez-Reverte and Arce are only two of many authors who have launched successful and lucrative careers in this ever-growing niche market of Golden Age cultural repatriation. Others include María López Villarquide (*La catedrática*, a novel about Queen Isabel's female tutor who would eventually become Spain's first female tenured professor in Salamanca), Luis García Jambrina (*El manuscrito de fuego*, a thriller set in the sixteenth-century court of Charles V), and the notable case of José Luis Corral, a professor of medieval Spanish history in Zaragoza and author of several historical novels that include the *Los Austrias* series, *Trafalgar*, *Numancia*, and *El Cid*.

While beyond the scope of this book, it should be acknowledged that this mode of repatriating the Golden Age through historical fiction emerges at the same time that a broader cultural interest in historical fiction has captured the Spanish cultural imaginary, even if the majority of critical attention regarding this phenomenon has been paid to its function in the process of recovering memories of the Civil War and the repressed voices of the Franco regime's victims. If we understand this trend in popular culture as a partial response to the deferral of justice, truth, and cultural reconciliation, the fact that popular historical fiction has also expanded the scope of its inquiry to include the Spanish Golden Age suggests that a deeper epistemological process is occurring in contemporary Spain.

This process, as we have seen, is highly mediated and impossible to separate cleanly from the discursive media currents of globalization. Regardless of what codes and conventions from other languages and cultures penetrate the Spanish historical novel, however, the publishing industry would have its readers consider the genre an aesthetically pleasurable means of acquiring access to national history. This approach to marketing is neatly encapsulated by *Planeta de libros*, an online distributor in Spain: *Viaja cientos de años atrás en el tiempo con las mejores novelas históricas. Entra y transpórtate a otras épocas para conocer la historia* [Travel back in time with the best historical novels. Enter and be transported to other eras to learn history].[14] Despite the site's reference to the global (*planeta*), its focus on Spanish publications and heavy use of first-person plural pronouns in its marketing (*nuestra historia, nuestro siglo de oro*, etc.) is indicative of both the Spanish readership it targets and the very Spanishness of the history revealed in its category of *novela histórica*, which currently counts 647 titles in its catalogue. Whether in film, television, or literature, Spain's interest in accessing its past via historical fiction continues to rise.

Whether voiced by contemporary Spaniards, transition figures like Pilar Miró, the Franco regime, the Generation of 1898 and subsequent scholars like Menéndez Pidal, nineteenth-century *casticistas* and Romantic neomedievalists, or even early modern artists like Guillén de Castro and Lope de Vega (and the noble patrons who funded them), nostalgic calls for a return to an earlier Golden Age of cultural splendor and national-identitarian clarity inevitably consist of narratives voiced from an authorial present in reference to an irrecoverable imagined past. In this sense, what distinguishes this contemporary epistemology from these earlier narrators of national history is not the relationship between fiction and history, but rather the global sphere of discursive influence informing a mode of inquiry that is as old as the very idea of Spain itself.

14 https://www.planetadelibros.com/

Conclusion

The Spanish Golden Age and Empire, Then and Now

The process of "repatriating" Golden Age narratives through globalized discourses explained in the previous chapter intensified during the buildup to the year 1992, a year of cultural programming carefully crafted for the foreign gaze. After 14 years of constitutional democracy and economic growth, Spain prepared its return to the international cultural stage through a series of spectacles, including the World Expo in Sevilla and the Summer Olympic Games in Barcelona, that would invite the world to witness and celebrate its political and economic regeneration. 1992, of course, was also the 500-year anniversary of Christopher Columbus's first voyage to the Americas, an anniversary for which Spain had begun planning its cultural programming since as early as 1983, only months after Felipe González and the PSOE won majority rule in a popular election. By the time the PSOE would lose power in 1996, it had successfully established both the CNTC and the Instituto Cervantes, two institutional pillars of contemporary Spain's public investment in Golden Age cultural patrimony.

Amid the preparations for 1992, a fascinating discursive battle developed among Spanish intellectuals and politicians, in which the government's promotion of the anniversary was perceived by many as historical revisionism meant to sanitize the injustices and atrocities of imperial conquest and colonization while still preserving pride in Spain's privileged place in world history. The discourse of state-sponsored cultural programming substituted the terms "colonization" and "conquest," for example, with the more benign "discovery" and "encounter" in an effort to sanitize Spanish history and reconcile the nation's imperial identity with postcolonial reality. While that discourse dominated how Spain presented itself to the outside world, it did not reflect the diverse opinions of its people, many of whom treated the lexical dispute as a new battlefield in the culture wars that characterized the period.[1] As Walther Bernecker and Verónica Jaffé explain, attacks came from both the right (in defense of Spain's historical legacy) and the left (in support of a more honest reconciliation with the victims of colonization). Regardless of one's position in the polemic, it was clear that Spaniards were experiencing democracy in all its chaotic messiness, engaged in spirited debate over how to interpret its national history in the pages of a privatized free press. Less than two decades beforehand, this discursive battle would have been unimaginable.

While the 1992 events in Sevilla and Barcelona presented Spain as sleek, modern, and progressive, Madrid had also been named the year's official cultural capital city of Europe, and its programming for the international spotlight was decidedly more traditional. The climax of the capital city's year-long cultural celebration was an early summer spectacle in which an immense procession of over 300 performers navigated the city's oldest streets through the Puerta del Sol and into the Plaza Mayor, where an *Auto sacramental* was performed. The considerable resources dedicated to the event became yet another subject of public debate in these "culture wars," in which opinion columns in national newspapers constituted an important "theater" (as Carey Kasten describes it) for the conflict. A common thread in debates on the choice of the *Auto* was its cultural relevance in contemporary Spain: as a mode of baroque spectacle long since abandoned by the Church as a regular devotional practice, the community's acceptance of its validity would require educating the Spanish citizenry regarding the history, significance, and spiritual function of the tradition. In this case, a Golden Age discursive practice and cultural artifact (the *Auto*) required a kind of internal or domestic reconditioning if it were to be deemed an acceptable investment of resources. Notwithstanding these concerns and debates, the Madrid celebrations would contribute to Spain's national branding in 1992, in conjunction with the more forward-looking spectacles of Sevilla and Barcelona, as a dynamic and progressive democracy while claiming cultural *gravitas* through a sanitized presentation of its historical significance as an empire. Just as the early modern Hapsburgs had patronized court painters and mounted lavish baroque musical performances and theatrical spectacles to project imperial power, contemporary Spain continues to tap the legacy of the Golden Age as a cultural resource. As this book has shown, this resource has proven to be useful, reliable, and sustainable because it is truly renewable, as so many generations of Spaniards have articulated their

---

1 Pablo Carmona et al. examine Spain's late twentieth-century "culture wars" as a conservative political strategy borrowed from the divisive Reagan-era practice in the U.S.

experience of Spanishness through them, against them, or in dialogue with them, with each deployment informed by its predecessors.

Spain's posturing in the present through symbols of the past can be perceived in most appearances of the Golden Age patrimony treated in this book. These pages have relied primarily on inductive argumentation, for a simple reason: it is impossible to articulate a single, coherent agenda behind the diverse deployments of Golden Age narratives because, now more than ever, no national consensus of what they represent has endured politically or institutionally for very long in the democratic era. As the nation's population continues to grow more diverse and more politically polarized, it seems less likely than ever that a such consensus could be articulated in a way that accounts for the breadth and scope of its people's experiences. Even the most explicitly authoritarian articulations of the Spanish nation, such as those offered during the Franco regime while suppressing the articulation of contrary perspectives, were subject to being countered from without, through counter-deployments of Golden Age patrimony similar to Picasso's famous sketch of Don Quixote for the communist party in France. Instead of deducing a definitive cultural history, I have sought to reveal the complexities and complications of these narrative deployments, and thus their utility for reading contemporary Spain's discursive cacophony. This lack of consensus is of course not unique to Spain, nor is the cacophony's amplification in a digital age of social media that has empowered an unprecedentedly wide array of voices to be heard. The long list of challenges faced by Spaniards today—economic, political, environmental, social, cultural—shares many parallels with the problems of many developed countries. In this sense, tourist slogans notwithstanding, Spain is *not* different.

What *is* unique to Spain, I would argue, is the relationship that has developed between its people and its literary patrimony, whether we attribute that unique relationship to the nature of its cultural resources, to the resourcefulness and creativity of its deployers, or to anything else. The consistency and regularity with which the Spanish Golden Age has been redeployed over the course of Spain's turbulent political history, even as its articulation has come to be shaped by discursive forces from outside of the Iberian Peninsula, provides for scholars a heuristic tool whose pervasive, complex power and cultural authority have been the object of study in these pages. At every proverbial inflection point or watershed moment in Spanish history since the early modern period, one can analyze invocations of the Golden Age to penetrate the surface of chronological events and understand how Spaniards understood and felt about their experiences—with the understanding that the specific item of Golden Age patrimonial value selected for any given moment is not simply the early modern cultural artifact unsealed from an original or pristine state, but rather the evolved version of that artifact shaped by the accumulated cultural baggage of its prior uses. Ramiro de Maeztu's Don Juan, for example, is not simply an invocation of Tirso de Molina's original character, as if perfectly preserved and freshly unsealed in the twentieth century; Maeztu's Don Juan bears the scars of having been expatriated by the likes of Molière (theatrical comedy), Calzabigi (ballet), Byron (satirical verse narrative), and Mozart (opera), and of then having been repatriated by Zorilla in the nineteenth century, as a romanticized Don Juan subject to further re-interpretation by Azorín, Valle-Inclán, and others at the turn of the twentieth century. This tradition of revisiting literary tradition means that while Spain may not be different in terms of the challenges it faces, the negotiation of those challenges does feature a unique discursive battleground—the Spanish Golden Age—and thus a unique opportunity for scholars to understand and study those challenges and their negotiations, in all their diachronic and intercultural complexity.

Pivot: A Pan-Hispanic Cultural Empire?

Having posited this disclaimer of contemporary Spain's debatable cultural and identitarian coherence, the space of this concluding chapter seems opportune for zooming out to deduce common threads, even as we resist the urge to ascribe a consistent or coherent agency to them or to pretend that they speak for all Spaniards. For Hispanists, it is also worth considering the utility of a diachronic Spanish Golden Age for transatlantic studies, a field that for some time has identified the need to move Hispanism beyond institutionally reinforced divisions between Spanish and Latin American studies, but whose slow development has frustrated scholars like Sebastian Faber, Alejandro Mejías-López, and Abril Trigo. Like Joan Ramón Resina, these scholars have detected in transatlantic studies a potentially slippery slope: by presuming a pan-Hispanic field of cultural production oriented around a Castilian metropolis, transatlantic Hispanists risk echoing the same Eurocentric cultural narrative on which the field was founded a century ago, and arguably in contradistinction to which the field of Latin American literary and cultural studies would develop. While the latter field's decolonial turn implies a rejection of that narrative, important work remains to be done regarding the persistence of the empire's cultural residue in the postcolonial societies of its former colonies. I would argue that the Spanish Golden Age, the canonical epicenter of such imperial cultural narratives, is an ideal cultural space from which to begin such transatlantic work—especially in an era when, as the previous chapter suggests, Spain's repatriation of its cultural patrimony is subject to foreign discourses. This discursive interplay suggests that the cultural vestiges of the Spanish Empire in Latin America can teach us a great deal not only about the diverse ways in which Latin American cultures continue to understand their history as the colonized, but also about how those cultures now inform the repatriated narratives of the colonizers themselves.

One implicit thread of continuity running through the preceding chapters seems especially relevant to how the Spanish Golden Age can intersect with transatlantic studies: the Spanish deployments of Golden Age narratives studied here share an underlying tension between containment and dissemination, between inward cultural reflection and outward expansion, or even between autochthony and universality. In other words, the accumulated significance of Spanish Golden Age narratives speaks to a perpetual desire by Spaniards both to understand themselves as a national culture and to extend the reach and influence of that culture beyond its borders, as if to internally validate and legitimate itself through its adoption by and adaptation to foreign contexts. To be sure, this tendency is more readily observable in some eras than in others: the Franco dictatorship itself is typically studied as a regime of two phases (*primer franquismo/tardofranquismo*) that in many ways are distinguishable by the intensity with which the foreign consumption of its culture was desired. Regardless of any such historical fluctuations, however, the Instituto Cervantes and other contemporary Spanish cultural institutions offer strong evidence that Spain continues to invest in how its culture is disseminated and presented to a foreign gaze. Transatlantic Hispanic approaches to the Spanish Golden Age can elucidate Spain's instinct to extend and expand its cultural footprint, even in those instances where the foreign gaze is more specifically what bell hooks would call an oppositional gaze. This urge to expand and extend, in short, is less an ideology than an ontology of empire.

The claim that the very idea of Spain has always involved an imperialist urge to expand and extend itself is supported, I would argue, by the nation's pre-history and the earliest attempts to articulate an expansive idea of Spain in the fifteenth century. The ironic term *Reconquista*, for example, articulates a Castilian identity defined by the recovery of a unified Iberian Christendom that had never actually functioned as a proto-state before Al-Andalus. As such, *Reconquista* points to the fact that Castilian hegemony has always depended on an aspirational use of nostalgic cultural narrative—the same nostalgia embedded in the very term *Siglo de oro*—through which a coherent cultural identity might be forged. The idea of Spain therefore first emerged from the Middle Ages as a call for (re)conquest and expansion, and I would argue that the critical utility of the Spanish Golden Age stems from the insight it affords into the explicitly textual nature of that ontology.

As legend has it, Isabel la Católica asked Antonio de Nebrija ¿para qué sirve? [What purpose does it serve?] when he presented his *Gramática de la lengua castellana* [Grammar of the Castilian Language] to her in 1492. In a letter addressed to her later that year, Nebrija would recall that, as he struggled to articulate an answer to the Queen's simple question, the Bishop of Ávila stepped in to bluntly explain its purpose for him:

> después que vuestra Alteza metiesse debaxo de su iugo muchos pueblos bárbaros y naciones de peregrinas lenguas, y con el vencimiento aquellos ternían necessidad de recebir las leies quel vencedor pone al vencido, y con ellas nuestra lengua, entonces, por esta mi arte, podrían venir en el conocimiento della [...]. (Nebrija, 14)

> [after your Highness holds under her yoke many barbarian people and nations of disparate languages, and with their conquest they would need to receive the laws that the conqueror imposes on the conquered, and with them our language, therefore, through my treatise, they may come to know it [...].]

This justification, beyond its naked embrace of Spain's appetite for conquest in the new world, demonstrates that Nebrija was explicitly aware of how all of Spain's forthcoming imperial transactions—conquest, colonization, exploitation, and destruction—would be accompanied by discursive or textual representations and articulations of their justification. The *Gramática* is thus both a seminal moment in establishing a national Spanish language and a discursive cornerstone of the Spanish Empire, as if destiny must be made manifest through its articulation and reception.

Nebrija's famous assertion that language and empire are inextricably linked ("siempre la lengua fue compañera del imperio" [11]) [language was always companion to empire] is vital to a full and diachronic understanding of Iberoamerican cultural exchange, including of course where the Spanish Golden Age is engaged as cultural patrimony. His voice echoes in a number of discourses emanating from Spain over the subsequent centuries tied to notions of a shared Hispanic cultural and linguistic heritage, including the politically fraught efforts to strengthen transatlantic ties in 1892 and 1992—centenary celebrations ostensibly intended to commemorate the first voyage of Christopher Columbus to the "New World," but that also coincided with publication anniversaries of Nebrija's seminal text. Since the turn of the current century, Spain has engaged with Latin America in ways that certainly are far removed from early modern conquest and cultural colonization, but Nebrija's original textual-transactional paradigm nonetheless haunts current pan-Hispanic and transatlantic cultural exchange.

The *Reconquista*'s successful narrativization consolidated Christian power and identity, through the militarization of its religious orders, the proto-nationalization of its institutions, and even an articulation of Catholic faith that developed myths like that of "Santiago Matamoros." This proto-nationalist narrative featured an ethical dimension—repelling the Muslim Other in defense of Christianity while saving the souls of the "convertible" non-Christian Iberians—around which the monarchy's subjects could be rallied to construct something called "España." As William Childers argues in his book *Transnational Cervantes*, this ideological programming of the colonial subject began in Spain itself before it was exported to the New World, and continued to form the Spanish citizenry for the duration of the Spanish Empire even as it also shaped the formation of colonial societies abroad. The same irony inherent in the term *Reconquista* could also be said of the Franco regime's engagement with the Spanish Golden Age centuries later: its ideological program of essentialist, homogenizing cultural nostalgia was also based on a monolithic and fascistic reading of national history, which it in turn leveraged to create an altogether novel modern fascist state capable of withstanding the forces of liberal democracy and free market capitalism that had overrun similar projects in Italy and Germany. Franco's narrative projection of the past and vision for the future promised a Spain purged of its peripheries and margins, through the erasure of its religious, ethnic, and ideological others, both early modern and modern. It also demonstrated that, regardless of the isolationist policies it instituted, falangist nationalism was no less tied to this imperial ontology than were Isabel and her husband.

If we accept the premise that the emergent idea of Spain of the waning Middle Ages was an aspirational narrative meant to rally the expanding subjects and resources of Castile to a common project of *Reconquista*, it is logical that this narrative could be morphed into imperial aspirations when Spain pivoted from Iberian to American conquest and colonization.[2] Henry Kamen's claim that the Spanish Empire was more myth than reality[3] reinforces the discursive nature of this imperial Spanish ontology: despite the unsustainably complicated and costly maintenance of control over its territories, the historical narratives of Spain passed down to its citizens in the centuries since the early modern period will invariably recall first the empire's vast expanse and geopolitical footprint through such elegiac

---

2 William Childers's *Transnational Cervantes* draws similar parallels between the colonial project of the Spanish Empire and Spain's "internal colonization," in effect a cultural program within Spain to inculcate an ideology of Castilian hegemony among the various regions united by Ferdinand and Isabel in the fifteenth century.

3 See Kamen's *Imagining Spain*.

descriptors as "the empire on which the sun never set." These discursive affirmations of imperial achievement have been memorialized in ways that the empire's collapse was not. When the gradual *desengaño* of discovering the illusory nature of empire had taken root in the seventeenth century, and as the reality of the Spanish Empire's geopolitical decline became apparent, the Spanish Golden Age was over as an historical period. As we have seen, however, its magnetic pull as an object of cultural nostalgia had only just begun.

If the idea of Spain emerged in ways inextricably tied to empire, it should come as no surprise that the preternatural disposition toward imperial expansion would remain perceptible in at least some of its patrimonial usages of Golden Age narratives throughout the centuries. Alda Blanco's description of a Spanish national "imperial consciousness" (1) through the nineteenth century, to which she attributes Spain's acquisition and defense of territories in North Africa well into the twentieth century, supports the notion that a kind of imperial identity or ontology is intrinsic to the very idea of Spain (at least as it was understood by those in power). So too does Claire Mar-Molinero's identification of a Spanish/Castilian linguistic empire that is now asserting itself in the realm of language policy within Spain (particularly among conservatives opposed to the PSOE's notion that Spain is a "nation of nations") and in Spain's efforts, through vehicles like the international Asociación de Academias de la Lengua Española [Association of Academies of the Spanish Language] and the Instituto Cervantes, to control international linguistic standards and the teaching of Spanish as a foreign language. While that inherent will-to-empire was no longer possible to be made geopolitically manifest after the Spanish–American War, I would argue that the further study of contemporary utilizations of Golden Age patrimony, particularly in a transatlantic context, will reveal that it does emerge in many instances as a kind of cultural imperialism in keeping with this scholarship.

This notion of a cultural *Hispania* or pan-Hispanic world featuring Castilian hegemony—a claim to a persistent Spanish cultural authority over its former colonies, especially in Latin America—certainly does not account for all contemporary Golden Age deployments within Spain, in all their cacophonic diversity. Beyond those noted in previous chapters of this study, many more examples of satirical deployments can be found in which the Spanish Golden Age is a tool for cultural critique and even deprecation of nationalistic pride, along the lines of Juan Goytisolo's op-ed decrying the state's complicity in persistent racial tribalism (*Fuenteovejuna, señor*). A viral video of a "trap" musical piece (*Velaske, yo soi guapa?*) animates Velázquez's *Las meninas* to critique how the ostensible social privilege of the Princess Mariana of Austria is undercut by her gender's function in early modern Europe as an object of political and economic exchange.[4] A 2011 stage production of *La dama boba* by Pie Izquierdo (Madrid) reduces Lope's *comedia* to a simplistic love story in order to capture the imagination (and hold the attention) of young children. In *Siglo de Oro, Siglo de Ahora*, the Madrid-based experimental theater troupe Ron Lalá satirizes the problems of contemporary Spain by drawing parallels with similar problems in the Golden Age, deploying a pastiche of sardonic cultural references to the period. None of these examples of Golden Age deployments reflect the imperial ontology described above.

In fact, the last of these examples is instructive regarding this thread of imperial ontology emanating from state-sponsored cultural programming. Ron Lalá, however irreverent and satirical their work may be, has recently collaborated with the CNTC to bring *En un lugar del Quijote* [*Somewhere in the Quixote*] to theater venues across western Europe—an institutional pairing that juxtaposes polar-opposite uses of the Spanish Golden Age that likely would have scandalized the CNTC's original leadership. The invitation for the small theatrical troupe to participate in the exporting of the Golden Age internationally alongside the publicly funded CNTC came after the surprising success of *Siglo de Oro, Siglo de Ahora* in Madrid. Notwithstanding their penchant for satire, Ron Lalá's collaboration with the CNTC is indicative of how, especially during an era of economic austerity and hence scarce funding for cultural programming, very different artistic visions and interpretations of Golden Age artifacts are often consolidated or synergized as they participate in a shared, economically precarious cultural ecosystem. As a result, one could argue, the inward-looking satire of Ron Lalá contributes to an outward-looking, expansion-minded CNTC—making for strange bedfellows that are enlisted due to their shared goal to engage twenty-first-century audiences through redeployments of the Spanish Golden Age. What these production companies, cultural institutions, and artists share is an acknowledgement of the Golden Age's magnetism, along with a desire to further expand its cultural influence on a global scale. This expansive dynamic merits further attention, and a full understanding of it requires an examination both of the global forces shaping it today and of the historical roots underlying it—particularly as they pertain to Latin America.

4 https://www.youtube.com/watch?v=Il6p2-40-Fo

The Spanish Empire, Then and Now

It is well known that the "boom" of early modern Spanish theater during the latter decades of the sixteenth century coincided with the colonization of the Americas, and that the *Comedia* was soon appropriated by the Empire as a tool for projecting Spanish cultural splendor and for contributing to the cultural evangelization and colonization of the empire's *amerindio* subjects. Spanish theater was an important agent of the empire, a vehicle for evangelical Spanish religious orders and even for the Spanish state to teach *la lengua castellana* [the Castilian language], to present Spain's historical and religious narratives to indigenous peoples, and to foster mutual cultural understanding. After the conquest, popular Spanish drama served important ceremonial courtly and evangelical functions and stimulated colonial cultural expression and development. Any history of colonial Latin American theater will invariably invoke figures like Sor Juana Inés de la Cruz and Juan Ruiz de Alarcón as exemplary colonial subjects who mastered the discourses of the popular Spanish *Comedia* in order to contribute to what we now know as the canon of Spanish Golden Age theater. To be sure, ample scholarship has argued against reading either of these colonial playwrights as merely derivative of the Spanish tradition, but it seems clear that both writers developed a keen awareness of the *Comedia*'s conventions and formulae, based upon their formative cultural experiences as colonial subjects.

It is also well known that today, Spain is making perhaps its most concerted effort *since* the colonial period to foster international appreciation of Golden Age patrimony beyond its own national borders, as part of a broader effort to disseminate Spanish culture around the world. In both cases, the *Comedia* is used as a symbol of Spanishness, as a metonym for Spanish cultural splendor, and as a means of promoting an appreciation for that splendor that can ultimately be linked to economic interests. Unless one reads these parallels between early modern and contemporary uses of the *Comedia* as mere coincidence, it is with good reason that we examine the contemporary, publicly funded programming of *Comedia* performance with eyes wide open to the possibility that they constitute a new kind of cultural imperialism, or at least evidence of what I am calling a Spanish imperial ontology. Contemporary Iberoamerican intercultural exchange should therefore be studied diachronically as well, as the services rendered by Spanish Golden Age theater as an agent of the early modern empire can help us to better understand how contemporary Spanish cultural institutions are using the patrimony of *teatro clásico* to foster interest in and appreciation for the Spanish brand, or for all things *Made in Spain*.

Spanish state-sponsored cultural programming occurring in Latin America today, particularly in the form of *Comedia* performance, is directed primarily through the leadership of the CNTC, a state institution underwritten through Spain's Ministerio de Cultura y Deporte.[5] Its explicit mission is to support "la recuperación, preservación, producción y difusión del patrimonio teatral anterior al siglo XX, con especial atención al Siglo de Oro y a la prosodia del verso clásico" [the recovery, preservation, and diffusion of pre-20th century theatrical patrimony, with special attention to the Golden Age and to the prosody of classical verse].[6] This mission statement's implicit double-vision, from which the Compañía's work can be said to be both inward and outward looking, reflects the tension between containment/preservation and expansion/dissemination described as an imperial ontology above: within Spain, the CNTC was founded to *recuperar* and to *preservar* the cultural patrimony of the *Comedia*, and to *producir* adaptations of early modern playtexts for a contemporary Spanish public that had become disenchanted with the Spanish Golden Age after the Franco regime. While the dictatorship did in principle support *Comedia* performance in its broader project to return Spain to its glorious cultural past, it did not invest in cultural institutions that would foster a coherently curated performance history along the lines of England's famous Royal Shakespeare Company. In other words, the regime drew upon the *Comedia* for ideological and propagandistic support, but without serious regard for fostering its appreciation among new generations of Spaniards, which it had taken for granted. As a result, the *Comedia* entered Spain's transition to democracy as ideologically associated with a *franquista* vision of traditional Spanish cultural values and, not surprisingly, as a cultural tradition of little interest to a newly liberated public eager to experiment and experience new modes of popular expression to which their access had been suppressed or even blocked for decades.

The CNTC was deemed a necessary intervention in 1986 primarily because of how Felipe González's Socialist government understood its role in the realm of cultural governance: to remedy the consequences of four decades of *franquista* cultural programming, in which the regime had successfully appropriated the *Comedia* and all things *Siglo de oro* as portals to a primeval

---

5 It is worth noting that prior to the PSOE's return to power in 2018, the distribution of ministerial offices had included Education as a companion to Culture (Ministerio de Educación, Cultura y Deporte). The significant investment in international outreach via Golden Age patrimony that preceded this change in political power, like the initiatives *Laboratorio América* and *Mi primer clásico*, might be tied to the administration of educational and cultural ministries within the same unit.

6 http://teatroclasico.mcu.es/la-comp/que-es-la-cntc/

Hispanidad or national essence, or as a cultural Eden to which the *generalíssimo* would lead Spain's return. A transition to democracy meant, unfortunately for classical theater enthusiasts, a transition away from the preferred theatrical tradition of the regime. But because theatrical performance is a form of cultural patrimony that requires organization, infrastructure, and continuity, after 11 years of democracy the neglected *Comedia* was seen as an endangered cultural species. In many ways, establishing the CNTC was not unlike efforts by the Second Republic to foster appreciation of the *Comedia* in the 1930s, through *misiones pedagógicas* like Federico García Lorca's itinerant theater company La Barraca.

The success of the CNTC exceeded all expectations and it remains a strong, healthy, and diverse institution more than 30 years after its founding. Through the many twists and turns of its history, some caused by leadership turnover and others by larger national economic and political forces, it has managed to maintain consistent critical praise and a stable national presence through a comprehensive program of productions across Spain. Its success bolstered the standing of the Festival de Teatro Clásico de Almagro (where the CNTC regularly receives top billing) and has inspired smaller private companies to adopt the *Comedia* in their repertoires. The CNTC has even expanded its programming to include Joven Clásico, a second company specifically designed to train fresh young talent with greater flexibility and artistic license than was originally afforded to the CNTC. Buoyed by a broader cultural nostalgia for the *Siglo de oro* that Spain has carefully nurtured with cultural programming to commemorate every conceivable *aniversario* or *centenario* that it can think of, the Compañía has proven to be a wise investment.

The initial focus of the CNTC when it was founded in 1986 was necessarily domestic—an urgent call to preserve a form of cultural patrimony that had informed Spanish national identities for centuries, but that depended on continued theatrical practice in an era when public demand would need to be re-stimulated by a reinvigorated, state-sponsored supply of cultural production. Since the turn of the twenty-first century, however, that focus has shifted notably to its other, more outward-looking mission: the *difusión del patrimonio teatral* [diffusion of theatrical patrimony] beyond Spain. The domestic success of the CNTC in reviving enthusiasm for Spanish classical theater for two decades, coupled with Spain's own economic prosperity heading into the new century, resulted in a well-funded and stable cultural institution with a deep roster of directors, actors, and technicians well equipped to extend the *Comedia*'s cultural footprint on a global scale.

In 2011, leadership of the CNTC was handed over to its current director, Helena Pimenta. Spain's economic crisis was in full bloom, with the Zapatero government only months away from losing power to Mariano Rajoy's Partido Popular, and with austerity measures threatening to limit the company's funding. What is perhaps most remarkable about this campaign to widen the CNTC's geographical footprint is the fact that was undertaken during such austere times. Pimenta's appointment was made in an era of financial crisis that has resulted in a precipitous decline in government spending for the arts and all other forms of cultural programming. As the crisis has persisted, the CNTC has attempted to do more with less, which has in turn fostered a change in culture within the company regarding how it treats its dramatic raw materials. While the company's original approach prioritized preservation over access, its own success and government austerity have converged to reverse that order of priority, and to expand the range of publics to whom the *Comedia* is to be made more accessible. The CNTC can now say that the problem that had inspired its foundation in the first place, Spain's lack of a classical performance tradition, has been remedied substantially after three successful decades of hard work; the appointment of Pimenta signaled an institutional pivot to a younger generation of theater practitioners with a more expansive agenda.

Despite—or perhaps because of—this economic crisis, press releases surrounding the announcement of Pimenta's leadership emphasized the beginning of a new, more expansionist mission for the CNTC. The Compañía would broaden its repertoire both geographically and chronologically, by incorporating "classical" works written outside of Spain (including William Shakespeare, Carlo Goldoni, and Charles Perrault) and through promises to adapt plays written before and even well after the Spanish Golden Age, including José Zorrilla's *Don Juan Tenorio*, in an effort to broaden the scope of the nebulous term *teatro clásico*. This project of repertoire expansion also included adaptations of texts not originally composed for the stage, such as *Don Quixote*, Quevedo's *Sueños*, and the *Romancero del Cid*, and eclectic new arrangements of textual fragments creatively packaged for theatrical performance with titles like *La voz de nuestros clásicos* [The voice of our classics], *Barrio de las letras* [Neighborhood of Letters], and *Préstame tus palabras* [Lend me your words]. Redefining *teatro clásico* in this way, which perhaps would be more accurately called *cultura clásica teatralizada* [theatricalized classical culture], reflects a more flexible approach to a cultural institution that spent much of its earlier years debating textual authenticity and establishing conservative parameters for curating and preserving the *Comedia* in its "purest" form. In effect, the CNTC faced economic austerity by shifting its mission from the preservation of an endangered cultural species to the creative search for new ways to attract spectators to new kinds of textual transactions, even as skyrocketing unemployment promised to limit the paying public's disposable income.

In addition to such freshly packaged programming, the CNTC has also become increasingly reliant on collaboration with other groups, both in Spain and abroad. Collaborations with Nao d'Amores, Rakatá, and Ron Lalá are now regular and allow offerings to increase in number and scope. As noted above, Ron Lalá was originally only marginally interested in the *Siglo de oro* as a means for delivering a fresh angle for contemporary cultural critique; its collaboration with the CNTC in recent years has focused especially on Cervantes, in the spectacle cited above (*En un lugar del Quijote*) and more recently in *Cervantina*, which bills itself as *Versiones y diversiones sobre textos de Cervantes* [Versions and diversions of Cervantes's texts] and borrows creatively from his verse, prose, and dramatic corpus.

More importantly, the 2011 "reboot" of the CNTC would feature more touring throughout Spain and abroad, with performances stretching from Ireland to India. A subsequent push for foreign outreach began in 2016 with the *Proyecto Europa*, a program of several productions to be performed in Italy, Germany, and Austria, as well as in several sites in North Africa. Included in this geographically ambitious programming is a consistent performance itinerary in Latin America, an agenda that was nominally included in the CNTC's original mission statement but only occasionally pursued with vigor, such as when Adolfo Marsillach took his production of Calderón's *El médico de su honra* to Buenos Aires in 1986. A series of conferences and reunions with theater practitioners from all over the Spanish-speaking world, including the *Foro sobre la producción escénica en Iberoamérica* [Forum on Scenic Production in Iberian America] in Argentina in 2011, allowed the CNTC to extend its international presence through professional networks. These exchanges would foster co-productions and collaborations in both Spain and Latin America that continue to this day, including the initiatives *Mi primer clásico* and *Laboratorio América*, meant to stimulate interest in the *Comedia* among young Latin Americans. It would also foster ties to Latin American companies that would bring them back to Spain, especially in venues like the international festival in Almagro. Alongside this programming, Pimenta dispatched CNTC productions to performance venues in its most comprehensive Latin American tour to date, with stops including Mexico, Argentina, Colombia, and Paraguay.

When presented as Director in 2011, Pimenta described Latin America as "un ámbito natural de difusión" [a natural place for diffusion], and we are left to interpret this *naturaleza* [nature] as owing to the shared historical and linguistic ties between Spain and its former colonies. The Compañía's reaction to economic crisis, in other words, was to look to Latin American audiences and theater practitioners as resources, which supports the notion that Nebrija's original textual-transactional paradigm remains a valid lens through which to study contemporary Iberoamerican cultural exchange. While Pimenta's perspective on Latin America as an *ámbito natural de difusión* is of course quite different from Columbus's first letters to the Spanish monarchs, in which he noted the rich natural and human resources that Spain could exploit, echoes of the underlying transactional paradigm do persist. Both Pimenta and Columbus survey the Latin American landscape and see opportunity for growth and expansion according to the interests of the Spanish state, and both see such benefits as somehow "natural."

This systemic effort to bring Spanish classical theater to its former colonies depends on institutional support from the Spanish state in order to make such outreach possible. The CNTC is now working with the Instituto Cervantes to create opportunities and logistical support for bringing the *Comedia* to every corner of the globe. The Instituto Cervantes, another state-supported organization with an explicit "evangelical" mission of disseminating Spanish culture and language instruction, has previously focused its efforts beyond the Spanish-speaking world, but the same collaborative spirit that now informs the CNTC-Instituto Cervantes relationship applies to how Pimenta's company has engaged with the various Latin American academies and theater associations with whom it has collaborated to raise the *Comedia*'s profile in the region. In turn, an increasing number of Latin American theater groups have coordinated with the CNTC and the Instituto Cervantes to bring productions across the pond to Spain's summer circuit of theater festivals, including the premiere venue in Almagro. The fact that the Instituto Cervantes has been an enthusiastic, state-supported partner institution with the CNTC suggests that they work toward common interests, and that the CNTC now identifies with the same mission of cultural outreach as the Instituto, which has been characterized by scholars like Claire Mar-Molinero as a project of cultural and linguistic imperialism (77).

Siglo de oro, Siglo de ahora

This shift in CNTC emphasis toward outreach makes sense when considered in the diachronic context of the Spanish Golden Age described in this book. The case can be made that the CNTC and partner institutions approach expansion into Latin America not as *conquistadores*, but in ways that do echo Spain's first efforts to harvest Latin America for its own gain, and that reflect Spain's imperial ontology. The goals of the CNTC are surely far less ethically problematic than were those of Carlos V, but when put in the context of the other cultural initiatives of the Instituto Cervantes—to establish standards and norms of Spanish language usage and pedagogy, and to attract new consumers for Spanish cultural production—the case can be made that the

CNTC participates in a new kind of cultural colonialism. Beyond noting the obvious connection with missionary uses of the *Comedia* during the colonial period to disseminate *castellano* and promote the Christian faith in indigenous communities, we do well to recall Nebrija's words as we study how language and culture—what we might call "soft power"—are features of contemporary Iberoamerican exchange, just as they were essential ingredients of the early modern Spanish imperial and colonial project.

While it would be unfair to equate Pimenta's perspective on Latin America as somehow parallel to Columbus's first letters to the Spanish monarchs, in which he noted the rich natural and human resources that Spain could exploit, the case can be made that there are some parallels, insofar as both Pimenta and Colombus see Latin America as a resource to be exploited or mined for the sake of Spanish prosperity. The parallels between the fifteenth and twenty-first centuries become clearer when we also take into account that Spain is now the second largest foreign investor in Latin America.[7] The Spanish Empire once depended on its ability to mine Latin American natural resources to sustain its ever-rising financial obligations, and beginning in the 1990s, Spanish banks and corporations began aggressively investing in the region again as a strategy for economic growth as it positioned itself within the European Union. A decade later, as the Spanish economy approached the tipping point of its crisis and needed to assure Europe of its capacity to survive without the kind of long-term bailouts that had crippled the economies of Greece and Italy, the turn to Latin America as economic resource was (as Helena Pimenta might say) "natural." If we are to take the plots of many early modern *comedias* as evidence, Spanish society experienced similar anxiety as its socioeconomic stability was shaken by the flood of currency from the Americas and the emergence of a new class of wealthy Spanish and *indio* subjects lacking the blue-blood pedigree of the traditional nobility; contemporary Spain has also experienced socioeconomic anxiety related to immigration from Latin America.[8] When Spain's banking system faced collapse at the beginning of the economic crisis of 2008, Latin American investment by Spanish banks like Santander and Bankia was by most accounts a key factor in preventing an even worse financial disaster. In 2012, Prime Minister Mariano Rajoy called on Latin America to return the transactional favor by shifting its own investment strategies away from Asia and towards Spain. Transatlantic investment in both directions has become

---

7 See Elena Martínez and Francisco Jareño for a detailed analysis of Spain's recent increase in economic investment in Latin America.

8 Laura Bass addresses this early modern anxiety in her article "The Economics of Representation in Lope de Vega's *La dama boba*."

a strategy for economic growth that would enhance Spain's standing among its European neighbors, not unlike how early modern transatlantic economic activity informed the perception of Spanish power among its European imperial rivals. In all of these cases, then and now, Spain's gaze across the Atlantic has seen Latin America as a resource to which claims of economic and cultural sovereignty are implicitly seen as its manifest destiny.

It is therefore tempting to see Spain's twenty-first-century economic ties to Latin America as neocolonial, but the current political chaos of the former colonizer is a reminder that democracy, for all its ugliness, does ensure that these cultural and economic ties will not be subject to the whims of a single absolutist voice or master narrative. In the Helena Pimenta era of the CNTC, for example, this interest has expanded beyond the simple prospect of bringing Spanish productions across the Atlantic, and into the fostering of partnerships that would yield transatlantic collaboration for years to come. Marsillach's 1986 tour, like Federico García Lorca's production of Lope de Vega's *La dama boba* in Buenos Aires in 1934, followed the spirit of a *misión pedagógica*, in which Spanish experts would bring their cultural artifacts to a Latin American audience with a clear and hierarchical distinction between the colonizer and the colonized. Pimenta's postcolonial collaboration, by contrast, aims to stimulate both knowledge and passion for *el teatro clásico español*—knowledge that will facilitate autochthonous Latin American productions in the future, and passion that will allow those productions to be economically viable.

A key moment in this effort came in 2014, when the CNTC produced Fernando de Rojas's *Los áspides de Cleopatra* in collaboration with Argentina's Complejo Teatral de Buenos Aires for Spain's International Classical Theater Festival in Almagro. In terms that Nebrija would surely have appreciated, Pimenta described this project to the newspaper *El país* as "la transformación del verso español en Latinoamérica a través del tiempo" [the transformation of Spanish verse in Latin America across time].[9] The professionalization and training of young Argentine actors and technicians of this collaborative, known as *Laboratorio América*, is indeed a postcolonial textual transaction, insofar as colonial hierarchies and zero-sum notions of wealth and power are replaced by what George Yúdice would call a paradigm of "expediency," in which all parties are enriched. Pimenta was quoted in *El país* as seeing *Laboratorio América* as a model for the sustainability of classical theater performance in an era in which economic austerity is the new normal: "Está claro que reducen los costes de forma importante y multiplican los talentos" [It is clear that they reduce costs substantially and multiply the talent pool] (Intxausti).

---

9 See Aurora Intxausti's article in *El País*, "Un Siglo de Oro con acento porteño."

While mitigating such material and economic concerns is presented as a benefit of these transatlantic cultural collaborations, there are of course less practical and more idealistic reasons for pursuing them. Pimenta highlights that her collaborative work is of the greatest benefit not to the CNTC but to Spanish *teatro clásico* itself, as it is enriched by the increased global capacity of the Spanish-speaking world to perform it. "Tenemos 4.000 textos que son un tesoro y muchos de ellos llevan demasiados años sin representarse" [We have 4,000 texts that are a treasure and many of them have gone too many years without being performed] (Intxausti). By including Latin America in its call for expansion, the CNTC appears to now see the region less as a colony and more as a partner with a shared cultural patrimony. This collaborative spirit opens up the possibility that, even if the shadow of Nebrija's original transactional paradigm remains relevant to the diachronic context in which contemporary Iberoamerican cultural exchange should be considered, its implicit hierarchy (colonizer/colonized) is no longer the only lens through which it must be analyzed. In this case, the *prosodia del verso clásico* [prosody of classical verse] whose preservation is explicitly featured in the CNTC's mission statement is transformed through the voices of postcolonial subjects in a performance celebrated at the Almagro festival, which in the world of *teatro clásico* constitutes the very seat of Spain's imagined cultural empire.

To be sure, this transaction is ripe for postcolonial critique, as the CNTC's training of Latin American theater practitioners can be said to suffer a kind of re-colonization through the process of being carefully trained by state-sponsored experts of the former colonizer. For Pimenta, however, this exchange is more than a unidirectional "mining" of colonized resources, but rather something both mutually beneficial and truly transformational: "No hay que olvidar que emergen nuevas miradas sobre el común patrimonio dramatúrgico" [One mustn't forget that new visions emerge of our common dramaturgical patrimony] (Intxausti). In the specific case of her production of *Los áspides de Cleopatra*, Pimenta characterizes its *otra mirada* as "la del extraordinario acento porteño" [that of the extraordinary *porteño* accent] (Intxausti). Therefore, while a healthy skepticism is needed to remain sensitive to echoes of Nebrija as they emerge, we might also see the shared cultural patrimony of the Spanish Empire as a means to better understand the postcolonial experience on both sides of the Atlantic.

This question might seem valid from an Iberian perspective, but of course it does not account for the perspective of the formerly colonized, nor does it address the concerns voiced by scholars that transatlantic Hispanism risks repeating Eurocentric cultural narratives similar to those on which the field was founded. For those artists, writers, and state-sponsored cultural programmers in Latin America that have chosen to engage with Spanish government cultural outreach in this way, it would be reasonable to assume that their choice to participate indicates an alignment of interests with the CNTC, the Instituto Cervantes, and other Spanish cultural institutions—or at a minimum, that the opportunities afforded by this collaboration are worth any potential problems that they might engender, be they professional, cultural, political, or otherwise.

In fact, determining just what those problems might be would be an important first step in developing a transatlantic approach to studying the diachronic Spanish Golden Age. It is also a step that is conspicuously absent in current scholarship on Latin American literary and cultural studies, and for very good reason in light of critical developments within that field that began in the latter decades of the twentieth century, only to intensify since, especially in the context of the field's postcolonial and more recent "decolonial" theoretical turns. While these developments have empowered Latin American studies to address issues hitherto ignored by Eurocentric Hispanism, they have also directed scholarly attention away from the kinds of questions that such a transatlantic approach to the Spanish Golden Age would engage. The ways in which some postcolonial subjects participate in the continued circulation and deployment of Spanish Golden Age narratives has simply not been an object of sustained critical focus among Latin Americanists, and it remains to be discovered to what extent the treatment of such subjects might complement, deepen, or (perhaps) contest a prevailing mode of scholarship that, like contemporary Spanish cultural studies, extends a "presentist" (to borrow again from Mariscal) privilege to "original" contemporary cultural production.

In an era in which the well-worn breaches separating Peninsular Spanish and Latin American Studies remain institutionally ensconced, there could be no better time than the present to pursue a fresh angle into the persistence of what is often called the colonial matrix of power embedded in the very intellectual DNA of Hispanism. Being armed with what we now understand about Golden Age patrimony and the history of its operationalization since the Golden Age in Spain, including about how they constitute powerful tools for both the affirmation and the subversion of the colonial matrix, we are better situated to approach the presence of these narratives in the Americas in all their complexity. Especially given the fraught relationships between the peoples and governments of many Latin American nations since the end of the Spanish Empire, this approach promises to offer a unique angle from which to analyze state-sponsored cultural programming in the region, including the *misiones pedagógicas* and other colonizing paradigms for promoting cultural unity that persist to this day, and which often invoke the Spanish Golden Age and its diachronically accumulated claims to human universality. In this context, uses and deployments of Spanish Golden Age narratives in postcolonial Latin America can be studied not as a unifying and culturally monolithic *espejo enterrado* [buried mirror], as Carlos Fuentes might call it, but as the countless fragments that remain after such a mirror has been shattered, with each piece refracting a unique perspective that is as important for us to study as any other.

Bibliography

Abad Nebot, Francisco. "Sobre el concepto literario de 'Siglo de Oro': Su origen y su crisis." *Anuario de estudios filológicos* 9 (1986): 13–22.
Albert, Manuel J. "La revuelta de las mujeres: Vecinos de Fuente Obejuna representan la obra de Lope de Vega." *El País*, August 27, 2004.
Allen, John Jay. *Don Quixote: Hero or Fool? A Study in Narrative Technique*. Gainesville, FL: University of Florida Press, 1969.
Alonso de Santos, José Luis. "Por qué leer hoy El *Quijote*." *Diario de Cádiz*, August 18, 2015. https://www.diariodecadiz.es/opinion/articulos/leer-hoy-Quijote_0_945205551.html.
Altschul, Nadia R., and Bradley J. Nelson. "Transatlantic Discordances: The Problem of Philology." *Hispanic Issues On Line* 2 (2007): 55–64.
Anonymous. *Lazarillo de Tormes*. Edited by Joseph V. Ricapito. Madrid: Cátedra, 1978.
Anonymous. *Poema de Mio Cid*. Edited by Pedro M. Cátedra. Barcelona: Planeta, 1985.
Anderson, Benedict. *Imagined Communities: Reflections on the Origin and Spread of Nationalism*. London: Verso, 1983.
Arbaiza, Diana. *The Spirit of Hispanism: Commerce, Culture, and Identity across the Atlantic, 1875–1936*. Notre Dame, IN: University of Notre Dame Press, 2020.
Arce, Juan Carlos. *Melibea no quiere ser mujer*. Barcelona: Planeta, 1991.
Ares López, Daniel. "Imagined Continuities: The Story of El Cid as a Post-9/11 War on Terror Narrative in Filmax/José Pozo's Animated Feature Film *El Cid. La Leyenda*." *Studies in Spanish and Latin American Cinemas* 11.1 (2014): 43–59.
Astrana Marín, Luis. *Vida ejemplar y heroica de Miguel de Cervantes Saavedra*. Madrid: Reus, 1958.
Avalle-Arce, Juan Bautista. *Deslindes cervantinos*. Madrid: Ediciones de historia, geografía y arte, 1961.
——. *Don Quijote como forma de vida*. Madrid: Castalia, 1976.
Bailey, Matthew. "From Latin Chronicle to Hollywood Extravaganza: The Young Cid Stirs Hearts." *Société Rencesvals* 22.1/4 (2001): 89–102.
Bakhtin, Mikhail. *The Dialogic Imagination: Four Essays by M. M. Bakhtin*. Austin, TX: University of Texas Press, 1997.
Balfour, Sebastian and Alejandro Quiroga. *The Reinvention of Spain: Nation and Identity since Democracy*. Oxford: Oxford University Press, 2007.

Balfour, Sebastian. "The concept of historical revisionism: Spain since the 1930s." *International Journal of Iberian Studies* 21.3 (2008): 179–87. DOI: 10.1386/ijis.21.3.179/1.
Bass, Laura. "The Economics of Representation in Lope de Vega's *La dama boba*." *Bulletin of Spanish Studies* 83.6 (2006): 771–87.
Baudrillard, Jean. "The Precession of Simulacra." In *Media and Cultural Studies: Keyworks*, edited by Meenakshi Gigi Durham and Douglas M. Kellner, 453–81. Oxford: Blackwell, 2001.
Bayliss, Robert. "Lope enamorado: Patrimonio cultural y cine posnacional." *Hispania* 98.4 (2015): 714–25.
———. "What *Don Quixote* Means (Today)." *Comparative Literature Studies* 43.4 (2007): 382–97.
Becker-Cantarino, Barbara. "The Rediscovery of Spain in Enlightened and Romantic Germany." *Monatshefte* 72.2 (1980): 121–34. http://www.jstor.org/stable/30157058.
Bernabéu-López, Amparo, and Rafael Rocamora Abellán. "De 'Spain Is Different' a 'I Need Spain.' La función apelativa en campañas turísticas españolas." *Gran Tour: Revista de Investigaciones Turísticas* 2 (2010): 83–100.
Bernecker, Walther L. and Jaffé, Verónica. "El aniversario del 'descubrimiento' de América en el conflicto de opiniones." *Ibero-amerikanisches Archiv* 18.3–4 (1992): 501–20.
Beswick, Jaine. *Regional Nationalism in Spain: Language Use and Ethnic Identity in Galicia*. Vol. 5. Clevedon: Multilingual Matters, 2007.
Bhabha, Homi. *The Location of Culture*. New York: Routledge, 1990.
Billig, Michael. *Banal Nationalism*. London: Sage Publications, 1995.
Blanco, Alda. "Spain at the Crossroads: Imperial Nostalgia or Modern Colonialism?" *A contra corriente* 5.1 (2007): 1–11.
Blecua, Alberto. "El concepto de Siglo de Oro." In *Historia literaria/Historia de la literatura*, edited by Leonardo Romero Tobar, 115–60. Zaragoza: Prensas Universitarias de Zaragoza, 2004.
Bloom, Harold. *How to Read and Why*. New York: Simon & Schuster, 2000.
Blue, Scott. A. "Meaning, Intention, and Application: Speech Act Theory in the Hermeneutics of Francis Watson and Kevin J. Vanhoozer." *Trinity Journal* 23.2 (2002): 161–84.
Blue, William R. "Politics in Lope de Vega's Fuenteovejuna." *Hispanic Review* 59.3 (1991): 295–315.
Bourdieu, Pierre. *Distinction: A Social Critique of the Judgement of Taste*. Harvard: Routledge and Kagan Paul Ltd, 1984.
———. "The Forms of Capital." In *Handbook of Theory and Research for the Sociology of Education*, edited by J. G. Richardson, 241–58. New York: Greenwood Press, 1986.
Brantlinger, Patrick. "Cultural Studies versus the New Historicism." In *English Studies/Cultural Studies: Institutionalizing Dissent*, edited by Isaiah Smithson and Nancy Ruff, 43–58. Champaign, IL: University of Illinois Press, 1994.
Britt-Arredondo, Christopher. *Quixotism: The Imaginative Denial of Spain's Loss of Empire*. Albany, NY: State University of New York Press, 2005.
Bryman, Alan. *The Disneyization of Society*. London: Sage Publications, 2004.

Buffery, Helena, editor. *Stages of Exile: Spanish Republican Exile Theatre and Performance*. Bern: Peter Lang, 2011.
Burningham, Bruce. *Tilting Cervantes: Baroque Reflections on Postmodern Culture*. Nashville, TN: Vanderbilt University Press, 2008.
Butler, Judith. *Excitable Speech: A Politics of the Performative*. New York: Routledge, 1997.
Byrd, Suzanne. *La Fuenteovejuna de Federico García Lorca*. Madrid: Pliegos, 1984.
Cantor, Paul. "Stephen Greenblatt's New Historicist Vision." *Academic Questions* 6.4 (1993): 21–36.
Cardenal, Ana S., et al. "Echo-Chambers in Online News Consumption: Evidence from Survey and Navigation Data in Spain." *European Journal of Communication* 34.4 (2019): 360–76. DOI:10.1177/0267323119844409.
Carmona, Pablo, Beatriz García, and Almudena Sánchez. *Spanish Neocon. La revuelta neoconservadora en la derecha española*. Madrid: Traficantes de Sueños, 2012.
Casalduero, Joaquín. *Sentido y forma del Quijote*. Madrid: Ínsula, 1949.
Cascardi, Anthony J. *Ideologies of History in the Spanish Golden Age*. University Park, PA: Penn State University Press, 2004.
Cascardi, Anthony J., editor. *The Cambridge Companion to Cervantes*. Cambridge: Cambridge University Press, 2002.
Castillo, David and William Eggington. "Hispanism(s) Briefly: A Reflection on the State of the Discipline." *Hispanic Issues Online* 1 (2006): 47–52.
Castro, Américo. *El pensamiento de Cervantes*. Edited by Julio Rodríguez Puértolas. Barcelona: Noguer, 1972.
———. *España en su historia. Cristianos, moros y judíos*. Buenos Aires: Editorial Losada, 1948.
Castro y Bellvis, Guillén de. *Las mocedades del Cid*. Edited by Stefano Arata. Barcelona: Crític, 2015.
Cervantes Saavedra, Miguel de. *Don Quixote*. Translated by Edith Grossman. New York: Ecco/Harper, 2003.
———. *Don Quijote de la Mancha, adaptación de Arturo Pérez-Reverte*. Madrid: RAE/Santillana, 2014.
———. *El ingenioso hidalgo Don Quixote de la Mancha*. Edited by Joaquín Ibarra. Edición facsímile. Real Academia Española, 2016.
Childers, William. "Bruce R. Burningham. *Tilting Cervantes: Baroque Reflections on Postmodern Culture*." *Cervantes* 29.2 (2009): 236–40.
———. *Transnational Cervantes*. Toronto: University of Toronto Press, 2006.
Close, Anthony. *The Romantic Approach to Don Quixote*. Cambridge: Cambridge University Press, 1978.
Cohen, Walter. *Drama of a Nation: Public Theater in Renaissance England and Spain*. Ithaca, NY: Cornell University Press, 1985.
Colmeiro, José. *Peripheral Visions/Global Sounds: From Galicia to the World*. Liverpool: Liverpool University Press, 2017.
Corral, José Luís. *El Cid*. Barcelona: Edhasa, 2003.
———. *Los Austrias: El vuelo del águila*. Barcelona: Planeta, 2016.
———. *Numancia*. Barcelona: Edhasa, 2006.
———. *Trafalgar*. Barcelona: Edhasa, 2001.
Crane, Diana, Nobuko Kawashima, and Ken'ichi Kawasaki, editors. *Global Culture: Media, Arts, Policy, and Globalization*. New York: Taylor and Francis, 2002.

Crumbaugh, Justin. *Destination Dictatorship: The Spectacle of Spain's Tourist Boom and the Reinvention of Difference*. Albany, NY: State University of New York Press, 2010.

Cucó Giner, Alfons. "Los nacionalismos periféricos: el caso valenciano." In *El siglo XX: balance y perspectivas: V Congreso de la Asociación de Historia Contemporánea*. Valencia: Facultat de Geografia i Història. Departament d'Història Contemporània, 2000.

Cvetkovich, Ann and Douglas Kellner, editors. *Articulating the Global and the Local: Globalization and Cultural Studies*. Boulder, CO: Westview Press, 2007.

Delgado, Luisa Elena. "La nación (in)vertebrada: razones para un debate." *Revista de estudios hispánicos* 37.2 (2003): 319-40.

——. *La nación singular: La cultura del consenso y la fantasía de la normalidad democrática española (1996-2011)*. Madrid: Siglo XXI de España Editores, 2014.

Díez Borque, José María. *Teatro y fiesta en el barroco: España e Iberoamérica*. Barcelona: Ediciones del Serbal, 1986.

Donnell, Sidney. *Feminizing the Enemy: Imperial Spain, Transvestite Drama, and the Crisis of Masculinity*. Lewisburg, PA: Bucknell University Press, 2003.

During, Simon, editor. *Cultural Studies: A Critical Introduction*. New York: Routledge, 2005.

Eggington, William. "*Quixote*, Colbert and the Reality of Fiction." *New York Times*, September 25, 2011. http://opinionator.blogs.nytimes.com/2011/09/25/quixote-colbert-and-the-reality-of-fiction.

——. *The Theater of Truth: The Ideology of (Neo) Baroque Aesthetics*. Stanford, CA: Stanford University Press, 2010.

Enjuto-Rangel, Cecilia, Sebastiaan Faber, Pedro García-Caro, and Robert Patrick Newcomb, editors. *Transatlantic Studies: Latin America, Iberia, and Africa*. Liverpool: Liverpool University Press, 2019.

Escobar, Juan de, and Martín Gregorio de Zabala. *Romancero, e historia del muy valeroso Caballero el Cid Ruy Diaz de Bivar*. México: Frente de Afirmación Hispanista A.C., 2017.

Esteve del Valle, Marc and Julia Costa López. "Reconquest 2.0: The Spanish Far Right and the Mobilization of Historical Memory during the 2019 Elections." *European Politics and Society* 24.4 (2023): 494-517.

Faber, Sebastiaan. "Economies of Prestige: The Place of Iberian Studies in the American University." *Hispanic Research Journal* 9.1 (2008): 7-32.

Fernández, Esther. "La justiciar está en la mujer: De *Fuente Ovejuna* a los feminicidios de Ciudad Juárez." In *Dialogos en las tablas: Últimas tendencias de la puesta en escena del teatro clásico español*, edited by Maria Bastianes, Esther Fernandez, and Purificacio Mascarell, 141-53. Kassel: Edition Reichenberger, 2014.

Fernández, Esther and Martínez-Carazo, Christina. "Mirar y desear: la construcción del personaje femenino en *El perro del hortelano* de Lope de Vega y de Pilar Miró." *Bulletin of Spanish Studies* LXXXIII.3 (2006): 315-28.

Fernández, James D. "'Longfellow's Law': The Place of Latin America and Spain in US Hispanism, circa 1915." In *Spain in America: The Origins of Hispanism in the United States*, edited by Richard L. Kagan, 123-41. Champaign, IL: University of Illinois Press, 2002.

Fernández y González, Manuel. *Cid Rodrigo de Vivar (el Cid Campeador): novela histórica original*. Madrid: Urbano Manini, 1875.

Fernández-Morera, Darío. "The Myth of the Andalusian Paradise." *The Intercollegiate Review* 41.2 (Fall 2006): 21–31.

Fletcher, Richard. *The Quest for El Cid*. London: Century Hutchinson, 1989.

Franco, Francisco. *Pensamiento politico de Franco: Antología*. Madrid: Servicio Infomativo Español, 1964.

Froldi, Rinaldo. *Lope de Vega y la formación de la comedia: en torno a la tradición dramática valenciana y al primer teatro de Lope*. Vol. 249. Madrid: Anaya, 1968.

Fuchs, Barbara. *Passing for Spain: Cervantes and the Fictions of Identity*. Champaign, IL: University of Illinois Press, 2010.

Fuentes, Carlos. *Cervantes o la crítica de la lectura*. México: Editorial Joaquín Mortiz, 1983.

Ganelin, Charles. *Rewriting Theatre: The "Comedia" and the Nineteenth-Century "Refundición."* Lewisburg, PA: Bucknell University Press, 1994.

García, Olalla. *El taller de los libros prohibidos*. Madrid: Ediciones B, 2018.

García Jambrina, Luís. *El manuscrito de fuego*. Madrid: Espasa Calpe, 2018.

García-Martín, Elena. "Fuente Obejuna hoy: Participación popular en la ficción histórica de Lope." In *Actas del congreso "El Siglo de Oro en el Nuevo Milenio,"* edited by Carlos Mata and Miguel Zugasti, 777–88. Pamplona: EUNSA, 2005.

———. *Rural Revisions of Golden Age Drama: Performance of History, Production of Space*. Lewisburg, PA: Bucknell University Press, 2017.

Garrusta, Marc Gil and Subirana, Jaume. "Francoist Purging of Nomenclature in Barcelona: Communion, Wishes and Beliefs." *International Journal of Iberian Studies* 34.3 (2021): 253–74.

Gasta, Chad. "The Politics of Agriculture: Dramatizing Agrarian Plight in Lope's *Fuenteovejuna*." *Bulletin of the Comediantes* 55.1 (2003): 9–21.

Geertz, Clifford. *The Interpretation of Cultures*. New York: Basic Books, 1973.

Gilbert-Santamaría, Donald. *Writers on the Market: Consuming Literature in Early Seventeenth-Century Spain*. Lewisburg, PA: Bucknell University Press, 2005.

Gillespie, Richard, and Caroline Gray, eds. *Contesting Spain? The Dynamics of Nationalist Movements in Catalonia and the Basque Country*. New York: Routledge, 2015.

Giroux, Henri. "Animating Youth: The Disnification of Children's Culture." *Socialist Review* 24.3 (1995): 23–55.

Goytisolo, Juan. "Fuenteovejuna, señor." *Journal of Spanish Cultural Studies* 3.1 (2002): 9–13.

Greenblatt, Stephen. *Renaissance Self-Fashioning: From More to Shakespeare*. Chicago: University of Chicago Press, 1980.

Greer, Margaret Rich. "Thine and Mine: The Spanish 'Golden Age' and Early Modern Studies." *PMLA* 126.1 (2011): 217–24.

Grieve, Patricia E. *The Eve of Spain: Myths of Origins in the History of Christian, Muslim, and Jewish Conflict*. Baltimore, MD: Johns Hopkins University Press, 2009.

Grossberg, Lawrence. *Bringing It All Back Home: Essays on Cultural Studies*. Durham, NC: Duke University Press, 1997.

Harbison, Robert. *The Built, the Unbuilt, and the Unbuildable: In Pursuit of Architectural Meaning*. Cambridge, MA: MIT Press, 1993.

Hirsch, E. D. "Meaning and Significance Reinterpreted." *Critical Inquiry* 11.2 (1984): 202–25.
Huerta, Teresa. "Tiempo de iniciativa en la Fuenteovejuna de García Lorca." *Hispania* 80.3 (1997): 480–87.
Hutcheon, Linda. *A Theory of Adaptation*. New York: Routledge, 2006.
Intxausti, Aurora. "Un Siglo de Oro con acento porteño." *El País*, January 13, 2014.
Jancovich, M. "'The Purest Knight of All': Nation, History, and Representation in El Cid (1960)." *Cinema Journal* 40.1 (2000): 79–103.
Jauralde Pou, Pablo. "Cervantes and the Philological School." Translated by Anne J. Cruz. In *Cervantes and His Postmodern Constituencies*, edited by Carroll B. Johnson and Anne J. Cruz, 109–15. New York: Garland, 1999.
Jauss, Hans Robert. "Literary History as a Challenge to Literary Theory." In *New Directions in Literary History*, edited by Ralph Cohen, 11–41. Routledge, 2002.
Johnson, Carroll B. *Cervantes and the Material World*. Champaign, IL: University of Illinois Press, 2000.
———. *Don Quixote: The Quest for Modern Fiction*. Long Grove, IL: Waveland Press, 1990.
Jordan, Barry and Rikki Morgan-Tamosunas, editors. *Contemporary Spanish Cultural Studies*. London: Arnold, 2000.
Kamen, Henry. *Imagining Spain: Historical Myth and National Identity*. New Haven, CT: Yale University Press, 2008.
———. *The Disinherited: The Exiles who Created Spanish Culture*. London: Penguin, 2008.
Kasten, Carey. *Cultural Politics of 20th-Century Spanish Theater: Representing the Auto Sacramental*. Lewisburg, PA: Bucknell University Press, 2012.
Ketelaar, Eric. "Muniments and Monuments: The Dawn of Archives as Cultural Patrimony." *Archival Science* 7.4 (2007): 343–57.
Kinder, Marsha. *Blood Cinema: The Reconstruction of National Identity in Spain*. Berkeley, CA: University of California Press, 1993.
Kirschner, Teresa. *El protagonista colectivo en Fuenteovejuna de Lope de Vega*. Salamanca: Ediciones Universidad de Salamanca, D.L. 1979.
Kraidy, Marwan M. "Globalization of Culture through the Media." In *Encyclopedia of Communication and Information*, Vol. 2, edited by J. R. Schement, 359–63. New York, NY: Macmillan Reference USA, 2002. Retrieved from http://repository.upenn.edu/asc_papers/325.
Labanyi, Jo, editor. *Constructing Identity in Contemporary Spain: Theoretical Debates and Cultural Practice*. Oxford: Oxford University Press, 2002.
Laguna, Ana María G. *Cervantes and the Pictorial Imagination: A Study on the Power of Images and Images of Power in Works by Cervantes*. Lewisburg, PA: Bucknell University Press, 2009.
Larson, Catherine. "Original and Borrowed Words in Guillén de Castro's *Las mocedades del* Cid." In *New Historicism and the Comedia: Poetics, Politics and Praxis*, edited by José A. Madrigal, 167–80. Boulder, CO: Society of Spanish and Spanish-American Studies, 1997.
Lash, Scott and Celia Lury. *Global Culture Industry: The Mediation of Things*. Malden, MA: Polity, 2007.
Lauer, A. Robert. "The Recovery of the Repressed: A Neohistorical Reading of Fuenteovejuna." In *New Historicism and the Comedia: Poetics, Politics and Praxis*,

edited by José A. Madrigal, 15-28. Boulder, CO: Society of Spanish and Spanish-American Studies, 1997.

Lefevere, André and Susan Bassnet. *Constructing Cultures: Essays on Literary Translation*. Clevedon: Multilingual Matters, 2011.

Levinson, Brett. *The Ends of Literature: The Latin American "Boom" in the Neoliberal Marketplace*. Stanford, CA: Stanford University Press, 2002.

Lippard, Lucy R. *The Lure of the Local: Senses of Place in a Multicentered Society*. New York: New Press, 1997.

Livingston, Robert Eric. "Glocal Knowledges: Agency and Place in Literary Studies." *PMLA* 116.1 (2001): 145-57.

Lopez Villarquide, María. *La catedrática*. Madrid: Espasa Calpe, 2018.

Lorenzo, Luciano García. "Teatro clásico e iniciativa pública." *Arbor* 177 (2004): 545-60.

Lucía Megías, José Manuel. *De los libros de caballerías manuscritos al Quijote*. Madrid: Ediciones SIAL, 2004.

——. *Leer el Quijote en imágenes: hacia una teoría de los modelos iconográficos*. Barcelona: Calambur Editorial, 2006.

Luzón, Javier Moreno, and Xosé M. Núñez Seixas. "Los símbolos nacionales en la España constitucional (1978-2017): Un consenso precario." In *La España constitucional (1978-2018). Trayectorias y perspectivas*, edited by Benigno Pendás, 381-94. Madrid: Centro de Estudios Políticos y Constitucionales, 2018.

MacLeod, Nicola E. "The Placeless Festival: Identity and Place in the Post-Modern Festival." In *Festivals, Tourism and Social Change: Remaking Worlds*, edited by David Picard and Mike Robinson, 222-37. Clevedon: Channel View Publications, 2006.

Maeztu, Ramiro de. *Defensa de la hispanidad*. Madrid: Gráfica Universal, 1934.

——. *Don Quijote, Don Juan y la Celestina: ensayos de simpatia*. Madrid: Espasa Calpe, 1926.

Mancing, Howard. *Don Quixote: A Reference Guide*. Westport: Greenwood, 2006.

Mar-Molinero, Clare. "The European Linguistic Legacy in a Global Era: Linguistic Imperialism, Spanish and the *Instituto Cervantes*." In *Language Ideologies, Policies and Practices*, edited by Clare Mar-Molinero and Patrick Stevenson, 76-88. London: Palgrave Macmillan, 2006.

Maravall, José Antonio. *La cultura del barroco: Análisis de una estructura histórica*. Barcelona: Editora Ariel, 1975.

Marín, Nicolás. "Decadencia y siglo de oro." Alicante: Biblioteca Virtual Miguel de Cervantes, 2006.

Mariscal, George. "Can Cultural Studies Speak Spanish?" In *Companion to Cultural Studies*, edited by Toby Miller, 232-45. Oxford: Blackwell, 2001.

——. *Contradictory Subjects: Quevedo, Cervantes, and Seventeenth-Century Spanish Culture*. Ithaca, NY: Cornell University Press, 1991.

Martí, Alejandro. "La huella del Siglo de Oro en las calles de Valencia." https://www.lasprovincias.es/planes/huella-siglo-20190820171802-nt.html.

Martín-Estudillo, Luis and Nicholas Spadaccini. "Introduction." *Hispanic Issues On Line* 2006. 7-12. http://spanport.cla.umn.edu/publications/HispanicIssues/hispanic-issuesonline/hispanic%20issues%20online-1.htm/introduction.pdf.

Martínez, Elena and Jareño, Francisco. "Foreign Investment by Spain in Latin America: Brazil, Argentina and Mexico." *Applied Econometrics and International Development* 14.2 (2014): 129–44.

Mayhew, Jonathan. "Was Lorca a Poetic Thinker?" *Romance Quarterly* 58.4 (2011): 367–88.

McClennen, Sophia A. *The Dialectics of Exile: Nation, Time, Language, and Space in Hispanic Literatures*. West Lafayette, IN: Purdue University Press, 2004.

McCrary, William C. "Fuenteovejuna: Its Platonic Vision and Execution." *Studies in Philology* 58 (1961): 179–92.

McKendrick, Melveena. *Theatre in Spain 1490–1700*. Cambridge: Cambridge University Press, 1989.

McLuhan, Marshall and Bruce R. Powers. *The Global Village: Transformations in World Life and Media in the 21st Century*. Oxford: Oxford University Press, 1989.

Mejías-Lopez, Alejandro. "Hispanic Studies and the Legacy of Empire." In *Empire's End: Transnational Connections in the Hispanic World*, edited by Akiko Tsuchiya and William G. Acree Jr., 204–21. Nashville, TN: Vanderbilt University Press, 2016.

Meléndez y Pelayo, Marcelino. *Historia de las ideas estéticas en España*. Santander: Ediciones de la Universidad de Cantabria, 2010.

Menor, Cristina Moreiras. *La estela del tiempo: imagen e historicidad en el cine español contemporáneo*. Madrid: Iberoamericana, 2011.

———. "Regionalismo crítico y la reevaluación de la tradición en la España contemporánea." *Arizona Journal of Hispanic Cultural Studies* 7.1 (2003): 195–210.

Mooers, Colin Peter, editor. *The New Imperialists: Ideologies of Empire*. Oxford: Oneworld, 2006.

Montero Reguera, José. *El Quijote y la crítica contemporánea*. Alcalá de Henares: Centro de Estudios Cervantinos, 1997.

Montrose, Louis. "New Historicisms." In *Redrawing the Boundaries: The Transformation of English and American Literary Studies*, edited by Giles Gunn and Stephen Greenblatt, 393–418. New York: MLA.

Moore, Molly. "After Machismo's Long Reign, Women Gain in Spain." *Washington Post*, October 7, 2006. https://www.washingtonpost.com/archive/politics/2006/10/07/after-machismos-long-reign-women-gain-in-spain/e6cdb3a0-b26b-4dea-9013-6d6e21d83e13/.

Morley, David and Kevin Robins. *Spaces of Identity: Global Media, Electronic Landscapes and Cultural Boundaries*. London: Routledge, 1995.

Mujica, Barbara. "Golden Age/Early Modern Theater: *Comedia* Studies at the End of the Century." *Hispania* 82.3 (1999): 397–407.

Myers, D. G. "New Historicism in Literary Studies." *Academic Questions* 2.1 (1989): 27–36.

Nebrija, Antonio de. *Gramática de la lengua castellana*. Barcelona: Red Ediciones, 2019.

Nirenberg, David, *Communities of Violence: Persecution of Minorities in the Middle Ages*. Princeton, NJ: Princeton University Press, 1996.

O'Connor, Thomas Austin. *Love in the "Corral": Conjugal Spirituality and Anti-Theatrical Polemic in Early Modern Spain*. Oxford: Peter Lang, 2000.

Oechler, Christopher C. "Dictating Aesthetic and Political Legitimacy through Golden Age Theater: Fuente Ovejuna at the Teatro Español, Directed by Cayetano Luca de Tena (1944)." *Hispanic Review* 86.4 (2018): 439-61.

Ortega y Gasset, José. *Meditaciones del* Quijote. Madrid: Residencia de Estudiantes, 1914.

Osborne, Peter. "The Postconceptual Condition: Or, the Cultural Logic of High Capitalism Today." *Radical Philosophy* 184 (2014): 19-27.

Paffey, Darren J. and Mar-Molinero, Clare. "Globalisation, Linguistic Norms and Language Authorities: Spain and the Panhispanic Language Policy." In *Spanish in the United States and Other Contact Environments: Sociolinguistics, Ideology and Pedagogy*, edited by Manel Lacorte and Jennifer Leeman, 159-73. Madrid: Iberoamericana; Vervuert, 2009.

Parker, Alexander. "The Approach to the Spanish Drama of Golden Age." *Tulane Drama Review* 4.1 (1959): 42-59.

Parker, Jason T. "Recruiting the Literary Tradition: Lope de Vega's Fuenteovejuna as Cultural Weapon during the Spanish Civil War." *Bulletin of the Comediantes* 62.1 (2010): 123-43.

Parr, James. "A Modest Proposal: That We Use Alternatives to Borrowing (Renaissance, Baroque, Golden Age) and Leveling (Early Modern) in Periodization." *Hispania* 84.3 (2001): 406-16.

———. *Don Quixote: An Anatomy of Subversive Discourse*. Madrid: Juan de la Cuesta, 1988.

Pérez Isasi, Santiago. "The Limits of 'Spanishness' in Nineteenth-Century Spanish Literary History." *Bulletin of Hispanic Studies* 90.3 (2013): 167-87.

Pérez-Reverete, Arturo. *El capitán Alatriste*. Madrid: Santillana, 1996.

———. *Sidi*. Barcelona: Alfaguara, 2019.

Pidal, Ramón Menéndez, and Pedro Muguruza. *La España del Cid*. Madrid: Espasa Calpe, 1969.

Quiroga, Alejandro. *Football and National Identities in Spain: The Strange Death of Don Quixote*. New York: Palgrave Macmillan, 2013.

Ratcliffe, Marjorie. "Powerless or Empowered? Women in Guillén de Castro's *Las mocedades del Cid* and *Las hazañas del Cid*." *Bulletin of the Comediantes*, 44.2 (1992): 261-67.

Resina, Joan Ramón. "Whose Hispanism? Cultural Trauma, Disciplined Memory, and Symbolic Dominance." *Hispanic Issues* 30 (2005): 160-88.

Rico, Francisco. "Lectores y detractores del 'Quijote.'" *El País*, July 11, 2015. https://cultura.elpais.com/cultura/2015/07/09/actualidad/1436443437_420316.html.

Riley, E. C. "*Don Quixote*: From Text to Icon." *Bulletin of the Cervantes Society of America* 8 (1988): 103-15.

Riquer, Martín de. *Aproximación al Quijote*. Barcelona: Salvat, 1970.

———. *Para leer a Cervantes*. Barcelona: Acantilado, 2003.

Rodríguez Cepeda, Enrique. "Los *Quijotes* de siglo XVIII a(1). La imprenta de Manuel Martín." *Bulletin of the Cervantes Society of America* (1988): 61-104. http://www.h-net.org/~cervantes/csa/artics88/rodrigue.htm.

Rodríguez-Marcos, Javier. "Sanchos que intentan ser Quijotes." *El País*, December 1, 2014. https://elpais.com/cultura/2014/11/26/babelia/1417012930_193899.html.

Rodríguez-Solás, David. *Teatros nacionales republicanos: la Segunda República y el teatro clásico español*. Madrid: Iberoamericana; Vervuert, 2014.

Rosenblat, Ángel. *La lengua del Quijote*. Madrid: Gredos, 1995.
Russell, P. E. "*Don Quixote* as a Funny Book." *Modern Language Review* 64.2 (1969): 312–26.
Santo-Tomás, Enrique García. "Lope de Vega and the Arts of the Nation." *Modern Philology* 111.2 (2013): 329–37.
Schmidt, Rachel Lynn. *Critical Images: The Canonization of Don Quixote through Illustrated Editions of the Eighteenth Century*. Montreal: McGill-Queen's University Press, 1999.
Serrano, Jorge Sáiz. "Pervivencias escolares de narrativa nacional española: Reconquista, Reyes Católicos e Imperio en libros de texto de historia y en relatos de estudiantes." *Historia y memoria de la educación* 6 (2017): 165–201.
Schwartz, Kessel. "A Falangist View of Golden Age Literature." *Hispania* 49.2 (1966): 206–10.
Sebold, Russell P. "Un David español, o 'galán divino': el Cid contrarreformista de Guillén de Castro." In *Homage to J. H. Mill, in memoriam*, 217–42. Bloomington, IN: Indiana University Press, 1968.
Shapiro, Johanna and Lloyd Rucker. "The Don Quixote Effect." *Families, Systems and Health* 22.4 (2004): 445–52.
Simerka, Barbara. *Discourses of Empire: Counter-Epic Literature in Early Modern Spain*. University Park, PA: Penn State Press, 2003.
Smith, Colin. *The Making of the Poema de mio Cid*. Cambridge: Cambridge University Press, 1983.
Smith, Paul Julian. *The Moderns: Time, Space, and Subjectivity in Contemporary Spanish Culture*. Oxford: Oxford University Press, 2000.
Smith, Sue Favinger. "Ancient Artist: Developing an Art Career after 50." http://ancientartist.typepad.com/ancient_artist_developing/2009/06/the-Quixote-effect.html.
Spitzer, Leo. "Linguistic Perspectivism in the Don *Quijote*." In *Linguistics and Literary History: Essays in Stylistics*, 41–85. Princeton, NJ: Princeton University Press, 1948.
Sreberny, Annabelle. "The Global and the Local in International Communications." In *Media and Cultural Studies: Keyworks*, edited by Meenakshi Gigi Durham and Douglas M. Kellner, 604–25. Oxford: Blackwell, 2001.
Storm, Eric. "The Problems of the Spanish Nation-Building Process around 1900." *National Identities* 6.2 (2004): 143–57.
Ticknor, George. *History of Spanish Literature*. Vol. 3. Boston, MA: Houghton, Mifflin, 1863.
Trapiello, Andrés. *Al morir don Quijote*. Barcelona: Destinos, 2004.
——. *Don Quijote de la Mancha, puesto en castellano actual íntegra y fielmente*. Barcelona: Destinos, 2015.
——. *El final de Sancho Panza y otras suertes*. Barcelona: Destinos, 2014.
Trigo, Abril. "Transatlantic Studies and the Geopolitics of Hispanism." In *Transatlantic Studies: Latin America, Iberia, and Africa*, edited by Cecilia Enjuto-Rangel, Sebastiaan Faber, Pedro García-Caro, and Robert Newcomb, 66–75. Liverpool: Liverpool University Press, 2019.
Unamuno, Miguel de. *Del sentimiento trágico de la vida*, 6th edition. Buenos Aires: Losada, 1964.

———. *Vida de Don Quijote y Sancho* [1905]. Edited by Alberto Navarro. Madrid: Cátedra, 1988.

Urbina, Eduardo and Fernando González Moreno. "Iconografía textual del *Quijote*: Principales aportaciones para las ediciones ilustradas del Siglo XIX." In *Literatura ilustrada decimonónica: 57 perspectivas*, edited by Borja Rodríguez Gutiérrez and Raquel Gutiérrez Sebastián, 315–26. PUbliCan, Ediciones de la Universidad de Cantabria, 2011.

Valdés, Ramón, and Elena Di Pinto. "Lope, aún mejor en 2015." https://www.elmundo.es/cultura/2015/01/08/54ae3f4522601d21278b456c.html.

Vega Carpio, Félix Lope de. *Arte nuevo de hacer comedias en este tiempo*, edited by Felipe B. Pedraza Jiménez and Pedro Conde Parrado. Cuenca, Spain: Ediciones de la Universidad de Castilla-La Mancha, 2015.

———. *Fuenteovejuna*. Madrid: Cátedra, 1993.

———. *La dama boba*. Madrid: Espasa Calpe, 2010.

———. *La villana de Getafe*. Barcelona: Red Ediciones, 2022.

———. *Mujeres y criados*. Madrid: Gredos, 2014.

Vélez-Sainz, Julio, and Nieves Romero-Díaz, editors. *Cervantes and/on/in the New World*. Newark, DE: Juan de la Cuesta, 2007.

Vidal, César. *Diccionario del Quijote: la obra para entender uno de los libros esenciales de la cultura universal*. Madrid: Planeta, 2007.

Villena, Fernando de. *Relox de peregrinos*. Granada: Caja General de Ahorros y Monte de Piedad de Granada, 1988.

Wang, Sam. "A Familial Relation? Spain and Latin America in the 21st Century." Council on Hemispheric Affairs, 2016. https://coha.org/a-familial-relation-spain-and-latin-america-in-the-21st-century/.

Weber, Allison. "Golden Age or Early Modern: What's in a Name?" *PMLA* 126.1 (2011): 225–32.

Weimer, Christopher. "The Politics of Adaptation: *Fuenteovejuna* in Pinochet's Chile." In *Echoes and Inscriptions: Comparative Approaches to Early Modern Spanish Literatures*, edited by Barbara Simerka, 234–49. Lewisburg, PA: Bucknell University Press, 2000.

Weiner, Jack. "Lope de Vega's *Fuenteovejuna* under Tsars, Commissars, and the Second Spanish Republic (1931–1939)." *Annali Istituto Universitario Orientale* 43.1 (1982): 167–223.

Wheeler, Duncan. *Golden Age Drama in Contemporary Spain: The Comedia on Page, Stage, and Screen*. Cardiff: University of Wales Press, 2012.

Williams, Raymond. *Marxism and Literature*. Oxford: Oxford University Press, 1977.

Winkler, Martin M. "Mythic and Cinematic Traditions in Anthony Mann's *El Cid*." *Mosaic* 26.3 (1993): 89–111.

Wright, Elizabeth R. *Pilgrimage to Patronage: Lope de Vega and the Court of Phillip III, 1598–1621*. Lewisburg, PA: Bucknell University Press, 2001.

Young. R. V. "New Historicism: Literature and the Will to Power." *Intercollegiate Review* 31.1 (1995): 3–14.

Yúdice, George. *The Expediency of Culture: Uses of Culture in the Global Era*. Durham, NC: Duke University Press, 2003.

Zukin, Sharon. *Landscapes of Power: From Detroit to Disney World*. Berkeley: University of California Press, 1993.

Index

Al-Andalus 22, 121, 141
Almagro (International Classical Theater Festival) 5, 28, 41-42, 51, 69, 81, 148, 150, 151, 153, 154
Azorín 9, 89, 140

Bourdieu, Pierre 5, 13, 48-49

Calderón de la Barca, Pedro 12n12, 43, 48, 64, 66, 67, 72, 150
Cascardi, Anthony 24, 60, 62, 84n2, 85, 127, 129
Castro, Américo 92, 121, 131
Castro y Bellvis, Guillén de 21-23, 37, 50, 51, 55, 56, 114, 121, 126-30, 131-33, 135
Catalonia 14, 18, 46, 47, 50, 53-54, 59, 72, 88, 112, 120
Cervantes Saavedra, Miguel de 1, 5, 9, 12, 15-16, 17, 18, 26, 30, 32, 33, 36-37, 38, 43, 45, 48, 51, 60, 74, 79, 83, 84-96, 98, 100-4, 106-10, 111, 119-20, 133, 134, 143, 150
   Don Quixote 1, 4, 6, 15-16, 24, 30, 33, 36-37, 43, 49, 63, 66, 79, 83, 84-98, 100-7, 109-10, 111-12, 115, 116, 117, 119, 120, 133, 134, 139, 149
Cervantistas (Cervantismo) 84, 92-93, 96
Cid (Rodrigo de Vivar) 21-24, 37-38, 85, 94, 111, 113-16, 118-34, 149
código de honor 21, 31, 51, 63, 77, 114, 117, 131
colonialism 11, 19, 36, 107, 110, 115, 137, 140-42, 143, 146, 152, 153-56
Columbus, Christopher 91, 137, 142, 151, 152

Compañía Nacional de Teatro Clásico (CNTC) 5, 13, 28, 30, 36, 43, 48, 69, 71-73, 74, 116, 137, 145, 147-55
Crisis de 1898 9, 63, 89-91, 94, 101, 130
cultural memory 15, 25, 113, 126, 127, 130-34
culture wars 24, 29, 34, 48, 106, 137-38

Delgado, Luisa Elena 2, 13, 19, 50
Díez Borque, José María 25
Disney 6, 21, 32, 37, 38, 115, 118-25
Donkey Xote 6, 32, 98, 118-21, 123, 124

Filmax 6, 21, 23, 32, 98, 118, 120, 121, 124, 132-33
Franco, Francisco 6, 9, 10, 13, 19, 22, 24-25, 30, 35, 38, 44, 46, 52, 62, 66, 67, 68, 69, 70-71, 74, 82, 83, 91, 92, 94, 95, 102, 111, 114-16, 126, 133, 143, 147
franquismo (Francoism) 6, 13, 24, 35-36, 41, 44, 63-69, 74-76, 81, 90, 91, 94, 114, 116, 125, 135, 139, 141, 143, 147

García Lorca, Federico 64-66, 70, 71, 73, 148, 153
Generation of 1898 4, 89, 90, 100, 101, 130, 131, 135
globalization 6, 18, 28-29, 94, 110, 113, 114, 115, 119-20, 121, 125, 134, 135, 137

Hispania 53, 144
Hispanidad 22, 25, 36, 63, 148
Hispanism 8, 9, 15, 18, 19, 25, 27, 55, 99-101, 140, 154-56
historical fiction 30, 32-33, 38, 63, 112-14, 130-35

historical memory 3, 13, 33, 47, 113, 133, 135
Hollywood 22–24, 31–32, 94, 98, 112, 117–18, 125, 126, 128
Hutcheon, Linda 17, 20–21, 23–24, 27

Iborra, Manuel 31, 74–75
Instituto Cervantes 5, 10, 96, 105–10, 111, 137, 141, 144, 151, 155

Kamen, Henry 11, 24, 38, 66, 143

Lazarillo de Tormes 31, 117–18, 132, 133
Lefevere, André 3–4, 16
limpieza de sangre (blood purity) 22
Lope de Vega *see* Vega Carpio, Félix Lope de

Maeztu, Ramiro de 91, 140
Man of La Mancha 94–95, 98, 115
Maravall, José Antonio 24–25, 93
Menéndez Pidal, Ramón 125, 126, 130–31, 132, 133, 135
El Ministerio del Tiempo 33, 38, 113, 132–34
Miró, Pilar 26n17, 30–31, 73–74, 117, 135
Molina, Tirso de 32, 66, 140
Morisco expulsion 22, 100, 101–3

nationalism 17–20, 29, 30, 34, 35, 36, 37, 38, 44–47, 48, 49, 50, 51, 52, 53, 55, 59, 60, 63, 66–68, 78, 81, 82, 88–92, 99–101, 109, 110, 113, 115, 120, 121, 126, 131, 132, 143, 144
Nebrija, Antonio de 107, 109, 142, 150–52, 153, 154
New Historicism 16–19, 23–28, 99

Ortega y Gasset, José 9, 90

Partido Popular (PP) 68, 103, 149
Partido Socialista de Obreros Españoles (PSOE) 2, 69, 71, 73, 103, 116, 124, 137, 144, 147
Pérez-Reverte, Arturo 33, 112, 134
philology 1, 6, 10, 16, 22, 24, 54, 73, 91–96, 98–103, 106, 111, 113, 115, 130
Pozo, José 6, 21, 115, 118, 119–21, 124–26

Quevedo, Francisco de 12, 51, 149

Real Academia Española (RAE) 5, 9, 84, 87, 96, 106–10, 111, 112, 113, 130
Reconquista 36–37, 53, 111, 121–23, 126, 141, 143
Romanticism 7, 8, 24, 81, 88–91, 92–94, 99–100, 101, 102, 110, 117, 119, 120, 130, 135, 140
RTVE (Radio Televisión Española) 4, 23, 30, 31, 33, 51, 63, 69–70, 97, 112, 116–17, 132

Second Republic 47, 63, 64, 66, 69, 125n10, 148
simulacra 98, 101–2, 109
"Spain is Different" 82, 94, 139
Spanish-American War 9, 89, 91, 130, 144
Spanish Civil War 5, 9, 13, 14, 24, 47, 48, 50, 62, 63, 66–69, 70, 94, 125n10, 131, 135
Spanish Empire 10, 11, 88, 107–10, 129, 133, 137, 138, 140–46, 152, 154, 155

tourism 20, 29, 30, 34, 37, 41, 42, 59, 81–84, 88, 93–96, 102, 104–5, 116, 139
Trapiello, Andrés 97, 112, 113

Una, Grande y Libre 67, 94
Unamuno, Miguel de 1–2, 4, 8, 9, 10, 15, 17, 26–27, 36, 64, 65, 90, 100

Vega Carpio, Félix Lope de 13, 18, 22, 31, 33–36, 38–39, 41–81, 133, 135, 153
 Arte nuevo de hacer comedias en este tiempo 38–39, 61
 La dama boba 31, 74–75, 117, 145, 153
 Fuenteovejuna 13, 34, 41, 42, 59–66, 68, 70, 72, 76–78, 81, 127, 131, 145
 El perro del hortelano 31, 35, 59, 73–74, 117
Velázquez, Diego de 43, 48, 132, 144
Vox 14, 34, 35, 47

Wheeler, Duncan 26, 30, 52, 67, 74, 116

Zapatero, José Luis Rodríguez 13, 75, 76, 100, 103, 119–20, 123, 124, 148–49

www.ingramcontent.com/pod-product-compliance
Lightning Source LLC
Chambersburg PA
CBHW050122020526
44112CB00035B/2357